GREEK LEADERS

GREEK LEADERS

BY

LESLIE WHITE HOPKINSON

UNDER THE EDITORSHIP OF
WILLIAM SCOTT FERGUSON

Essay Index Reprint Series

BOOKS FOR LIBRARIES PRESS
FREEPORT, NEW YORK

STANDARD BOOK NUMBER:
8369-0017-0

LIBRARY OF CONGRESS CATALOG CARD NUMBER:
75-76904

PRINTED IN THE UNITED STATES OF AMERICA

CONTENTS

ACKNOWLEDGMENTS

In trying to present in one short and readable volume the results of the best scholarship applied to eleven different subjects, I have of course had to consult a great number and variety of authorities, more than it is practicable to enumerate here. My obligations, however, to the various translators upon whom I have so freely drawn must be acknowledged in more detail.

The version of Plutarch is "that commonly known as Dryden's," revised and edited by Arthur Hugh Clough. Those of Thucydides and Plato (the *Banquet*) are Jowett's, while the passages from Plato's *Apology* and *Phœdo* are taken from an anonymous translation published in 1879 under the title of "Socrates," with an introduction by Professor W. W. Goodwin. For the extracts from the orations of Demosthenes I am greatly indebted to Mr. Pickard-Cambridge's *Demosthenes and the Last Days of Greek Freedom* (G. P. Putman's Sons). As for the metrical versions of Solon's poems, those in rhymed hexameters and in blank verse are taken from Mr. F. G. Kenyon's translation of Aristotle's *Constitution of Athens* (G. Bell & Sons, Ltd.); the passage beginning, "Solon surely was a dreamer," occurs in Clough's Plutarch (*Life of Solon*); while the elegiacs are an experiment of my own. In quoting the *Clouds* of Aristophanes I have taken the great liberty of combining the standard translation of Mr. B. B. Rogers (G. Bell & Sons, Ltd.) with that introduced by Mr. A. D. Godley in his *Socrates and Athenian Society*. For all these I wish to express my thanks.

L. W. H.

INTRODUCTION

THIS book is especially designed for use, in conjunction with a textbook, in high-school classes in ancient history. It bases its claim for consideration in this connection primarily on the fact that it consists of biographies of manageable length which combine attractive literary form with real merit as history.

It is hoped that *Greek Leaders* may find a place in that select group of books which, being complementary to the textbook used by the class, are as indispensable to the schools as is the textbook itself. Ideally such books should be in the hands of every pupil; but since this is not always practicable, it is now generally recognized that there should be at least one copy of them in the school library for every five pupils in the class. The teacher must have available such a number of copies of these books that pupils may be able to do the reading assigned by him without jostling one another. Nothing dampens the ardor for reading of students of history so quickly as inability or time-consuming difficulty in "getting the books."

The reasons for the existence of "collateral reading" in connection with history instruction in high schools and academies are generally recognized. One of them, however, has, I venture to think, been insufficiently emphasized. Perhaps it applies peculiarly in the field of ancient history. There circumstances have brought it about that writers of textbooks, forced not only to include in one volume of fixed dimensions the history of Greece and Rome and the history of the Near East and the early Middle Ages, but also to enrich their narrative of events by taking account

of social, economic, and cultural developments, have been
unable to furnish more than well-proportioned summaries.
Such *manuels* afford an excellent basis for classroom work,
and they have been found indispensable in the teaching of
history both in America and Europe. But they are commonly not good samples of history writing. They do not
dwell long enough on situations and actors, or on societies
and forces, to give the imagination a fair chance to con-
struct plots or visualize communities. In them there is no
room for eloquence, no opportunity to linger Herodotus-
wise on pleasant bypaths, no space to register the ups and
downs of affairs. All is inexorable quick-march. They are,
therefore, condemned in advance to be rarely or never
interesting. They are too compact for that. In the schools
of France they are taken as the point of departure, not so
much for analyses by the question-and-answer method, as
for oral narratives developed with the literary and dramatic
skill for which French teachers are distinguished. Thereby the French pupil is introduced to real history. In America this introduction must be, and commonly is, made
through collateral reading.

It is, therefore, important in the highest degree that the
books by which the textbook is supplemented should be
chosen, both as regards type and individual volume, with
the utmost care. Yet of one kind of work the choice is inevitable, as is shown by the accord in this particular, so
seldom secured in other matters, of school teachers and
college examiners: *biography* must form an essential part
of the collateral reading of pupils taking up the study of
ancient history in their secondary-school course. It is not
biography of the child's story order, where the persons and
not the times, the epochless, nationless, timeless heroes and
heroines are the objects of interest, that is demanded. Nor
is it biography, like Plutarch's, where incidents and policies

are indifferent in themselves so long as they betray character. The biography that is sought has this in common with all biography that it subordinates tendencies, movements, enterprises, collaborators to a dominant personality in a way that makes them intelligible and interesting, especially to boys and girls; but it differs from the varieties of biography already described in that it gives seriousness and significance to its subjects by exhibiting them at work on the most momentous problems of their own people, state, and age.

How well the eleven Greek biographies included in this particular volume meet justified demands may be left to the reader to decide. They have the advantage over biographical passages from extended histories that a whole has over a fragment, over biographical sketches from encyclopædias that an essay has over a *résumé*. They will probably be found much more serviceable in school use than one detailed biography of equal length. They are written by an accomplished teacher, and for that very reason, perhaps, are not written down to the assumed level of children. "One reason," writes Professor Henry Johnson in his authoritative work on the *Teaching of History*, "why American estimates of the ability of children to cope with history are lower than similar European estimates is the American habit of translating history so largely into the reading vocabulary of children."

WILLIAM SCOTT FERGUSON.

GREEK LEADERS

SOLON

(Died 559? B.C.)

THEY say that Solon, coming to Crœsus at his request, was in the same condition as an inland man when first he goes to see the sea; for as he fancies every river he meets with to be the ocean, so Solon, as he passed through the court, and saw a great many nobles richly dressed, and proudly attended with a multitude of guards and footboys, thought every one had been the king, till he was brought to Crœsus, who was decked with every possible rarity and curiosity, in ornaments of jewels, purple and gold, that could make a grand and gorgeous spectacle of him. Now when Solon came before him and seemed not at all surprised, . . . he commanded them to open all his treasure-houses and carry him to see his sumptuous furniture and luxuries, though he did not wish it; . . . and when he returned from viewing all, Crœsus asked him if ever he had known a happier man than he. And when Solon answered that he had known one Tellus, a fellow-citizen of his own, and told him that this Tellus had been an honest man, had had good children, a competent estate, and died bravely in battle for his country, Crœsus took him for an ill-bred fellow and a fool. . . . He asked him, however, again, if besides Tellus, he knew any other man more happy. And Solon replying, Yes, Cleobis and Biton, who were loving brothers and extremely dutiful sons to their mother, and when the oxen delayed her, harnessed themselves to the wagon and drew her to Hera's temple, her neighbors all calling her happy, and she herself rejoicing; then, after sacrificing and feasting, they went to rest, and never rose again, but died in the midst of their honor a painless and tranquil death. "What," said Crœsus, angrily, "and dost thou not reckon us amongst the happy men at all?" Solon, unwilling either to flatter or exasperate him more, replied, "The gods, O King, have given the Greeks all other gifts in moderate degree, and so our wisdom,

too, is a cheerful and homely, not a noble and kingly wisdom, . . .
and him only to whom the divinity has continued happiness unto
the end, we call happy." . . . So at this time Crœsus despised
Solon, but when he was overcome by Cyrus, had lost his city, was
taken alive, condemned to be burnt, and laid bound upon the pile
. . . he cried out as loud as he possibly could three times, "O Solon!"
and Cyrus being surprised . . . Crœsus told him the whole story.
. . . When this was told Cyrus . . . he not only freed Crœsus from
punishment but honored him as long as he lived, and Solon had
the glory, by the same saying, to save one king and instruct
another.

That the visit of Solon to Crœsus never happened — since
Solon died, a very old man, in Athens, just as Crœsus
was coming to the throne of Lydia — Plutarch, who relates
it, knew as well as we do; "but," says he, "I cannot reject
so famous and well-attested a narrative, and, what is more,
so agreeable to Solon's temper and so worthy his wisdom
and greatness of mind, because, forsooth, it does not agree
with some chronological laws." For the same reasons it
should be included in any modern life of Solon, and for another also: it is so characteristic, not only of Solon himself,
but of his time and race.[1] For in the seventh and even in
the early sixth century, the average European Greek was
still a frugal, rustic, homely sort of fellow. His idea of warfare was to put on as much armor as he could conveniently
carry, march out a few miles to the nearest piece of good
flat ground, whack away all day at some hundreds of simi-
larly equipped neighbors from across the ridge, and go comfortably home at night. His idea of wealth was a good farm,
a fruitful olive orchard, or a range of upland pastures dotted
with flocks. His towns were small and poor, his clothes were
homespun, his meals were few and spare. But if, through
outlawry or adventurous spirit, he took to the sea and the

[1] The idea that the gods are jealous of extreme prosperity, apart from wrong-doing,
belongs rather to the time of Herodotus (fifth century) whose story Plutarch condenses.

chances of the new trade with Asia, he might, traveling inland from the already sophisticated Ionian cities, come in contact with an unheard-of luxury and splendor, an unimagined softness of living, a dazzling profusion of gold and silver ornaments, of rich and dainty dishes, and, strangest of all, with the elaborate military and political organization of a great Oriental state. Solon, the first citizen of Athens, member of her wealthiest and most aristocratic class, merchant and traveler moreover, could be at Sardis but a country cousin come to town, a sight-seer, condescendingly expected to gape and exclaim at the wonders spread before his eyes.

But Solon does not gape; the country cousin keeps his head. The characteristic attitude of the thoughtful Greek before all this overwhelming wealth and power is cool, grave, independent. His sense of proportion — by which the surpassing beauties of his art and literature are to be shaped — is somehow shocked and displeased by this overweening prosperity; he feels that the gods love it not, and, in no fanatical or puritanical spirit, he turns away in search of that middle road which leads to simple comfort of body and a cheerful, healthy spirit. "Nothing too much," "Moderation in all things" — these are the characteristic sayings of the famous Seven Sages of Hellas, of whom Solon has left by far the greatest mark.

Solon, son of Execestides, was born in the latter half of the seventh century, during the rule of the feudal aristocracy which had held uninterrupted sway over Attica ever since the abolition of the original monarchy. To this aristocracy of mingled birth and wealth — for the latter, being counted almost entirely in land and its products, was practically limited to the nobles — Solon himself belonged, being, indeed, a member of the most ancient and famous house of the Medontids, descendants of Codrus. It seems therefore at first sight rather surprising that the first thing we know about his life should be that he was a merchant. Plutarch, writing some seven hundred years later, has to apologize for his hero's being "in trade," explaining that in his time "merchandise was a noble calling, which brought home the good things which the barbarous nations enjoyed, was the occasion of friendships with their kings, and a great source of experience." Why it held this honored position, Plutarch does not inquire, but the fact is that when the luxuries of the East first began to tempt the Greeks they had nothing to exchange for them but the products of their soil — especially olive oil; and, as the nobles were the only large landholders, they alone had any surplus to exploit and so became the only merchants on a large scale. Most of them, of course, remained country squires, but the more enterprising were attracted not only by the "good things," but by the "great source of experience," and of these was Solon.

Among the results of his trading voyages was a thorough acquaintance with the literary culture of the Ionian cities, then so much in advance of European Greece, and a mastery of the prevailing form of verse, the elegy. Written prose was not yet developed; what a man wished to say in lasting form or to a larger audience than his voice would reach, he put into elegiac verse. So the first appearance of Solon in Athenian history is as the author of a stirring poem, urging his fellow-citizens to "re-take" Salamis. When and how Salamis had been lost, history does not tell us, but the position of the island made it inevitably a bone of contention between Athens and Megara, and the latter state under her able tyrant, Theagenes, may well have been strong enough to wrest away the prize. To Athens, however, the possession of the island was a matter not only of pride, but of necessity if she were to become a commercial state; a rival seated right athwart her very harbor mouth could block her indefinitely. Athens was then, of course, unconscious enough of her destiny, but it is possible that Solon, who knew the conditions of trade and navigation at first hand, and who was later to do so much to foster Athenian commerce, may have foreseen its needs. At all events, he put great fire into his elegy, of which only brief fragments have come down to us: —

I come as a herald, self-sent, from Salamis, beautiful island,
And the message I bring to your ears, I have turned it into a song.

. . . .

Country and name would I change, be known as a man of Siciné,
Nay, Pholegandrian even, rather than all men should say,
Pointing in scorn, "There goes one of the cowardly, lazy Athenians,
Who let Salamis slip through their fingers, when it was theirs for
    a blow."

. . . .

On then to Salamis, brothers! Let us fight for the beautiful island,
Flinging afar from us, ever, the weight of unbearable shame!

That this poem, recited, according to tradition, by its author in the market-place, succeeded in its object seems probable from the great prestige it brought to Solon, who is also, rather more doubtfully, credited with having been the actual leader of the resulting expedition. His reputation was yet heightened by the poems — pamphlets, as they would be in our day — in which, turning now to internal affairs, he set forth the evils which threatened the community and the spirit in which they must be met.

I see, and my heart is woe, as my eyes behold the afflictions
That weigh on the ancient home of the sacred Ionian race.
Not in the mind of Zeus and the rest of the blessèd Immortals,
Not in their will can it be, that our city should perish away,
While over it spreadeth her hands, protecting, the guardian-
    goddess,
Pallas Athené, Zeus-born, and wardeth all ill from its gates.

Ay, but within are the foes — the nobles who spoil and destroy it;
Greedy for gold are they all, and cruel and false the officials
Over whose guilty heads punishment waiteth to fall.
Bridle and measure they know not; never enough have they feasted,
Still by their unjust deeds piling up wealth for themselves;
Pickers and stealers they are, nor spare they the Gods or the
    People;
Holy the temple of Justice, — they care for it never a whit.
Ay, but she sits in her shrine, patient and silently waiting,
Knowing all things that are done, waiting to strike, in good time.
Such is the festering wound that eateth the strength of the city;
Slavery is it, no less, that holdeth her fast in its grip.
But ever on slavery's heels come strife, and the worst of all warfare,
Laying full low in her streets many a beautiful youth.
So in the city — but lo! far in the land of the stranger,
There toil her poorest, bearing the chains and the brand of the
    slave.
Thus spreads the evil afar — chamber nor court can conceal it;
Would one be blind to its presence, vainly at home will he hide.

These are the words that my soul bids me say to the people of
    Athens:
Evil the fate of the city wheresoever Misgovernment reigns.
Only Good Rule bringeth peace; she layeth in chains the ill-doer,
Tameth the fierce, putteth bound to the hunger of ravening greed;
Under her touch fall withered the blood-red blossoms of Até;
She maketh the crooked ways straight and stayeth the clamor of
    strife.

Well might a patriotic Athenian be distressed as he looked
around him. What was actually happening, as we can now
see, was that Greece was passing out of her "Middle Ages"
— answering in many ways to those of Europe 2000 years
later — into her "modern" period, and that the transition
was, like all such, a time of disturbance, suffering, and bewilderment. In some states the process was being hastened
and smoothed by the temporary expedient of a "tyranny,"
whereby a brilliant and masterful despot like Periander of
Corinth could arbitrarily enforce order, suppress civil strife,

curb the pride of the nobility, relieve the poor, and encourage trade. Athens, however, came late in the procession. Her nobles had been faithfully supported, not opposed or betrayed, by their vassals, in crushing Cylon's attempt to seize the government, and though they had yielded something to the spirit of the time in permitting Draco to draw up a written code of laws, they were still practically undisturbed in their position as the owners of the soil, the controllers of traffic, the fountain of justice, and the governors of the state.

A few generations back, all this had been accepted as in the natural order of things, nor had it been, in practice, very hard to bear. The small husbandman might be but a tenant paying his "sixth-part" in kind, but just because his payment was of that sort his landlord had no temptation to press for arrears when a bad harvest had made payment impossible. What would be the use of arrears of perishable stuff, grown only to be eaten? A bad season was a visitation of the gods, to be borne philosophically by landlord and tenant alike. And even if the *seigneur* were heartless enough to wish to evict a man with whom he had grown up and who stood to him much as a Highland clansman to his chief, why should he do so? Where would he get another husbandman to till the vacated farm? And if the Eupatrid was content to take his luck as he found it, so, on the whole, was the farmer. His chief might bully him, but without the protection of that chief he would be helpless and alone, at the mercy of every stray marauder.

During the seventh century, however, and especially toward its end, conditions were changing. As the state grew stronger, and with it the idea of public law,[1] feudal

---

[1] Under a *feudal* system, landlords and tenants are directly responsible to each other only. Tenants owe service to their landlords and landlords owe protection and justice to their tenants. If a tenant is wronged, he brings his case before the landlord's court. Under a system of *public law*, both landlords and tenants are responsible to the state and their cases are tried alike in the state courts.

protection became less necessary and feudal loyalty a menace instead of a help to public order. At the same time the growth of commerce brought new tastes and needs. Articles of luxury were in demand and must be *bought*. The old system of barter was no longer sufficient — for the first time, money was introduced into Greece. That meant the end of the patriarchal age. Henceforward, the tenant was not primarily a humble friend and dependent; he was an instrument of wealth. By his means the noble must raise crops not only for his own use but for exchange with these new stuffs and jewels and furnishings that the ships were bringing in from the East. If he failed, he must pay the penalty, pay with his own person or those of his children, for as a slave he became a marketable commodity. His place in the field might be taken by some one from that increased population which commerce was bringing in its wake, or by some luckless man of the middle class who had been led away by the craze for a higher scale of living, had borrowed at the ruinous rate of interest which the scarcity of money made inevitable, and found himself a hopeless debtor, thankful for a means of livelihood on any terms.

It is now easy to see how all these causes together — the exaction of feudal dues when there was no longer need of feudal protection, the dying out of the old personal relation between landlord and tenant, the rise in the scale of living, the use of money, and the resultant degradation of free farmers into "villeins" and "villeins" into slaves — had brought about a condition of great misery among the bulk of the population. And when we remember that another result of commerce was the creation of a class, still small, but becoming noticeable, of free and prosperous tradesmen and craftsmen, whose condition presented a sharp contrast to that of the agricultural laborers, and, finally, that this was an age of great intellectual awakening throughout

-Hellas, we do not wonder that this misery found voice in a most threatening discontent.

Alarmed at the blackness of the gathering storm, the Eupatrids turned to Solon. He was a popular hero, the winner of Salamis; he was a poet, at a time when the halo of divine inspiration still hovered about that title; he was a modern sort of man, who had traveled, and seen how other cities managed their affairs; he was a reformer who had expressed in the strongest terms the exasperation of the poor: —

But ye who have store of good, who are sated and overflow,
Restrain your swelling soul, and still it and keep it low:
Let the heart that is great within you be trained in a lowlier way;
Ye shall not have all at your will, and we will not forever obey. —

And yet he was, after all, one of themselves, an aristocrat *pur sang*, who could be trusted not to betray his own order into the hands of the hungry mob. So they elected him not only archon, but "lawgiver," with extraordinary powers for a year (B.C. 594–93 or 592–91).

The laws of Solon are set forth in every textbook and need not be detailed here. The most crying need, of course, was the social one, and it was met by the first and most drastic reform. At one stroke, all outstanding debts were canceled, all slaves for debt were set free, and even, by what means we know not, those who had been sold away into foreign parts were ransomed and brought home. No wonder that the memory of this great deliverance was preserved in Athens by a festival the very name of which, *Seisachtheia* — the Casting-off of Burdens — is a cry of joy. Moreover, the dark load, once lifted, was never again to be imposed. A law, never repealed, forbade henceforth an Athenian to pledge himself, his children, or his womenfolk as security for debt. To appreciate this reform we

must realize that the legal right of the rich to enslave the
poor lasted for centuries longer in other Greek cities, and
in some forms survived into modern times.

The other laws attributed to Solon which come under
the general head of "social" are for the most part such as
are found in most codes of the period. Some, such as those
limiting the size of landed estates and granting a man without sons the right to dispose of his property by will, tended
to check the great clan and family holdings and encourage
an independent peasantry; some, such as the bounties on
wolves' heads, recall the rustic, pastoral character which
still dominated Attica; while that, on the contrary, forbid-
ding a woman to go out unattended at night, shows the
creeping in of that Oriental feeling about women which was
to become one of the most unfortunate features of Athenian life.

Solon's principal commercial reform, the substitution of
the Euboic for the Æginetan coinage, was of the greatest
future consequence, because it tied up Athens with the
Ionian cities and the wealth of Asia behind them instead
of with her rivals and neighbors of the Peloponnesus. It
thus prepared the way for that rich Ionic culture which
made Athens "the eye of Hellas," and at the same time,
by fostering a much livelier and more profitable commerce
than could prevail under the old provincial system, provided careers for men who did not like to live, even in
personal freedom, under the overshadowing dominance of
the landed gentry; henceforth commerce and democracy
went hand in hand.

As to the political reforms of Solon, there is much difference of opinion among scholars. It seems pretty clear
that he did not create the classification of citizens according to property, but he may have been the first to use it as
a political, not merely military, rating. By his social and

economic reforms, moreover, he not only made it much easier for a man to rise, by acquiring wealth and (probably) putting it into land, into the higher classes, but increased enormously the numbers of the lowest, the free laborers. Thus whether he was the first to admit these, the Thetes, into the Assembly, or whether, as a small and weak class, they already possessed a nominal but almost useless right to attend it, he unquestionably made them a power in the state. It is true that they proposed no laws, but they voted on measures laid before them by the Council of Four Hundred, and they almost certainly shared in the election of the magistrates. Moreover, by the establishment of the Heliæa, the great popular jury courts to which all citizens were eligible by lot, and by which judicial decisions of magistrates were scrutinized when exception was taken to them, Solon completed the control of the people over its officers and took the first steps toward Athenian democracy.

Yet he was obviously no democrat. His task, as he conceived it, had been to free the commons from intolerable oppression and to give them sufficient power to protect themselves from any repetition of it. To put the actual direction of the state into their hands was as far from his plan as to redistribute the lands of Attica equally among the citizens. Such confiscation and redivision was no unheard-of thing in Greece, and many among the people clamored for it and were bitterly disappointed to find themselves left, both politically and economically, in a distinctly inferior and subordinate position. The noble creditors and *seigneurs*, on the other hand, were far from pleased at the curtailment of their incomes and of their personal control over their tenants. In short, nobody was satisfied, and that, in Solon's opinion, was the best proof that he had followed the path of justice and moderation, the true "middle way."

The truth of this view of Solon's policy [says Aristotle] is established alike by the common consent of all [centuries later] and by the mention which he has himself made of it in his poems. Thus: —

"I gave to the mass of the people such rank as befitted their need,
I took not away their honour, and I granted naught to their greed;
But those who were rich in power, who in wealth were glorious
    and great,
I bethought me that naught should befall them unworthy their
    splendor and state;
And I stood with my shield outstretched, and both were safe in
    its sight,
And I would not that either should triumph, when the triumph was
    not with right."

Again he declares how the mass of the people ought to be treated: —

"But thus will the people best the voice of their leaders obey,
When neither too slack is the rein, nor violence holdeth sway;
For satiety breedeth a child, the presumption that spurns control,
When riches too great are poured upon men of unbalanced soul."

And again elsewhere he speaks about the persons who wished to redistribute the land: —

"So they came in search of plunder, and their cravings knew no
    bound,
Every one among them deeming endless wealth would here be
    found,
And that I with glozing smoothness hid a cruel mind within.
Fondly then and vainly dreamt they; now they raise an angry din,
And they glare askance in anger, and the light within their eyes
Burns with hostile flames upon me, yet therein no justice lies.
All I promised, fully wrought I with the gods at hand to cheer,
Naught beyond of folly ventured. Never to my soul was dear
With a tyrant's force to govern, nor to see the good and base
Side by side in equal portion share the rich home of our race."

Once more he speaks of the destitution of the poorer classes and of those who before were in servitude, but were released owing to the Seisachtheia: —

"Wherefore I freed the racked and tortured crowd
From all the evils that beset their lot,

Thou, when slow time brings justice in its train,
O mighty mother of the Olympian gods,
Dark Earth, thou best canst witness, from whose breast
I swept the pillars broad-cast planted there,
And made thee free who hadst been slave of yore.
And many a man whom fraud or law had sold
Far from his God-built land, an outcast slave,
I brought again to Athens; yea, and some,
Exiles from home through debt's oppressive load,
Speaking no more the dear Athenian tongue,
But wandering far and wide, I brought again;
And those that here in vilest slavery
Crouched 'neath a master's frown, I set them free.
Thus might and right were yoked in harmony,
Since by the force of law I won my ends
And kept my promise. Equal laws I gave
To evil and to good, with even hand
Drawing straight justice for the lot of each.
But had another held the goad as I,
One in whose heart was guile and greediness,
He had not kept the people back from strife.
For had I granted, now what pleased the one,
Then what their foes devised within their hearts,
Of many a man this state had been bereft.
Therefore I took me strength from every side,
And turned at bay, like wolf among the hounds."

Satisfied, then, that he had done what he could and given
the Athenians, as he said, "the best laws they could take,"
Solon now decided that what his new machinery most
needed was to be let alone, and that so long as he was in
Athens there would be no end to the demands for additions
and amendments. Having therefore seen to the publica-
tion of his laws on wooden cylinders, framed and set in public places, and having secured an oath from the Council
and the magistrates to observe them, he bought a trading
vessel and betook himself once more to his travels. A pleasant time he must have had of it, slipping along in his little
ship, half "tramp," half yacht, from port to port, as far

east and south as the mouths of the Nile and thence, on
the return voyage, to Cyprus, and north again to the Ionian
cities, with an inland trip, for aught we know, to Sardis and
its splendors, although no Crœsus, alas! was there as yet to
receive him. Everywhere the genial sage was welcomed and
honored, everywhere he studied and observed, and left behind some tradition of his wise sayings and tactful manners.

"For, always roaming with a hungry heart," he might
have said with Tennyson's Ulysses, —

> Much have I seen and known; cities of men,
> And manners, climates, councils, governments;
> Myself not least, but honored of them all.

After some ten years of this agreeable vacation, Solon
returned, to find that his hope of having made a permanent settlement of the troubles of his native city had
proved vain. His social and monetary reforms, indeed,
stood firm; the emancipated peasants remained free, and
the new coinage circulated, but politically all was in confusion. Not only did district once more lift up its hand
against district and class against class; but new parties
had arisen. The crime-shadowed Alcmæonidæ, recalled from
exile by Solon's act of amnesty, but forever set apart, by
the curse upon them, from their social equals, provided
a captain, Megacles, for the solid middle class, the "men
of the Shore," who backed the Solonian compromise. The
country squires, the "die-hards" of the Tory party, gathered their forces under one Lycurgus, and determined to
win back their lost privileges. And finally a third party
appeared, that of the hillmen, the poor shepherds, the un-
satisfied "sixth-parters," the unsuccessful and the radicals
who had dreamed of a new heaven and a new earth and
found themselves bound to the same old routine of hard
work and hard fare in the same old world, after all. They
lacked but a leader, and found him at about the time, it

would seem, of Solon's return, in a brilliant young kinsman
and friend of his, Pisistratus, who had just won great ac-
claim by the taking of Nisæa in a new war with Megara.

Solon, according to Plutarch, was one of the first to suspect the designs of the popular hero, and tried first to dis-
suade him from them, and then, in opposing in the Assembly the proposal to grant him a bodyguard, to warn the
citizens against the coming *coup d'état.* "But observing,"
says Plutarch, "the poor men bent to gratify Pisistratus,
and tumultuous, and the rich fearful and getting out of
harm's way, he departed, saying he was wiser than some and
stouter than others; wiser than those that did not understand the design, stouter than those that, though they under-
stood it, were afraid to oppose the tyranny." When Pisistratus did seize the Acropolis, the city was all in an uproar
and Megacles with all his family took to flight, "but Solon,
though he was now very old, and had none to back him,
yet came into the market-place and made a speech to the
citizens, partly blaming their inadvertency and meanness
of spirit, and in part urging and exhorting them not thus
tamely to lose their liberty; and likewise then spoke that
memorable saying, that, before, it was an easier task to
stop the rising tyranny, but now the greater and more
glorious action to destroy it. . . . But all being afraid to
side with him, he returned home, and, taking his arms, he
brought them out and laid them in the porch before his
door, with these words: 'I have done my part to maintain
my country and my laws,' and then he busied himself no
more." Living in retirement, he continued to express his
mind in poems, telling his countrymen, —

> If now you suffer, do not blame the Powers,
> For they are good, and all the fault was ours.
> All the strongholds you put into his hands,
> And now his slaves must do what he commands, —

and replying to those who asked in what he trusted for protection, that he dared speak so boldly, "To my old age." Indeed, however, Pisistratus seems to have had only respect and good will for the brave old man, and even to have paid him court and sought his counsel during the year or two that remained of Solon's life.

Thus the revolution and consequent tyranny that Solon had made it his chief work to avert came to pass even within his lifetime. He had only postponed for a few years a period which Athens, like so many other Greek states, had to pass through before her people were ready to assume the management of their own affairs. Was his work then, after all, so very valuable? Would he not have deserved better his title of Wise Man if he had taken the advice of his friends, assumed, as he was generally expected to do, the supreme power, and himself seen to the execution of his own reforms? To some critics the answer is obvious. He was, they say, a man of high character and valuable ideas, a man deserving all respect for his modesty and disinterestedness, but, after all, essentially a theorist, a "scholar in politics," not a man of action. Pisistratus is the man for them, with his fearless, unscrupulous resourcefulness, his wide-sweeping, imaginative plans, his firm, yet not unkindly hand upon the reins of government. Yet, while granting that much of Solon's work was quickly undone, and much else would doubtless have been done before long anyway, one may hold that perhaps his greatest legacy to Athens was this very refusal to rule over her. Solon was a pleasant, social man, of what Plutarch, with the Stoic ideal in mind, calls "soft" morals; he believed in compromises, he was always ready to learn from experience, he "got on" with everybody. But certain beliefs he held absolutely, and he lived up to them. He believed in divine justice, in the certain retribution overhanging all "violence" — whether usurpation of power or

proud and insolent use of the wealth and power that one
has. To break the fundamental law of his state, to make
himself her despot, was to him such a crime of violence, one
which neither men nor gods would forgive. He felt the
criticism of "practical" men. "Solon was a dreamer," he
makes them say —

Solon surely was a dreamer, and a man of simple mind;
When the gods would give him fortune, he of his own will declined.
When the net was full of fishes, over-heavy thinking it,
He declined to haul it up, through want of heart and want of wit.
Had I but that chance of riches and of kingship for one day,
I would give my skin for flaying and my house to die away —

but he was unshaken: —

                    . . . that I spared my land
And withheld from usurpation and from violence my hand,
And forbore to fix a stain and a disgrace on my good name,
I regret not; I believe that it will be my chiefest fame.

Who shall say that this is not, indeed, his chiefest fame,
and that the example he thus set of respect for law, of personal disinterestedness, of absolute reliance upon fundamental principles, was not, in its influence upon the eager,
aspiring youth of Athens, who learned his verses in their
schools and saw his figure receding, age after age, through
an ever more magnifying haze of tradition and veneration,
the most precious legacy he could leave to his dear city?

THEMISTOCLES

(Died 460? B.C.)

You have never considered what manner of men are these Athenians. . . . They are revolutionary, equally quick in the conception and in the execution of every new plan, while you are conservative. . . . They are bold beyond their strength, they run risks which prudence would condemn; and in the midst of misfortune they are full of hope. . . . They are impetuous, and you are dilatory; they are always abroad, and you are always at home. . . . When conquerors, they pursue their victory to the utmost; when defeated, they fall back the least. . . . With them alone to hope is to have, for they lose not a moment in the execution of an idea. . . . None enjoy their good things less, because they are always seeking for more.

Speech of the Corinthian envoys at Sparta.

And in the matter of education, whereas they [the Spartans] from early youth are always undergoing laborious exercises to make them brave, we live at ease, and yet are equally ready to face the perils which they face. . . . If then we prefer to meet danger with a light heart and without laborious training, and with a courage which is gained by habit and not enforced by law, are we not greatly the gainers? . . . For we have a peculiar power of thinking before we act and of acting too, whereas other men are courageous from ignorance but hesitate upon reflection. . . . To sum up: I say that Athens is the School of Hellas, and that the individual Athenian in his own person seems to have the power of adapting himself to the most varied forms of action with the utmost versatility and grace.

Funeral Speech of Pericles.

For Themistocles was a man whose natural force was unmistakable; this was the quality for which he was distinguished above all other men; from his own native acuteness, and without any study either before or at the time, he was the ablest judge of the course to be pursued in a sudden emergency, and could best

divine what was likely to happen in the remotest future. Whatever
he had in hand he had the power of explaining to others, and even
where he had no experience he was quite competent to form a
sufficient judgment; no one could foresee with equal clearness the
good or evil intent which was hidden in the future. In a word,
Themistocles, by natural power of mind and with the least preparation, was of all men the best able to extemporize the right thing
to be done.

No one can read these extracts from Thucydides without
realizing that whatever else he was or was not, Themistocles
was a typical Athenian. The same thing strikes us the moment we compare him with his most famous contemporaries.
Aristides, so far as we know him, might as well have been a
Roman, or an Englishman. Personally, he belongs with
Washington. Leonidas takes his place among national
heroes like William Wallace and Arnold von Winkelried —
men who "made way for liberty and died." But for Themistocles, as for Pericles, there was but one parent-state possible. And as Pericles represents, on the whole, the ideal
Athenian at the brief, ever-glorious moment when Athens
poised herself on the pinnacle of her fame, so Themistocles
typifies the generation that toiled and dared to place her
there.

Themistocles was born of obscure parents. The typical
quality of his Athenianism is all the more marked if the
story is true that his mother was an "outlander," for the
cosmopolitanism of Athens, the favor she then extended to
the strangers within her gates, was one of the most striking,
unusual, and successful features of her policy. At any rate,
the certain fact is that Themistocles was a self-made man,
obliged all through his political life to fight for his own hand,
helped by none of the social prestige or even party backing
which counted so much for his rivals.

About his youth, therefore, naturally nothing is recorded except the usual anecdotes that grow up around the memory of a great man — the schoolmaster who prophesied his future eminence, for good or for ill; the precocious taste for oratory, etc., etc. The general impression one gets is of an eager, ambitious boy, careless of the elegant accomplishments on which the social Greek set such store, but hungry for all knowledge and training which would fit him for public life.

Into this he must have plunged at the earliest opportunity and quickly forced his way to the front, for as he was "still young," as Plutarch says, at the battle of Marathon, where he fought in his tribal regiment, he must have held the office of archon (B.C. 493–92) at not much over the minimum age of thirty. At once he initiated the policy which was to be his life-work, the creation and upbuilding of the naval supremacy of Athens. The first step was to provide a suitable port in place of the wide unprotected strand of Phalerum. The assembly passed his measure for the fortification of the whole peninsula of the Piræus, and work was begun upon the wall, but interrupted by the first Persian invasion and not completed until after the second. During the interval, however, the windfall of the newly discovered silver-deposits at Laurium gave Themistocles an opportunity to take the next step forward — and a long one. Instead of dividing the profits among the citizens, after the good old childlike, hand to mouth fashion, the Assembly was persuaded to spend them on new ships, and two years later Athens had a navy surpassed by no Hellenic state except Syracuse and possibly Corcyra. In each case the Assembly's motive was jealousy of neighboring Ægina, but that of its leader, we may well believe, was much more comprehensive. Even before Datis and Artaphernes crossed the Ægean, his far-sighted eyes caught sight of Persian sails on the eastern horizon; after Marathon, Persian vengeance was only a matter of time.

So marked a change in policy could not, of course, be brought about without a hard struggle. "And henceforward," says Plutarch, "little by little, turning and drawing the city down towards the sea, in the belief that, whereas by land they were not a fit match for their next neighbors, with their ships they might be able to repel the Persians and command Greece, thus, as Plato says, from steady soldiers he turned them into mariners and seamen tossed about the sea, and gave occasion for the reproach against him, that he took away from the Athenians the spear and the shield, and bound them to the bench and the oar." Not only must the statesman who would do that meet the solid opposition of the army, led as at Marathon by Miltiades, but there was a social and economic question deeply involved as well. "Whether or no," Plutarch goes on, "he hereby injured the purity and *true balance of government* may be a question for philosophers" — in view of the fact that his policy actually did win Salamis and save Greece. At the time, however, Salamis was in the future, and the question was not academic but very actual. All that was best as well as what was worst in the conservative temper, all that held by the old pieties, the honorable past, the solid virtues of the farmer, the reliable vote of the citizen "with a stake in the country," shrank with instinctive foresight from the vision, however dimly perceived, of a new Athens, commercial, cosmopolitan, democratic, mobile as its own new element.

It was inevitable that Aristides, no reactionary, no hankerer after oligarchy, but a convinced and loyal constitutional democrat, should yet, just because of his own character and temperament, be the soul of this conservative opposition. All through their lives the two men were neces-

sarily coming into collision, for each was strong where the
other was weak and each instinctively distrusted his rival.
To Aristides, Themistocles was not only a dangerous inno-
vator and a rash counselor, but a man of uncertain character
and principles, a politician who played the game with sus-
piciously sticky fingers. To Themistocles, on the other
hand, Aristides must have been, for all his virtues, or all
the more because of them, an exasperating embodiment of
just that impervious, gentlemanly conservatism which stood
like a wall between him and every reform on which he had
set his heart. There is not only something so admirable
in the unflinching honor and perfect disinterestedness of
Aristides, but something so lovable in the generosity with
which he supported his rival in Greece's critical moment and,
with a long list of personal injuries to avenge, refrained from
word or deed which might embitter that rival's ultimate fall,[1]
that we are in some danger of forgetting that it was, after
all, the brain of Themistocles and not the heart of Aristides
which in those fateful years was indispensable to Athens,
to Greece, and to civilization.

During those dozen years Themistocles pursued one
great policy, made up of two distinct but closely interwoven
strands: the whole summed up in the words, *sea power*. To
transform Athens from a military state of average importance to the greatest naval power in Hellas, to commit her
absolutely to the great adventure of such a transformation,
equally to commit the Hellenic Alliance, against all their
tradition and what seemed their immediate interests, to the
policy of meeting and defeating Persia by sea, and to hold
them, once so committed, to their agreement — these were
the component parts of one great scheme, failure in which
would have meant the blotting out of Athens and of Greece
from history, while success in it placed Themistocles

---

[1] It is not certain, however, that Aristides was still living at that time.

deservedly in the position of the savior of his race. For
with magnificent self-confidence he carried the whole thing
through, practically single-handed. To the fulfillment of his
purpose everything was subordinated. When it was necessary to have a free hand in committing Athens to a great
navy, he gently but firmly removed his chief opponents,
Xanthippus and Aristides, by ostracism, from his path;
when the time came for Athens, once so committed, to face
the consequences with a united front, he was the first to
propose their recall. His much-abused "trickiness" was all
at the service of the cause: he "worked" the oracles to
encourage faint hearts; he scraped together from the most
secret hoards every last obol to maintain the fleet; he spread
broadcast on the rocky coast, like a modern advertising
agent, the appeals that might compromise, if they did not
win over, the Ionian contingents of the Persian armada;
and he ran the whole gamut of inducements, from patriotic
exhortation to naked bribery, which might persuade the
suspicious, anxious Peloponnesian admirals, fighting always
with one eye over the left shoulder on the harbors of home,
to stick together and save Greece.

Ambitious, sensitive, and irritable as he seems to have
been by nature, he fairly sank himself in this cause, yielding,
generously and promptly, his position as chief admiral of
the Allied fleet to the Spartan Eurybiades, and by tact and
patient pressure gaining a lasting influence over that me-
diocre but honest sailor. "Strike if you will, but listen!"
are the famous words with which he met the upraised staff
of the irritated commander-in-chief, and the anecdote typifies the selflessness of this whole period of his career.

The events themselves of the great year 480 are writ so
large in the history of Greece that they need no detailed
mention here, though Themistocles bore his part in all of
them. As strategus (and now Athens reaped the benefit of

that constitutional change which had recently reversed the
relative importance of strategus and polemarch) he commanded the Athenian forces in the futile allied expedition to
Tempe as well as the Athenian fleet during the combined
operations at Thermopylæ and Artemisium which ended
in the withdrawal to Salamis. He superintended the abandonment of Athens by her citizens. Finally, he exhausted
every means, legitimate and illegitimate, of bringing about
the decisive battle in the narrow seas.

The story of these last efforts is too characteristic as well
as famous to be omitted from any account of Themistocles.
When Xerxes had occupied Attica the sentiment of the
Allies became so overwhelmingly in favor of a retreat to the
Isthmus that some of the captains did not even wait for the
decision of the Council of War before hoisting sail, and only
nightfall held the ships at their moorings. To Themistocles
retreat meant a double tragedy — the certain abandonment
of Athens to her fate, and the great probability of a crushing
defeat for the whole fleet. It was with the latter argument
that he resolved to make one last effort. Going by night to
the admiral's flagship, he so wrought upon Eurybiades that
that sorely perplexed patriot reconvened the Council, and
Themistocles, without waiting for the formal putting of the
question, plunged at once into his plea. "At the games,"
scoffed the Corinthian admiral, "those who stand up
too soon are whipped for their pains." "Ay," flung back
Themistocles, "but those who start late win no crowns."
He was not going to waste time, however, in personal
squabbles; the one thing to do was to state the issue so
clearly that the dullest and most fearful could not fail to
see it. "Hear both ways," he said, "and set them in comparison. If thou engage battle at the Isthmus, thou wilt
fight in an open sea, into which it is no means convenient
for us that we fight, seeing that we have ships which are

heavier and fewer in number than those of the enemy. Then,
secondly, thou wilt give up to destruction Salamis and
Megara and Ægina, even if we have success in all else; for
with the fleet will come also the land army, and thus thou
wilt thyself lead them to the Peloponnesus." He then set
forth with the same precision the corresponding advantages of the opposite course, and ended by pointing out that
God helped those who helped themselves. Hitherto he had
wholly controlled his temper, but when the same Corinthian,
Adeimantos, dared to protest his vote, sneering at him as a
man without a country, his anger flamed as he declared that
Athens was on her ships, and, if deserted by her allies, would
sail away and seek new hearths and homes in the free West.
The threat accomplished more than the argument, the
decision was recalled, and Themistocles breathed again.

But not for long. A few days later the actual sight of the
enemy drawn up along the shore of Phalerum revived the
uneasiness of the Peloponnesians; their land force at the
Isthmus drew them like a magnet; and when Xerxes, dis-
posing his ships so as to block the straits on either side of
the islet of Psyttaleia, showed a purpose to prevent their
withdrawal, Eurybiades called yet another Council, and
Themistocles saw all his work to be done over again.

Never was he so typically himself as now, when with
absolute self-reliance he staked his all and his country's all
on a desperate throw which, had the outcome been other
than it was, would have handed his name down to all succeeding ages as that of the supreme traitor. Leaving the
Council, he dispatched a trusted slave to Xerxes himself,
with the message that the Greeks, weakened by divided
counsels, were on the point of breaking up in disorder, and
that by forcing them to an immediate battle he might win
an easy and complete victory. This done, Themistocles
slipped back into his place.

One can imagine the tense nerves with which he waited hour after hour while the night went by and the discussion — sound and fury, signifying nothing — raged around him. Suddenly he was called out into the darkness. Aristides, his old rival, sailing across from Ægina, had found his passage blocked by hostile ships, and, slipping through the cordon, had hastened with the tremendous news that the fleet was surrounded. Very significant is the relationship between these old enemies — in face of the supreme need every shred of rivalry and distrust has vanished. Aristides, never dreaming that his news is anything but calamitous, chooses to break it first to Themistocles; Themistocles, with absolute confidence not only in his rival, but in that rival's confidence in him, tells him the whole truth, and then, shrewdly guessing that his own assertion would be suspected, sends him in to the Council to announce his tidings. Even the testimony of Aristides the Just, however, could not convince the unwilling Peloponnesians that they were cornered at last, until a Tenian ship deserting from the enemy confirmed the news.

In the ever-memorable fight that followed, Themistocles, commanding the Athenian fleet, fought well and wisely, but the relative values of all concerned are best summed up by Simonides when he speaks of "that noble and famous victory, than which neither amongst the Greeks nor barbarians was ever known more glorious exploit on the seas, obtained by the joint valour indeed and zeal of all, but by the wisdom and sagacity of Themistocles."

Such, at the time, seems to have been the almost universal verdict of his contemporaries. Failing of due honor through the almost incredible childishness of his colleagues, who, as the story goes, voted each the first prize for valor to himself and the second to Themistocles, he was received at Sparta — a state certainly none too prone to recognize foreign merit — with such honors as she had never paid before. The olive wreath for valor she did indeed reserve for her own Eurybiades, but another "for ability and skill" was presented to the Athenian, together with the best chariot in Lacedæmon, and "having much commended him, they escorted him on his departure with three hundred picked men of the Spartans . . . as far as the boundaries of Tegea, and he is the only man of all we know to whom the Spartans gave escort on his way." And at the next Olympic games the spectators, Herodotus tells us, fairly turned their backs upon the contestants to gaze after Themistocles, to point him out one to another and to clap his every appearance.

Doubtless Themistocles enjoyed these compliments, though he might have preferred a free hand in following up the Persian fleet. That was his policy — to seize the moment of the enemy's demoralization, pursue him to the Hellespont, and by another crushing defeat at once cut off the retreat of the land army and give the signal for revolt to the Ionian cities. The scheme was too greatly daring for the stay-at-home Peloponnesians, and Themistocles himself realized that it would be foolhardy for the Athenians alone, who, in their elation over their recent achievement, were ready to undertake anything. So, for once, he held them back, and according to the legend — a pretty doubtful one — seized the opportunity to lay up for himself favor with Xerxes by sending him word of the threatened pursuit and of his own good service in discouraging it.

After the whole Persian army, however, had retired to Thessaly, apparently in full retreat homeward, the Confederates returned to the Themistoclean plan of rousing Ionia. But no sooner had Athens made ready for her share in an Asiatic campaign than the southward march of Mardonius, in the spring of 479, made her realize that a purely naval policy meant a second abandonment of Attica. Themistocles was ready for that, but Athens was not; in a sudden revulsion of feeling, she turned against the man who asked her to be more than human, and set Xanthippus in his place.

So it came about that Themistocles took no part — or none now visible — in the campaign of either Platæa or Mycale. In the creation and organization, moreover, of the Confederacy of Delos, which was to develop into the Athenian empire, Aristides was given full responsibility and credit. Nevertheless, when we realize that the marvelous expansion in power and wealth and all the arts of civilization which make the next fifty years of Athenian life unique in history would have been impossible, not only without that preponderance of naval force which Themistocles had insisted on, but without that conception of Athenian policy, — adventurous, daring, ambitious, "far-flung," in which he had educated his fellow-countrymen, we feel that to him more truly than to any other statesman or commander the Athenian empire was due.

Moreover, though out of office, Themistocles was far from inactive or uninfluential during these next years. The comparative insignificance of the archonship after it was filled by lot instead of choice left the field open to the unofficial popular leader, the "man of the town-meeting," and as such the ex-strategus swayed decisively the policy of his city. Once more there were two strands to that policy — a tactful but vigilant resistance to the tendency of Sparta to transmute her acknowledged leadership of continental Hellas into a supremacy, and the picking up again and working out of all those plans for the maritime, mercantile, and democratic development of Athens which had been perforce interrupted by the Persian war. And again the two strands were interwoven, for upon such development Sparta looked with jealous eyes. Even the fortification of the rebuilding city was hateful to her, and she sent envoys to remonstrate

against it. The well-known story of how Themistocles, as
one of the embassy sent in return, kept the Spartans in play
while men, women, and children raised the wall to a defensi-
ble height, and then boldly announced that Athens could
take care of herself and must henceforth be dealt with as an
equal, shows at once the quick assumption of such equality
on the part of Athens and the association of the challenge
to Spartan supremacy with the name of Themistocles. A
second and more resented check — for Sparta could hardly
have really expected Athens to consent to her own helplessness — was the successful resistance made by the same
Athenian, at the Council of the Delphic Amphictyony, to the
insidious proposal to expel from the League, in the name
of patriotism, those states — Thessaly, Thebes, even passive Argos — who had not joined in the resistance to Persia.
After this we hear of no more pleasant hospitalities extended
to Themistocles at Sparta.

The other half of his policy demanded equally the completion of his plan for the Piræus. The political effect of the
development and walling-in of this harbor is clearly brought
out by Plutarch, who says of Themistocles, that "he did
not only knead up, as Aristophanes says, the port and the
city into one, but made the city absolutely the dependant
and the adjunct of the port, and the land of the sea, which
increased the power and confidence of the people against
the nobility, the authority coming into the hands of boat-
swains and pilots."

One truth of which Themistocles had a firm grasp was the
close relation between naval power and naval commerce.
The new harbor was not a mere navy yard; it was built for
the merchant ships of Athens and all the world. But if
Athens was to be a world market she must have exports to
pay for her imports; therefore she must greatly increase her
industries; and, again therefore, she must encourage in

every way the settlement within her borders of foreign tradesmen and mechanics. It is in his relation to all these policies and their effects that we see Themistocles most plainly as the link between Cleisthenes and Pericles, the middle term of the three great founders of Athenian democracy.

The next stage in the life of Themistocles — his increasing unpopularity, culminating in ostracism — is tantalizingly obscure. Contributing causes we can dimly see — the vanity which led him to build beside his own house a shrine to Artemis, Wisest in Counsel; the mysteriously increasing fortune (he is said to have gone out of public life a hundred times as rich as when he entered it), which must have led to many a comparison with the austere integrity of Aristides; the sharp tongue which he could not restrain from stinging replies to undeserved reproaches, and which seemed yet more unpleasant compared with the delightful geniality of his rapidly rising young rival, Cimon; above all, perhaps, his advocacy of peace with Persia. Wise or not, it was consistent with his whole far-sighted, thoroughly thought-out scheme of commercial expansion, east and west. Persia was no longer dangerous to Athens; trade with the Orient, impossible while war lasted, was highly desirable for her. But Athens was too proud of the laurels Themistocles himself had won for her, of savior and protectress of the Asiatic Greeks, to check herself in full career while the Carian cities still felt the Persian yoke and Xerxes was free to gather new fleets in southern waters. Nor was the high-spirited Cimon, with the crowning victory of the Eurymedon yet to be won, likely to let himself be easily thwarted of the great prize of his career.

The test came in 472, and a potsherd bearing the name of Themistocles still exists to bear witness to the decision. The exiled statesman retired to Argos, and in the natural course

of things might expect to return before many years, like
Aristides before him, to the active and honorable service of
his country. A far different fate was reserved for him.

Pausanias, the victor of Platæa, had conspired not only
to overthrow the constitution of his native city, but to sell
her into the hands of the Great King. Seeing his old friend
Themistocles fretting bitterly in undeserved banishment,
he conceived the idea of gaining the assistance of the shrewd-
est brain in Greece. There is no evidence, there is no probability, that Themistocles took any part in this wretched
plot against Hellas, but his persistent policy of opposition
to Sparta may have involved him in the scheme to under-
mine her government. The undisputed fact that he had
been in correspondence with the traitor gave Sparta the
long-desired chance to get even with the man who had
blocked her ambition; she denounced him to Athens, his
enemies there took up the cry, and the Assembly voted
his arrest and summons before a general Council of the
Greeks.

His courage failed him. Perhaps he knew the jury would
be packed against him. At all events, he fled to Corcyra
and thence, pursued by both Spartan and Athenian officers,
to the wild country of Epirus, where, like a suppliant in old
heroic days, he flung himself down upon the hearth of a
personal enemy, King Admetus of the Molossians, and,
holding in his arms the King's infant son, made such a
claim upon Highland hospitality as could not be denied.
Thus he escaped his indignant fellow-citizens, who in his
absence condemned him as an outlaw and confiscated his
property, much of which, however, his friends managed to
smuggle out of the country and convey to him at Susa. For
thither, after many a thrilling adventure by land and sea,
the new Ulysses, as homeless, as resourceful, as "much-
enduring" as his prototype, finally betook himself — mak-

ing the last stage of his journey in a closed litter as an
Ionian beauty on her way to a courtier's harem!

A more dramatic meeting than that between the son and
successor of Xerxes and the Athenian who had foiled that
mighty monarch can hardly be imagined. That Persia knew
who had been her worst enemy is plain from the fact that
there was a price of two hundred talents on his head. But
with the same sure and daring calculation which had enabled
him to play and win the desperate game at Salamis, Themistocles resolved to place himself in the hands of no one less
than his greatest foe. Concealing his identity, of course,
from the King's officers, he sought an audience with
Artaxerxes, and an interesting light is thrown upon the
sense of personal dignity associated with the very name of
Greek, by the apologetic manner in which the chamberlain
explained to the Hellenic stranger that he could not be
admitted to the Great King's presence unless he were willing
to prostrate himself before him.

"When he was introduced to the King," says Plutarch,
'and had paid his reverence to him, he stood silent, till the
King commanding the interpreter to ask him who he was,
he replied: 'O King, I am Themistocles the Athenian,
driven into banishment by the Greeks. The evils that I
have done to the Persians are numerous; but my benefits to
them yet greater, in withholding the Greeks from pursuit,
so soon as the deliverance of my own country allowed me
to show kindness also to you. I come with a mind suited to
my present c⁻lamities; prepared alike for favors and for
anger; . . . If you save me, you will save your suppliant;
if otherwise, you will destroy an enemy of the Greeks.' "

Great was the delight of the King at this unexpected
good luck. In his very sleep, they say, he would cry out for
joy, "I have Themistocles the Athenian!" In the court
there was ill-will enough for the "subtle Greek serpent,"

but the royal favor was more than sufficient to protect him.
Mastering the Persian language, he became the chief counselor as well as the boon companion of Artaxerxes and even
received that highest mark of Oriental confidence, admission
to the women's quarters and conversation with the Queen-
mother. The revenues of three cities were granted him for
maintenance, and the story goes that, looking around at his
splendidly served table, he remarked to his family, "Children, we had been undone if we had not been undone."

That the Athenian in him was not so dead, however, as
he would believe, appears in the curious and rather touching little incident of the brazen statuette of a girl carrying
water which he saw in the temple of Cybele at Sardis and
recognized as one which he himself had set up at Athens in
the days before Persia was more, even to him, than a vague
cloud on the eastern horizon, the far-off days when he was
serving his city in the domestic office of water commissioner
and had this little image made out of the fines of citizens
convicted of tapping the town-pipes for their own use. One
feels the tightening around his heart as his youth rushed
back upon him, and the vision of Athens, the little homely
Athens of the days "before the war," swam before his eyes.
He would have bought the statue and sent it home, a mute
message to his estranged countrymen, but the Persian
governor scented treason, and he dropped the scheme.

So far, he had paid no price for all the honors that the
Great King showered upon him, for Asiatic affairs were
absorbing the sovereign's energies. At last, however, the
time came when Artaxerxes summoned him to aid in an
expedition against Greece. From this lowest depth of in-
famy, however, he was saved. Whether his own act or, as
the better version has it, a merciful illness rescued him from
the horrible dilemma into which fate and character had
driven him, will never be known, but he died suddenly at

Magnesia, and Greece had no more to fear than to hope from her greatest statesman.

Of the sixty-five years of Themistocles's life, most, as Plutarch says, had been spent "in politics and in the wars, in government and in command." Themistocles the statesman looms so large that it is not easy, out of the few scattered anecdotes preserved by ancient writers, to build up an image of Themistocles the man. At least, nothing that is told of his private life is inconsistent with what we know of his public one. Most of the tales turn on the keenness of his wit, of a dry, sardonic sort that must have made him more feared than loved, even when the retort was as well deserved as that with which he crushed the Seriphian who pointed out that the honors showered upon him were really meant for his city. "Doubtless," he replied, "I should have been no more famous if I had been of Seriphus than you, had you been of Athens." A sense of injustice seems to have embittered his most successful days. The Athenians, he said, "did not honor him or admire him, but made, as it were, a sort of plane-tree of him, sheltered themselves under him in bad weather and, as soon as it was fine, plucked his leaves and cut his branches." Such things he could not forgive or forget; when one who had snubbed tried to court him, he turned frigidly away with "Time, young man, has taught us both a lesson."

Yet, if not loved, he seems, before party strife reached its height, to have been respected by his fellow-citizens and in demand among them as an arbitrator in private suits, while as a magistrate he was inflexibly just. "Simonides," he said to his friend the poet, who was importuning him, "you would be no good poet if you wrote false measure, nor should I be a good magistrate if for favor I made false law." An attractive side to his nature is the domestic. The father of ten children, we catch a glimpse of him still surrounded by them in his exile, while at the height of his glory he chaffs his little boy as the most powerful person in Greece: "For the Athenians command the rest of Greece, I command the Athenians, your mother commands me, and you command your mother."

Altogether, he gradually shapes himself for us as a not unfamiliar, not unmodern type — a man of kindly instincts and cold manners, sensitive, irritable temper, a sincere desire to serve his country and an equally sincere wish to have that service duly acknowledged. If he was unscrupulous in his methods, he seems to have wronged no man, and his "graft" has probably been considerably exaggerated by hostile tradition. Yet there was a fatal flaw in the man. His character was not equal to his intellect. He could rise to a supreme occasion, his every faculty fused in the consuming flame of his patriotism, could dedicate himself to his country's service in the lofty spirit of that speech he made to the Athenians in the last moments before the battle at Salamis, bidding them remember that in all things there is a higher and a lower way, and it was for them to choose the higher. But the disinterestedness, the fortitude, the patience, the self-control which bore the test of Greece's "Annus Mirabilis," broke down under the continued strain of petty injustices and defeats and of the final undeserved charge. An embittered, disappointed man, he lost all faith in his country, all courage to plead his case before her. He turned his back upon his past, and the savior of Greece died a renegade, if not a traitor. His own time could not be expected to forgive him, but we who know what his work means for us can afford to pass merciful judgment on the man but for whom the Athens of Pericles, Phidias, and Sophocles could never have existed, and Greece itself would have been wiped out of the world's history.

PERICLES

(Died 429 B.C.)

PERICLES, the most famous if not the greatest statesman of Athens, was born under circumstances highly favorable to his career. The impressionable years of his boyhood were the years during which Athens became the savior of Hellas. The heroes of Marathon were those of his earliest childhood; as a lad he must have shared the family flight from home at the oncoming of the Persian host, have witnessed from the shores of Salamis, crowded with praying, trembling, exulting refugees, the Great Deliverance, and have returned to an Athens desolate to the outward view but more precious and glorious than ever in the eyes of her triumphant sons. And in the next year, at Mycale, his own father, Xanthippus, led the Athenian fleet in the victorious battle which freed Ionia from the Persian yoke. The passionate love of Athens, the unquenchable pride and faith in her as the rightful leader of Hellas, which beat in the pulses of his great Funeral Oration, spoken fifty years later when the shadows were gathering around his dear city and himself, became a part of his very life-blood during the great days of his youth.

In another sense, the birth of Pericles was very significant. His father was not only a general, but a prominent politician, who shared with Aristides the leadership of what, in distinction from the radicalism of Themistocles, may be called the liberal-conservative party — the old party of the "Coast." And his mother, Agariste, was the grand-niece of Cleisthenes, the second founder of Athenian democracy. Through her, Pericles became the political heir, the "rising hope," of the most brilliant, the most ambitious, and the most democratic of the noble families of Athens. Leadership was in the blood of the Alcmæonidæ; leadership by means of the democracy had become their settled family policy; from generation to generation — Cleisthenes, Pericles, Alcibiades — we see it taken up by men of differing degrees of wisdom and virtue but all bearing in some form the hall-mark of genius. It is very interesting, in following the career of Pericles, to see how the ambition, the daring, the radicalism, and the willingness to stoop to conquer which characterize his mother's family are obvious during the period of his youth and rise to power, while as an assured leader of mature years he becomes increasingly cautious and conservative, till like his father he finds his chief support among the steady business men of the middle class.

In yet a third way the circumstances of his youth influenced Pericles. While Athens was still — and was long to remain — one of the most religious communities in Hellas, devoted to the worship of the old gods, her liberal commercial policy and her increasing intercourse with the Ionian cities were bringing in the "new thought" which had already developed across the Ægean. "Philosophers," who combined the teaching of argumentation with that of the beginnings of natural science, found eager hearers among the more thoughtful youth of the city. Pericles, in particular, received a lasting impression from his teachers, Damon (himself, to be sure, an Athenian), Zeno, and, above all, the serene and lofty thinker, Anaxagoras of Clazomenæ, whose central belief that the universe is the creation of one Eternal Mind, became his pupil's innermost conviction, at once elevating his thoughts and freeing him from the host of childish superstitions which, before and after him, played such a disastrous part in Greek history. Two instances are enough to show the gulf which separated such men as

Pericles, intellectually, from the majority of their fellows: in 413 Nicias, the richest and most respected citizen of Athens, rejected the last chance of saving his army and himself rather than march on the morrow of an eclipse of the moon; eleven years earlier, Pericles, observing that the steersman of his ship was greatly perturbed by the oncoming of an eclipse of the sun, held up his cloak before the man's face so that he could not see and asked him if he saw any harm in that, "and he answering No, 'why,' said he, 'and what does that differ from this, only that what has caused that darkness there, is something greater than a cloak?'"

The public career of Pericles covers about forty years and falls into two roughly equal parts. During the first, from about 470 to about 450, he is preëminently the party leader; from the latter date until his fall in 430–29, he is the statesman, standing above parties, the uncrowned king of Athens. Again, the first or partisan period falls naturally into two pretty equal divisions — that of his apprenticeship to politics as the eager and able lieutenant of Ephialtes, followed, after the assassination of that victorious and deeply hated enthusiast, by that of his own unquestioned leadership of the democratic party.

The fall of Themistocles (472) had been brought about by a coalition of the conservative, or Cimonian, party and the Alcmæonidæ. Its end accomplished, however, the coalition, like most such, soon dissolved, the Alcmæonids resumed their democratic policy, and we see Pericles from the beginning to the end of his career following in the footsteps and carrying out the long-sighted plans of the man his house had helped to overthrow.

The time was ripe for a democratic advance. The Constitution of Cleisthenes, now forty years old, was in some respects like the English Reform Bill of 1832; it had accomplished a great change by transferring control from the aristocratic to the middle class, and the Athenian, like the English, middle class were inclined to think the reform an ideal one. Every Athenian citizen had the right to attend the Assembly and to vote on the measures prepared for its consideration by the Council; what more could he ask? To turn over the executive offices and the actual government of the state to artisans, peasants, and day-laborers, simply because they formed the majority of the population, would surely be the height of folly. Unluckily for persons of this way of thinking, Themistocles, by committing Athens to a maritime career, had made inevitable not only a steady increase in the numbers of the artisan class, — those engaged both in the shipbuilding trades and in the manufacture of articles for export, — but, as the ships were manned almost entirely from the two lower classes, had made those classes responsible for Athenian victories and Athenian empire. No wonder the men whose toil at the oar carried out the policies of their city were now clamoring for more voice in the decision of those policies.

Right athwart any movement in sympathy with this demand lay the solid bulk of the Areopagus, the bulwark of conservatism. Composed entirely of ex-archons, themselves necessarily belonging to the two upper classes (chiefly landed nobility and wealthy merchants), and armed with the right to veto any law on the ground of unconstitutionality, it presented, like the English House of Lords, which it in many ways resembles, a solid front of opposition to every constitutional reform. And just as in England there arose among exasperated Liberals the cry of "Mend it or end it!" so the Athenian radical leaders, Ephialtes and the young Pericles, realizing that none of their plans could be put through till this obstacle was out of their way, waged their first fierce campaign against the Areopagus.

The three-years absence of Cimon in Thrace gave them

an opportunity to make so much headway in rousing popular distrust, both of individual Areopagites, whom they prosecuted for fraud and abuse of office, and of the body as a whole, which they charged with conspiracy against the democracy, that the hero of the Eurymedon returned to a much altered community and was actually suspended from office and put on trial for having taken bribes not to attack Perdiccas. Pericles was one of the prosecuting attorneys, and the scandal went — for in Athens it was held scandalous for a woman to interfere in public affairs — that Elpinice, Cimon's clever elder sister who was supposed to supply what that gallant gentleman lacked in political intelligence, persuaded him to drop the case. The charge itself was so preposterous, however, that Pericles may well have preferred, for his own credit's and conscience's sake, not to press it; at all events, Cimon came off clear, was reëlected General, and for the moment was once more the most popular man in Athens.

Thus he was able, when Sparta in dire need sent for the help of Athens against her revolted Helots, to persuade the people "not to suffer Greece to be lamed, nor their own city to be deprived of her yoke-fellow." This generous and even magnanimous policy — for Sparta was not only a jealous rival, but under strong suspicion of being a treacherous ally — was warmly opposed by Ephialtes and Pericles, who maintained always the Themistoclean tradition of unsleeping hostility to the "natural enemy" of Athens. They must have got considerable consolation, however, from the departure not only of Cimon, but of his three thousand hoplites — for the heavy-armed troops, drawn from the solid yeomen of Attica, were the backbone of the conservative party. In their absence the city radicals had full swing, and this time they succeeded in bringing about a really great constitutional change, the transference of nearly all the functions of the Areopagus to the Council and the jury courts, so that from being the final arbiter on all questions of government and civic morals it sank to the position of a court for murder trials. By this success, moreover, the radicals pulled down their great opponent, for when the news of it reached Sparta, that city, realizing that her enemies were now in control of Athenian policy, began to mistrust Cimon's army, and sought a pretext for sending them home. The insult to so high-spirited a people was unbearable, and their wrath fell heavily upon the leader whose counsel had brought it upon them. Cimon was ostracized, and the reforms went merrily on.

The most important of these were the complete organization of the jury courts which Solon had instituted, and the payment of jurors, members of the Council, and almost all officials. At about the same time the archonship was opened to the third class — the artisans and small farmers. It was while these measures were being put through that Ephialtes was murdered, so that for good or for ill the responsibility for them has always been placed on Pericles. Both the merits and the motives of these decrees have been hotly debated by historians ancient and modern. It was freely charged that Pericles bought his popularity and power, outbidding the public-spirited generosity of the wealthy and free-handed Cimon by this expenditure of the city's money, enabling and encouraging the unfit to enter politics and law for a living. On the other hand, it is obvious that the throwing open of offices to the poorer citizens amounted to nothing unless they could afford to hold them, and that the whole elaborate system of jury courts, which required many hundreds of citizens to sit daily, would become a farce or an engine of oppression in the hands of the wealthy, unless the jurors were compensated for the loss of their earning-time. As the allowance was barely enough for a day's food, it seems absurd to call it a bribe. The real importance of the measure was its effect in completing and confirming the rule of the people, — a degree of self-government never before attained by any state, — and it is by the results of that rule that it should be judged.

So complete was the victory that the conservatives gave up the fight. Moreover, Sparta had so estranged them by her insult that they were willing to fall in with the Periclean policy of alliance with Argos and Thessaly and open enmity with Lacedæmon. All they asked as the price of their full support was that the war with Persia should also be kept up and Cyprus freed. To this the democrats made no objection, — the extension of naval power and of the trade that "followed the flag" was always welcome to the city laborers, — and so was launched the policy of *radical imperialism*, the effort of the Athenian people to win the leadership of continental Greece while fulfilling its task of clearing all Hellenic seas and coasts of the barbarians.

It was a vast and thrilling program — too vast, as events were to prove. Athens, in the pride of her prime, overestimated her own powers, and Pericles, whether or not against his better judgment, rode on the crest of the wave to temporary and dazzling victories, followed by inevitable loss. It is unnecessary to trace here the thick-crowding events of the next ten years. The crushing victory over the nearest rival, Ægina, the daring and romantic Egyptian expedition with its false dawn of success, the momentary check at Tanagra, lighted by its chivalrous episode of the sacrifice of Cimon's friends and his recall at the suggestion of Pericles, the conquest of Bœotians, Phocians, Locrians, the completion of the Long Walls, all placed Athens at a height of power which she was never to reach again. The price was too heavy. Athens had not the "man-power" to go on winning victories at such cost, and

Pericles was the first to realize the fact. The tide was turning: the Egyptian adventure ended in catastrophe; Cyprus was lost; in Greece all sides were war weary. In 450 Cimon, sent to Sparta to negotiate a peace, secured at least a five-year truce. To him that meant the concentration of Athens upon her historic task of fighting Persia, and Pericles consented to one more expedition. It was Cimon's last; he died in Cyprus, and the peace party, of which Pericles was now the recognized head, gained control of Athenian policy.

The "Peace of Callias" (448?) marked the end of the great fifty years' war between Greece and the Barbarians and left Athens practically mistress of the Ægean and the Propontis. The people, nourished on the tradition of undying pursuit of the national foe, were not over pleased, but Pericles knew when Athens had reached her limit, even in sea power. On land, he had to learn that she had passed it. A series of losses and revolts, emphasized by the disastrous defeat at Coronea, put her back almost to where she had been in 461. An actual attack on the city by a Spartan army was barely staved off, and in 446–45 a general peace for thirty years was concluded between Athens on the one side and the Peloponnesian League on the other. Athens kept Ægina and saved the indispensable Eubœa, but she lost Megara and all her land empire except the ever-faithful little friend, Platæa. Henceforth two facts were firmly established: that Greece could be united under no single power, but must remain divided into two more and more opposing factions, and that Athens must seek her greatness wholly upon the sea.

These two facts were the foundation stones of all the future foreign policy of Pericles. For fourteen years of peace and two of war he built upon them with a master hand. No more aggression, no more far-flung, alluring adventures. The task of Athens was to consolidate her island empire

and hold it firmly, even sternly, yet on the whole benevo-
lently; in Greece to maintain a front of dignified neutrality,
behind which she might gather all the resources necessary
for the universal conflict, the shattering of the Greek world,
which he saw as inevitable. Yet, while his strong sense of
reality made him keep this "dualism," this fundamental
conflict of Athenian and Spartan interests and civilizations
always in mind, there was another side of his nature, a lofty
idealism, which is perhaps his most attractive feature, and
which kept him hoping against hope for the possibility of a
nobler unity than the victory of either side could bring
about. Pan-Hellenism was the dream which once and again
he invited his fellow Greeks to share with him. After the
Peace of Callias, he sent word to all the Hellenic states
(except those of Sicily and Magna Græcia) that the great
Hellenic task had been completed and that it remained for
them to unite, through a Congress to which Athens invited
them, in restoring the temples of the gods, giving thanks by
votive offerings for the common deliverance, and keeping
the rescued seas free for all comers. It was a broad-minded
and high-minded suggestion, but it came from an Athens
at the height of her power and it fell upon ears deafened
by suspicion. Years later, Pericles thought he had found
another chance for the expression of this ideal in the great
scheme of a Pan-Hellenic re-founding of the destroyed city
of Sybaris. This time there was a brief response: Peloponnesians, Ionians, Athenians went forth rejoicing to found
the new city of brotherly love, but soon they fell a-quarrel-
ing, and Thurii became like any other faction-ridden town.
"The great deed was too great."

Another great dream, the fulfillment of which might have
saved Athens and in the end all Greece, seems never to have
occurred to Pericles. This was the widening of Athenian
citizenship so as to include the resident aliens who formed

so large and important a part of the city population, and, in some form or other, to take in on a basis of equal partnership the members of the Empire. So far from moving in this direction, the policy of Athens became increasingly narrow. It was one of the vices of the democracy that the more powerful and prosperous it became, the more jealously it guarded its privileges. Marriages with non-citizens, if not strictly legal, had been common and openly recognized, especially among the nobility, and some of Athens' most illustrious men — for instance, Miltiades and probably Themistocles — were children of such unions. Now, however (451), a law (perhaps an old one revived) was put in force, penalizing such marriages by declaring their children illegitimate. The motive — as well as the extent to which mixed marriages had been winked at — becomes clear when we see that on the occasion of a great gift of corn from Psammetichus of Egypt, to be divided equally among the citizens, the lists were purged of some five thousand names! The decree of 451, attributed to Pericles, was so shortsighted and so patently selfish that it is hard to believe that he did more than assent to its passage as one of the sops that even he must throw from time to time to the Demos. If so, he was justly punished.

As to the subject allies, the difference in status between them and the imperial city was even emphasized by one of Pericles's favorite measures, the planting of cleruchies, or colonies of Athenian citizens, in different parts of the empire. These served the double purpose of relieving the pressure of population at home and providing what were practically garrisons abroad, but they were as bitterly resented by the allies as they were popular at Athens.

Pericles was frankly imperialistic. He had no idea of lifting the allies to an equality with Athens; what he would do for them was to give them a mistress so surpassing in beauty,

in civilization, in private justice and individual liberty, as
well as in power and glory, that obedience to her should be
more profitable and delightful than freedom itself. Athens,
as he proudly declared in his greatest oration, was "the
school of Hellas," copying none but setting an example to
all. She had achieved, as he saw her, the reconciliation of
what no one state had ever combined, the greatest amount
of individual liberty, the greatest hospitality aud liberality
of spirit, with the most perfect obedience to law; the greatest ease and pleasantness of living with the highest degree
of military valor; the fullest control of the luxuries of all
the trading world with the most marked simplicity of taste
and manners. Therefore, he could say with quiet pride:
"No enemy who comes against her is indignant at the
reverses which he sustains at the hands of such a city; *no
subject complains that his masters are unworthy of him.*"

The key to his imperial policy is in those words. Nor was
the appeal of Athenian civilization without effect. However
restive the subject cities may have been, there was in each
a strong party which looked to Athens as its head and ex-
emplar, while individual "colonials," like Herodotus the
historian, left their native towns to merge themselves whole-
heartedly in the glory of Athens. Upon the finest minds in
the city itself the ideal of Pericles worked with compelling
force. Sophocles, not only the supreme tragic poet of the
time, but the very type of the moderate conservative, the
Greek ideal of serene piety and harmonious virtue, came
over completely to his side, and served as one of the Treas-
urers of the Delian League at the moment when that
League was definitely and openly converted into an Empire.
Andocides, Callias (the richest man in Athens), Phormio,
and among the younger men the ill-fated Nicias and
Lamachus were others among the conservatives who, seeing
that Pericles held a consistent policy and was the ruler, not

the puppet, of the mob, forgave his constitutional changes
for the sake of his glorification of Athens. One of his closest
friends and fellow-workers was Phidias, and together they
planned the most beautiful buildings and statues which the
world has ever known. After 2350 years the world is still
feeling about the mutilated remains of these works what
Plutarch felt when they were already 500 years old: "For
every particular piece of his work was immediately even at
that time, for its beauty and elegance, antique; and yet in
its vigor and freshness looks to this day as if it were just
executed. There is a sort of bloom of newness upon these
works of his, preserving them from the touch of time, as if
they had some perennial spirit and undying vitality mingled
in the composition of them." Well might Pericles say, "We
shall not be without witnesses; there are mighty monuments
of our power which will make us the wonder of succeeding
ages." Well might his final appeal to his fellow-countrymen
be "to fix their eyes upon the greatness of Athens until they
became filled with the love of her."

Over such an Athens, so beautiful, so proud, so busy,
prosperous, and joyous, Pericles now held undisputed sway.
As Thucydides says, her government, nominally the rule of
the people, was practically that of her first citizen. All the
threads of domestic and foreign policy were in his hands;
all important measures were prepared for the Assembly in
his closet. Year after year he was reëlected strategus and
put upon the principal building commissions. But his chief
power was unofficial — that of the leader of the Assembly.
Greatest of all *demagogues*, in the Greek sense of the word,
he was as far as possible from the type which the word sug-
gests to us. Economical, reserved, austere, he employed
neither the liberality nor the jovial manners of Cimon to
win popularity; if he ever yielded to the people it was with
the air of commanding them, and for the most part he did

command them.   He was not often seen in public; his
speeches were rare, carefully prepared, and irresistibly persuasive.   The adjective "Olympian" he may have won by
his lofty eloquence, but it is equally appropriate to his imperturbable serenity, the impersonal indifference with which
he lightly put aside the shafts of his enemies.   Plutarch tells
how once, being followed to his home at nightfall by a
loud-mouthed fellow who had been reviling him all day
in the market-place, he merely told one of his servants,
as he stepped inside, to take a light and see the man safe
home.

Another quality, which impressed his contemporaries
even more than it would ourselves, was his disinterestedness.   "Graft" was the typical vice of Greek statesmen,
even some of the greatest.   Themistocles was said to have increased his fortune a hundredfold during his political career;
Pericles died without having added one drachma to his
patrimony.   He did not even engage in legitimate business,
but gave his entire time to the state, leaving his private
affairs in the hands of one trusted slave-steward, who managed them with the most exact economy.

There is something so unusually harmonious about the
character of Pericles, such a balance of qualities, interests,
and accomplishments, that his personality is harder to
realize than one of more irregular outline.   It is like his
portrait bust, so serenely classic as to be almost unbeliev-
able.   Just as in regard to his looks it is quite a relief to
know that there *was* an irregularity, — the unusually high
head (concealed by the helmet) which was the favorite
object of jesters of the day, — so we turn gladly to that
trait which was indeed no defect, but an exception, in one
who was otherwise normal almost to a fault.   This was his
devoted affection for Aspasia.

In early life Pericles had married a cousin, by whom he

had two sons. The marriage proved uncongenial and was dissolved by mutual consent, Pericles, according to approved Athenian custom, providing another husband for his divorced wife. Shortly after, he established as mistress of his house a brilliant and accomplished woman whom, a few years before, he might have married legally. But Aspasia was from Miletus, and the unwise law of 451 made it impossible to give her more than the standing of what in European courts to-day is known as a "morganatic" wife. No union that we know of in Greek history, however, comes so near our modern ideal of domestic happiness as that of Pericles and Aspasia. As long as he lived she was not only his dearest friend and most trusted counselor, but she shared his intimacies with the most distinguished thinkers and artists of the day and gave to his hospitality the grace and charm of an accomplished hostess. Not only did the ablest men of Athens frequent her "salon" and profess themselves her pupils in eloquence and philosophy, but some even dared to bring their wives — an unheard-of innovation in Athenian social life. It is no wonder, perhaps, that conservative feeling, always particularly sensitive in what concerns the family, took alarm at these mixed gatherings and at the unsettling ideas about marriage and women's education which were said to be discussed at them; the "foreign woman" was more and more regarded as a danger to the good old ways of Athens, and when the enemies of Pericles finally gathered courage to attack him they chose his connection with her as the weakest spot in his armor.

The real animus of this attack was the exasperation of those who desired a more spirited foreign policy. For ten years the Peace of 446 had been strictly kept. The revolt of Samos, to be sure, had been put down promptly and sternly, but the Carians had been allowed to fall away, the Empire, so far from increasing in extent, had actually shrunk a little, and all dreams of western adventure had been absolutely frowned upon. In Greece the opposing forces of Empire and League were watching each other narrowly, but so far the balance of power had been kept, and as long as the "elder statesmen" of Athens, Sparta, and Corinth held the helm peace was likely to continue. This did not at all suit the restless spirits of the radical democracy, nor the capitalist merchants and manufacturers who desired extension of their trade. Joining forces with the remnant of the old aristocratic party, they tried to gain their object by a flank attack — to discredit Pericles through his friends. So strong a prejudice had been excited among the people — who, for all their radicalism in politics, were in religion and morals among the most conservative in Greece — by the free-thinking of the circle who met at Pericles' house, that all his influence was unable to save the blameless Anaxagoras from a death sentence which he escaped only by flight, or the supreme artist, Phidias, from an imprisonment during which he died. But when the blow fell upon Aspasia herself, Pericles, contrary to all his habits, appeared in court to plead for her, and the citizen jurors were amazed and abashed by the sight of their Olympian premier, whom no accusation had ever perturbed, no insult ruffled, bursting into a passion of tears when he faced the loss of the woman he loved more than life.

This turned the tide. The great middle party closed in solidly behind Pericles, and all immediate danger to his ascendancy was passed. But the days of peace were numbered. The quarrel between the two great naval states of Corinth and Corcyra put squarely up to Athens the decision as to which side she would take, and a decision either way, so delicate was the balance of power, was sure to bring on a general war. Pericles, who had kept the peace so long and well, was convinced that the hour had struck. Already he

was taking in sail for the storm he saw coming from the
Peloponnesus; a decree was passed to borrow no more
money from the treasury of Athena for the adornment of
her city. As decided as he was cautious, he would have had
Athens take her stand once for all by making a complete
alliance with Corcyra, but the people, not quite ready for
war with Corinth, compromised on a defensive one.

The next three years were ones of great tension. Athenian
marines fought Corinthians off the headlands of Corcyra
and Athenian hoplites defeated Peloponnesians outside the
walls of Potidæa, yet still the Thirty Years' Truce was
technically unbroken; Sparta shrank from giving the word
for a general conflagration, and hoped that if only Athens
were sufficiently impressed by the forces massing against
her, she might yield without fighting, as in 446. To any
such backward step Pericles was unalterably opposed. For
fourteen years Athens had kept her oaths and offered no
provocation to the Peloponnesians, but sooner than make
the smallest concession to their threat she would put all to
the hazard. To concede anything would be to concede all,
for it would put her in the attitude of a subject, not an
equal, of the Peloponnesian League, and the news that she
had stepped down from her high estate would be the death-
knell of her empire. So convinced was he that the time had
come for Athens to take a high hand and to speak with her
enemies in the gate, that he seized the occasion of a petty
border quarrel with Megara to hurl at her the famous
Decrees, shutting her out from the Athenian ports and
markets upon which her farmers absolutely depended. The
measure was so harsh, so aggressive, so out of all proportion to the provocation, that there were many protests
not only from the opposing party as such, but from conscientious Athenians who feared he was putting their city
in the wrong. Objection took shape in the absurd legend

which we see Aristophanes reviving years afterward in his "Peace": —

O most worthy sapient farmers, listen now and understand,
If you fain would learn the reason why it was she [Peace] left the
  land.
Phidias began the mischief, having come to grief and shame;
Pericles was next in order, fearing he might bear the blame,
Dreading much your hasty temper and your savage bull-dog
  ways;
So before misfortune reached him, he contrived a flame to raise,
By his Megara enactment setting all the world ablaze.

Against both scruple and slander, however, Pericles stood firm. Athens had thrown down the gauntlet; let come what would!

What came, the world knows to its cost. Pericles lived through only two years of the great war which was to end in the downfall of his city. During the first he maintained his leadership under one of the severest tests to which it could be put. As Themistocles had persuaded the Athenians to give up their city to the Persians and seek safety and victory behind the "wooden walls" of their fleet, so Pericles called upon them to sacrifice their farms and orchards, their cottages and villas, and, thronging within the impregnable Long Walls which secured their access to the sea, defy the enemy to deal them any real injury. "Let us give up lands and houses," he said, "but keep a watch over the city and the sea. We should not under any irritation at the loss of our property give battle to the Peloponnesians, who far outnumber us. Mourn not for houses or lands, but for men; men may give these, but these will not give men. If I thought you would listen to me, I would say to you: Go yourselves and destroy them, and thereby prove to the Peloponnesians that none of these things will move you. . . . Such is the power which the empire of the sea gives."

Bitter as was the experience, the Attic farmers stood it, getting some consolation from the naval raids which Pericles permitted upon the exposed coasts of their enemies. The defensive policy for which he stood was thoroughly sound and must in time have worn out the foe, but it put a tremendous strain upon his popularity, and an utterly unexpected calamity made the strain too great to bear. The awful disaster of the plague descended upon the overcrowded city, and when the black cloud lifted, Athens was changed forever. Not only was her population, cut down by one third, never again to reach its mark in 431, but the demoralization of those awful years had gone deep. It was a different Demos, more nervous, more fickle, more suspicious, and more cruel, which howled assent to the vengeful proposals of Cleon, from that which had felt itself at once convinced and ennobled by the eloquence of Pericles.

And in the catastrophe Pericles himself had gone down. In vain he pointed out that even in her agony Athens was winning the war; the people were frantic for peace and would have accepted any decent terms. Sparta's, however, were impossible, and Athens had to pluck up such spirit as she could and continue the war. But not under her great leader. The jackals gathered around the old lion, and a charge of embezzlement, — as absurd as that which he himself in his youth had furthered against Cimon, — was brought against him. He was suspended from office and ordered to produce his accounts for the whole fourteen years of his rule. At his trial he showed the high spirit which marked his whole career, and though he was fined, his bearing left a deep impression, so that after a few months the people called him back to office. But it was too late. Misfortunes had come thick upon him — his sister, his two legitimate sons, nearly all his nearest friends had been carried off by the plague, and he himself was sick to death.

As a first and last favor, he asked the people to legitimatize
his only remaining son, Aspasia's, and the request was
granted. He died in 429, telling his friends with his last
breath that his chief satisfaction was that he had caused
no Athenian to wear mourning.

Pericles was not a statesman of the first rank, but he
stands high in the second. He was not the creator of
Athenian democracy or Athenian empire; he was rather the
artist who molded them to their consummate form. Under
him each attained its height; after him each fell into confusion and decay. By these facts he must be judged.

What he thought of the Athenian democracy of his time
we have already seen, and posterity has, on the whole,
agreed with him. Severe criticism, both ancient and modern, has been made of his measures by which the whole body
of citizens, without distinction of rank or wealth or fitness,
became the supreme, irresponsible ruler of the state. Especially blamed has been his system of widespread public employment. At its height, this meant that a changing body
of many thousand citizens were in the direct pay of the
state, besides the multitude which prospered on steady
wages from the contractors for great public works. In short,
his policy was not only to enable the poorest man to take
his part in the management of the state, but to associate
the glory and power of Athens, in the minds of her citizens,
immediately with their own prosperity. This association
certainly had its bad side, encouraging a very ugly sort of
corporate selfishness and a desire for gainful adventure, but
during Pericles' life the evils were not very apparent, while
the result of the whole system was brilliantly attractive.
Nowhere before or since, in all the world, has there been
a free, self-governing community at once so intelligent, so
cultivated, so hospitable, tolerant, and humane. Never,

probably, has so delightful a life been possible as that of an Athenian citizen in the age of Pericles.

The weak point, politically, in this democracy was just that which made it so charming socially and that of which Pericles boasted, — it was made up of irresponsible amateurs. Where every office was refilled annually and nearly every one by lot, where there was no continuing body anywhere in the state, no group of responsible statesmen, and no real limit — though there existed certain checks — to the power of the Assembly, there could be no steadfast, far-seeing policy, and the state must be at the mercy of sudden gusts of passion, sudden discouragements, and the flattering tongues of self-seeking demagogues. This weakness, which became so tragically evident after the death of Pericles, was hardly noticeable during his life, so steady was his hand on the helm, so complete the confidence reposed in him. Yet in a sense we must own that Pericles was responsible for Cleon and for Cleophon.

As to the relation between Athens and her subjects, he had no doubt whatever. He was an imperialist, convinced and convincing. The Athenian Empire was no artificial creation, no prize of deliberate conquest. It had developed naturally, inevitably, out of the services of Athens, the needs and weaknesses of the Ionian cities, a voluntary accession here, a punitive expedition there. It was like the Indian Empire of Great Britain, a vast, complex, unquestionable fact. You might have twinges of conscience as to how it had been obtained, but there it was; what could you do about it? Thucydides, son of Melesias, and his little group of high-minded anti-imperialists certainly scored a point when they said that Athens, in employing for her own adornment the treasury of the Delian League, was behaving like a vain woman rigged out in borrowed jewels, and that the spectacle was an insult to the most deep-seated

instinct of every Greek, his love of independence. But what
policy had they to offer? To break up the Empire and
restore to every city its original status? Nobody dared suggest such a thing, and indeed to do so would have been
simply to invite Persia to devour them one by one. The
lame conclusion of the opposition was that the treasury
should be returned to Delos and the tribute money stored
up there for possible future war with Persia. Over against
such half-way measures the policy of Pericles stood out
consistent, definite, and unashamed. He did not condescend
to palliate it. "What you hold," he told the Athenians, "is,
to speak plainly, a tyranny; to take it perhaps was wrong,
but to let it go is unsafe."

A third criticism of Pericles sometimes made is that he
"steered Athens straight for the Peloponnesian War." It
might be truer to say that, seeing the storm coming and
mindful of the dangers of a lee shore, he steered his ship
straight for the open sea. Unquestionably he never shared
the generous faith of Cimon in the possibility of a real friendship between the leading states of Greece. He inherited the
Themistoclean suspicion of Sparta; he was always preparing
Athens for what he believed to be the inevitable conflict.
But up to the last moment he did nothing to bring that conflict on. His policy was strictly defensive, studiously correct, until the line-up had become so evident that no choice
was left to Athens but that between war and giving up her
empire. Then he struck, and struck hard. Moreover,
although the war turned out so fatally for Athens, there is
every indication that the military policy of Pericles, if persisted in, would have brought her through safe, if not victorious.

When all is said, however, we realize that it is not as
democrat, or empire builder, or general, that Pericles holds
his place in world history. His glory is that when we call

up a picture of the Acropolis in its perfect prime, when we look at what time has left us of the marbles of Phidias, when we read the "Antigone" of Sophocles or the "Alcestis" of Euripides, — in one word, when we think of *Athens,* we think of it as it was in the Age of Pericles.

ALCIBIADES

(Died 404 B.C.)

"They love, they hate, they cannot do without him."
ARISTOPHANES: *The Frogs.*

EVERY now and then in the world's history is born an
individual of the class that Carlyle calls "Heroes," and
Emerson, "Representative Men," — one who gathers up in
himself the best qualities of his age, who most completely
fulfills its needs and gives it a lift forward. In the history of
Athens such rank we should all assign to Pericles. But besides these there appear from time to time men and women
even more strongly individualized, men and women whose
personalities are so intensely vital, made up of elements
so rarely combined, that they fascinate not only their contemporaries but succeeding ages, to a degree out of all proportion to their actual worth or achievement. Such, for
instance, was Mary, Queen of Scots, in whose most doubtful
cause serious scholars and learned historians have down to
our own day shed their ink as obstinately and enthusiastically as gallant gentlemen of the sixteenth century
poured out their blood. Of such was Alcibiades. Nor is the
comparison with Mary Stuart so far-fetched as it looks at
first, for there is a great deal in common between the brilliant, beautiful, accomplished, and utterly unscrupulous
Athenian of the fifth century before Christ and the typical
characters of the Renaissance. Try to imagine Alcibiades
in the heavy, formal, luxurious atmosphere of the Roman
Empire, in the spiritualized barbarism of the Middle Ages,
or the tremendous fanaticisms and loyalties of the Wars of
Religion; — one feels him at once to be utterly out of place.

But Alcibiades discussing statecraft with Macchiavelli, matching his conscienceless ingenuity against Cæsar Borgia, dazzling the court of the superb Francis I, flattering and fascinating Elizabeth Tudor — who cannot see him in his element? For in Alcibiades as in the typical men of the Renaissance the central fact seems to have been the same, an enormously vital, all-demanding, all-devouring individuality, to which the world is its oyster, and an immense, inexhaustible power of enjoying life.

Alcibiades was well born. His father, Clinias, won fame as a gallant and generous officer at Artemisium; his mother belonged to the ancient race of the Alcmæonidæ. He was thus a relative of Pericles, who became one of his guardians when his father, unluckily for the boy, was slain at the battle of Coronea (447). From the first, therefore, all the doors of the social aristocracy, of that inner circle of clubs and family groups which, as in so many a modern community, underlay the political democracy, were open to him as of right. From earliest boyhood, moreover, he was marked out by an extraordinary beauty, which "bloomed with him in all the ages of his life, in his infancy, in his youth, and in his manhood; and in the peculiar character becoming to each of these periods gave him, in every one of them, a grace and a charm." [1] This charm attached itself to his very defects, and even his lisp and his youthful affectations of gait and manner were admired. One gets a glimpse of the young dandy in the lines in which, later, a poet[2] ridiculed his son: —

> That people may believe him like his father,
> He walks like one dissolved in luxury,
> Lets his robe trail behind him on the ground,
> Carelessly leans his head, and in his talk
> Affects to lisp.

[1] Plutarch.   [2] Archippus, quoted by Plutarch.

Earlier than this, however, the insatiable ambition, the craving for dominance which was to govern his life, had shown itself in many childish episodes, of which we may quote one from Plutarch: "As he played at dice in the street, being then but a child, a loaded cart came that way when it was his turn to throw; at first he called to the driver to stop, because he was to throw in the way over which the cart was to pass; but the man giving him no attention and driving on, when the rest of the boys divided and gave way, Alcibiades threw himself on his face before the cart, and, stretching himself out, bade the carter pass on now if he would; which so startled the man that he put back his horses, while all that saw it were terrified and, crying out, ran to assist Alcibiades." That he won the leadership among his "set" which he so craved is shown by the anecdote of his actually putting flute-playing out of fashion because, as a schoolboy, he absolutely refused to distort his face with it and ridiculed it as below the dignity of a free Athenian.

Rich, handsome, reckless, fascinating, it was no wonder that Alcibiades grew up the center of a swarm of flatterers, who applauded his most foolish and reckless acts and egged him on to yet greater extravagance. In the midst of even his most outrageous follies we catch gleams of that lovable grace which melted the hearts of his sternest critics. Thus, having really shocked all decent folk by boxing the ears, quite unprovoked and for fun, of a highly respectable citizen, he went to the gentleman's house early the next morning, threw off his mantle, and offered himself to be scourged for his offense. Whereupon the outraged citizen not only forgave him on the spot but soon after made him his son-in-law! The same mixture of charm and impudence seems to have succeeded equally with the daughter, for when, at last wearied out by the open disrespect with which her husband treated her, she returned to her family and sought a divorce, Alcibiades suddenly appeared in court, snatched her up, and carried her in his arms straight home through the crowded market-place — a Petruchio-like treatment which apparently won back her affection, for she remained with him till her death.

There was one friend of Alcibiades' youth who did not flatter him or urge him on to silly "stunts," one whose influence was so strong, so excellent, so earnestly exerted, so cemented by mutual affection and mutual benefits, that its failure to make any permanent change in his character is the strongest proof that there was something fundamentally rotten, something past saving, at the heart of that tempting fruit. This friend was Socrates, and history affords few more picturesque contrasts than that between the homely, sturdy, shabby, middle-aged philosopher and the exquisite, dandified boy who persistently sought his company and followed him on his conversational rounds. That the quick-flashing intellect and sense of humor of Alcibiades should have been delighted by the well-laid pitfalls and dialectic triumphs of the Socratic method, as practiced on unwary citizens, is no wonder, but it must have been real regard which made the spoiled darling of Athens submit to be run after, "as if he had been a fugitive slave," pulled back from unwholesome pleasures, scolded and humbled by the uncompromising moralist of the streets. At Potidæa the elder soldier stood beside the young one, rescued him, wounded, at his own risk, and, eager to encourage his more honorable ambitions, pressed his claims to the prize of valor. One may guess that Alcibiades' pride as well as his affection was gratified when, years after, in the rout at Delium, he was able to return the favor by saving the life of his old friend.

Not only in his home city was the young Alcibiades known. As the only competitor, be he private person or king, to put so many as seven chariots into the Olympian games, and as the winner, in one fell swoop, of the first, second, and fourth (or, according to Euripides, third) prizes, he was famous throughout Hellas, and received special honors and compliments from the Ephesians, the Chians, and the Lesbians.

A more exciting game, however, than chariot-racing, even at Olympia, was always going on in a Greek democracy, and to a man of ambition and self-confidence its fascination was irresistible. At an earlier age than was common in his world, Alcibiades began to make politics his chief interest. This was during the so-called Peace of Nicias, the very name of which was a constant irritant to his vanity. Everything, good and bad, about Alcibiades, his penetrating intellect, his power of quick decision, his instinct for what the Germans call *Realpolitik*, as well as his impatient contempt of the limitations of popular morality and religion, marked him out as the destined rival of Nicias, — Nicias the respectable, solid citizen, the pious, the conservative, the peace-loving, the man who could cast away the last remaining chance of salvation for his army and himself rather than disregard the omen of an eclipse of the moon; Nicias, whose qualities so completely satisfied the popular ideal of morality that after his incompetence and vacillation had wrecked the greatest enterprize on which Athens ever embarked, had brought a miserable death upon himself and thousands of his fellow-citizens, and opened the way to the downfall of his country, the general verdict seems to have been that of the critical, unsentimental Thucydides: "No one of the Hellenes in my time was less deserving of so miserable an end, for he lived in the practice of every virtue."

Characteristically, the first fruit of Alcibiades' ambition was a practical joke, played at the expense not merely of an individual but of one of the time-honored institutions of the state. For when the factions of Nicias, Alcibiades, and another young aristocrat, Phæax, were becoming a bit troublesome to the public peace, a certain Hyperbolus, an unimportant fellow generally laughed at for his impudence, proposed the ostracism of one of the rivals, and Alcibiades, by a neatly planned coalition of forces, turned the ostracism upon Hyperbolus himself — the first time this punishment, which had been worn like a badge of honor by such men as Aristides, was ever inflicted on a mean or obscure person.

One distinction of Nicias' particularly irritated Alcibiades, — that of being the special representative at Athens of Spartan interests, for the position of *proxenus* (something like our *consul*) of the Lacedæmonians was hereditary in his own family; he had lived up to its obligations by paying special attentions to the prisoners taken at Pylos, and, but for his youth, would have been the natural person for Sparta to employ in negotiating the peace, which should in his opinion have borne his name instead of that of Nicias.

Thus personal grievance against Sparta and personal jealousy of the head of the peace party combined with Alcibiades' own political judgment to make him more and more the leader of the opposing faction — that which, if not yet exactly a war party, yet looked with the greatest suspicion upon Sparta's behavior as a nominal ally, foresaw a fresh outbreak of the great duel as sooner or later inevitable, and urged the fostering of anti-Spartan alliances in the Peloponnesus which should at the same time increase the resources of Athens and remove the first shock of war as far as possible from her own borders. However sound his instinct in this matter — and the comparative harmlessness to Athens of the Spartan victory at Mantinea went far to prove it so — the means he employed to commit Athens to his policy were characteristically unscrupulous. For Sparta, alarmed by the rumors that Athens was contemplating an

Argive alliance, hastened to send envoys fully empowered
to settle all differences and head off a move so dangerous to
her interests. These envoys had already come before the
Council and made an excellent impression, when Alcibiades
privately assured them, as an hereditary friend of Sparta,
that it would be the greatest possible mistake for them to
tell the Assembly, before which they must go on the morrow, that they came with full powers, as the people would
then impose upon them to any extent. The dull-witted
Lacedæmonians fell promptly into the trap and stolidly
denied before the Assembly what they had affirmed to the
Council; all Nicias' fair hopes of a settlement were undone;
the people were furious at having been played with and,
after a little more fruitless negotiation at Sparta, formally
entered into a defensive alliance with Argos as a counter-
poise to Sparta's with Bœotia. Alcibiades, now elected a
general, devoted himself for the next few years to cementing
in every possible way the new Peloponnesian league, moving
about with a small force from city to city, strengthening the
democratic factions, everywhere favorable to Athens, and
matching his wits against the pro-Spartan oligarchical ones.
When the long-delayed hostilities between Sparta and
Argos finally broke out, and culminated in the great battle
of Mantinea (B.C. 418), Athens, though providing a contingent, was not seriously involved in the Argive defeat,
and even Sparta's success in forcing an alliance upon Argos
and setting up an oligarchy there was quickly undermined,
since no sooner was her back turned than the Demos rose
and, instigated and guided by Alcibiades, overturned the
new government, began in feverish haste to build long walls
to the sea, and once more courted the friendship of Athens.

The next important occasion on which Alcibiades and
Nicias came into direct conflict was the fateful decision
whether or not to make the Sicilian expedition. Everything

about the undertaking — its vastness, its novelty, its elements of huge risk and equally enormous profit — was of
the sort to appeal to Alcibiades. Grandiose visions of a
Mediterranean empire, in which Sicily should be a mere
storehouse and port of call, are said to have possessed his
mind and those of his followers, so that "You might see
great numbers sitting in the wrestling grounds and public
places, drawing on the ground the figure of the island and
the situation of Libya and Carthage." In vain did Nicias
exert all his influence in favor of caution, moderation, and
attention to internal affairs; in vain, even after the fatal
vote had been taken, and he himself had been assigned, with
Alcibiades and Lamachus, to the command of the expedition, did he make one last effort to induce his countrymen
to reconsider their decision. His pointed, not overtactful
allusions to his colleague as a showy, extravagant young man
who should not be given an opportunity of "indulging his
own magnificent tastes at the expense of the state," and his
accusation against him of packing the Assembly with the
younger citizens only brought Alcibiades to his feet with an
assurance so superb that it is no wonder it dominated his
audience. Accepting, instead of deprecating, the personal
charges of Nicias, he declared his very profusion a patriotic
service and his haughtiness a proof of superiority: —

Apart from the conventional honor paid to such successes [as
his at the Olympian games], the energy which is shown by them
creates an impression of power. At home, again, whenever I gain
distinction by providing choruses . . . to strangers these acts of
munificence are a new argument of our strength. There is some use
in the folly of a man who at his own cost benefits not only himself,
but the state. And where is the injustice if I, or anyone who feels
his own superiority to another, refuse to be on a level with him?
The unfortunate keep their misfortunes to themselves. We do
not expect to be recognized by our acquaintance when we are down
in the world, and on the same principle why should anyone com-
plain when treated with disdain by the more fortunate? He who

would have proper respect shown to him should himself show it toward others. I know that men of this lofty spirit, and all who have been in any way illustrious, are hated while they are alive . . . but that they leave behind them to after-ages a reputation which leads even those who are not of their family to claim kindred with them, and that they are the glory of their country, which regards them, not as aliens or as evil-doers, but as her own children, of whose character she is proud.[1]

Then, rapidly summing up his own services to the state in the matter of the Argive alliance, and running over the weaknesses of the Sicilian cities, he swept on to one of the clearest, most forcible, and most uncompromising statements of imperialist policy ever made: —

Like all other imperial powers, we have acquired our dominion by our readiness to assist anyone, whether Barbarian or Hellene, who may have invoked our aid. If we are all to sit still and do nothing . . . we shall add little to our empire and run a great risk of losing it altogether. *For mankind do not await the attack of a superior power; they anticipate it.* We cannot cut down an empire as we might a household; but having once gained our present position, *we must, while keeping a firm hold on some, contrive occasion against others; for if we are not rulers we shall be subjects.*[1]

The die was cast. Nicias' only remaining hope, that of discouraging the people by piling up the estimate of the necessary equipment, was met by a vote of confidence empowering the generals to raise as large a fleet and army as they thought best, and immediately the whole city was alive with preparation. All was excitement, confidence, and hope, when one morning the town awoke to find the Hermæ, the square stone posts with carved heads that stood guard at the door of every temple and almost every dwelling, mutilated, every one. To get some faint idea of the shock caused by this mysterious outrage, one should call up a memory or a picture of some Roman Catholic city in southern Europe and imagine the sudden discovery that

[1] Thucydides.

every crucifix or every little wayside shrine of the Madonna
had been wantonly defaced. Even so, there would hardly
be the sense of evil omen, the panic and universal suspicion
which descended upon Athens. In the effort to discover
the criminals, some evidence was extracted concerning the
mutilation of other statues by young men in a drunken
frolic, and also in regard to profane parodies, carried on in
private houses, of the sacred Eleusinian Mysteries. Alcibiades was implicated in these charges, his enemies seized
the occasion, and the fickle public, exasperated by fear and
bewilderment, turned violently against their favorite. The
soldiers and sailors of the expedition, however, stood by him
manfully, while the Argive and Mantinean auxiliaries flatly
declared that they were going to Sicily on his account only
and if he were ill-used would all go home instead. His
enemies thereupon changed their tactics and put up certain
speakers to urge that the expedition must not be delayed
on account of one man, but that the trial should be postponed until his return. In vain Alcibiades saw through the
ruse and demanded immediate opportunity to clear himself;
he was commanded to sail at once, with the accusation
hanging over his head.

After seeing off the fleet, the Athenians became more than
ever absorbed in the mystery of the mutilations and prof-
anations, which they became increasingly convinced had
some secret, treasonable meaning, and finally decided to
recall Alcibiades. The Salaminian galley, bearing the request "in the mildest terms" — for an arrest in the midst
of his army would have merely meant a mutiny — that he
would come back and stand trial, caught up with the fleet at
Catane, before anything important had been accomplished.
Whatever strand of genuine patriotism, whatever fiber of
honorable ambition may have been woven into the complex
web of Alcibiades' character, this treatment by his country-

men cut short off. Under greater, but not wholly unlike
provocation, he made the decision of Benedict Arnold. Up
to this moment of his career, selfish, reckless, unscrupulous
as he was, he had been an Athenian; henceforth, for many
a year, he was to be Alcibiades against the world.

"I will make them feel that I am alive." This, his sole
comment on hearing that the Assembly had convicted him
of sacrilege, condemned him to death, confiscated his property, and decreed a solemn curse upon his name, — that he
was, in short, legally dead, — may be said to have been his
motto for the next period of his life. Already, almost on the
instant of receiving his summons, he had automatically,
as it were, begun his revenge by betraying to Syracuse the
pro-Athenian party which he had fostered in Messina.
Starting back as if to obey the call to Athens, he slipped
ashore at Thurii and made his way to faithful Argos. The
atmosphere of that city, however, friendly alike to him and
to Athens, was much too neutral to be interesting; revenge
and dramatic effect both called him to Lacedæmon. Frankly,
without minimizing the injuries he had done the Spartan
cause, he offered to pay for them by services as great; as
frankly Sparta accepted his offer, and well was the pledge
redeemed. The two measures which more than any other
acts of Sparta caused her final victory and the ruin of
Athens were the timely aid sent to Syracuse and the permanent occupation of Decelea; both were undertaken by
the advice of Alcibiades.

At Sparta he amused himself and delighted his hosts by
showing how completely he could conform his habits to
theirs. "People who saw him wearing his hair close-cut,
bathing in cold water, eating coarse meal, and dining on
black broth, doubted, or rather could not believe, that he
ever had a cook in his house, or had ever seen a perfumer,

or had worn a mantle of Milesian purple. For he had, as it was observed, this peculiar talent and artifice for gaining men's affections, that he could at once comply with and really embrace and enter into their habits and ways of life, and change faster than the chameleon. . . . At Sparta, he was devoted to athletic exercises, was frugal and reserved; in Ionia, luxurious, gay, and indolent; in Thrace, always drinking; in Thessaly, ever on horseback; and when he lived with Tissaphernes, the Persian satrap, he exceeded the Persians themselves in magnificence and pomp."[1]

The opportunity to be Ionian — welcome enough, one may guess — soon presented itself. News of the terrible disaster at Syracuse was filtering through to the Athenian Allies in Ionia, and Chios, Lesbos, Cyzicus were growing restless, ready, if they could get a promise of Spartan aid, to desert a falling cause. Alcibiades threw his influence in favor of Chios, started off with a few ships, and, suppressing the news of a check which the Peloponnesian fleet had just received near Corinth, arrived in time to bring off the revolt in both Chios and the neighboring Erythræ and Clazomenæ. The whole Ionian empire of Athens hung in the balance. The blow, coming so close on the terrible failure in Sicily, was indeed staggering, but never had her ancient spirit risen more splendidly to an emergency. By incredible efforts she renewed her fleets; Samos, faithful to the bitter end, provided a rallying-point, and the last long phase of the war, the struggle, year in, year out, for the mastery of the Ægean Sea and the coast of Asia Minor, began in earnest. No need to follow its details. In the foreground, slipping to and fro like a weaver's shuttle from city to city, fleet to fleet, here stirring up an oligarchical revolution, there lending a hint or a push to some slow Spartan admiral, above all linking up the Peloponnesian cause with the vast resources and

[1] Plutarch.

awful prestige of Persia, flits the brilliant, restless figure of Alcibiades. And in the background looms ever the sinister shadow of that great barbarian power for the sake of whose aid all the free Greeks, first the Spartans and at last even the victors of Marathon and Salamis, are to come begging, cap in hand.

One Spartan admiral there was, the manly and honorable Lichas, who revolted in angry disgust from the disgraceful terms to which he found his country had consented and refused flatly to be a party to such a treaty. While he commanded, the relations between Spartans and Persians became somewhat strained, and Alcibiades, as prime mover of the alliance, found himself looked upon askance in the Spartan camp. He therefore withdrew into the interior and proceeded to make himself indispensable to Tissaphernes. "For this barbarian, not being himself sincere, but a lover of guile and wickedness, admired his address and wonderful ability. And, indeed, the charm of daily intercourse with him was more than any character could resist or any disposition escape. Even those who feared and envied him could not but take delight, and have a sort of kindness for him, when they saw him and were in his company. So that Tissaphernes, otherwise a cruel character and, above all other Persians, a hater of the Greeks, was yet so won by the flatteries of Alcibiades, that he set himself even to exceed him in responding to them. The most beautiful of his parks, containing salubrious streams and meadows, where he had built pavilions and places of retirement royally and exquisitely adorned, received by his direction the name of Alcibiades, and was always so called and so spoken of." [1]

Henceforth Alcibiades, having no more to hope from Sparta, ceased to consider her interest, but urged steadily upon Tissaphernes the advantages of a waiting game, keep-

[1] Plutarch.

ing the Spartans in play with promises and moderate advances of funds, but cutting down the pay of the fleet by one half, refusing aid to the revolted cities, and always postponing the arrival of that long-looked-for Phœnician armada which was to turn the scale of naval superiority. In short, his advice to the wily satrap was to play off Sparta against Athens at the least possible expense and trouble to himself — a counsel most congenial to the Oriental mind.

And now, in the midst of the "barbaric pearl and gold" of the Asiatic court where he trailed his robes in perfumed luxury, the mind of the Athenian exile began to turn towards home. Might he not make double use of this advice which Tissaphernes found so good, and begin to build upon it some credit with his countrymen? The one dread of the generals at Samos was that Phœnician fleet; if he could promise that it should never round the capes into the Ægean, might he not be held to have deserved well? His first tampering was with certain officers of his own class, to whom he appealed as a fellow-aristocrat, suggesting that they by an oligarchical revolution and he by his influence with the Persian should combine to save the city from impending ruin. At first all went well with the plot, in spite of the opposition of Phrynichus, one of the generals, who saw through it but, in his effort to discredit it, involved himself in such a maze of lies, betrayals, charges and countercharges, that the army might be excused for not understanding what it was all about. Pisander, going to Athens, started there the idea of a change in the constitution, the recall of Alcibiades, and a Persian alliance; so desperate was the situation that considerable support was found for the proposal, and Pisander himself was commissioned to see what terms could actually be got from Tissaphernes. But this was pushing the wily Oriental too far; now that Athens was ready to court him, he began to smile upon Sparta, and the negotiations fell through. Whatever part Alcibiades played in the matter,— and it is a very obscure one, — he lost his usefulness to the conspirators, who decided to go ahead without him. The result was the famous revolution which upset in a day the hundred-year-old constitution of Athens, and seated the Four Hundred, representing an imaginary Five Thousand, in absolute authority over that proud democracy. The real democracy, however, was not within the walls; it was at Samos, manning the fleet, and it rose as one man when the evil news was brought. Renewing oaths to the ancient constitution, the soldiers and sailors declared themselves independent of the new government and, as their first political act, recalled Alcibiades.

A new phase, the most honorable of his checkered life, now opened for Alcibiades. At no time did his many-sided character appear to better advantage. His revenge had been accomplished, his treason, forgiven, was put behind him; independent, clear-sighted as ever, he

> . . . bent his keen, untroubled gaze
> Home to the instant heart of things.

The soldiers clamored to be led home to put down the tyrants; he had but to yield to this insistence to return in triumph, at the head of a furious avenging army, to the city which had cast him out. Even the injuries he had inflicted upon Athens were hardly greater than the service he did her now, when, by the exercise of all his persuasive powers in public and in private, he prevailed upon the men to relinquish so mad a step, one which would have left all Ionia, the islands, and the Hellespont to fall without opposition into the enemy's hands. Pride, moreover, as well as patriotism, restrained him from going home, even after Athens herself, having overthrown the Four Hundred, not only desired but commanded him to return. Not as a grate-

ful, forgiven prodigal, but as a benefactor and savior of his
country, would Alcibiades see again his native city.

And as such did he at last revisit her, after a most successful campaign in the region of the Hellespont, whither
the Spartans, weary of the deceits of Tissaphernes and hoping better things from Pharnabazus, satrap of Phrygia,
had moved the seat of war. For a moment, indeed, Alcibiades was near falling a victim to his own vanity, for,
visiting Tissaphernes, to boast of the victory he had helped
Athens to win at Cynossema, he found his old friend decidedly cool and himself under arrest. Tissaphernes, in
fact, was in bad odor just then with the Great King, and
inclined to make the Athenian his scapegoat, but Alcibiades escaped his clutches and, rejoining the fleet, led it in
a sudden descent upon the Peloponnesians in the harbor of
Cyzicus, winning a smashing victory. Mindarus, the Spartan admiral, was slain, and Pharnabazus fled inland, whither
Alcibiades pursued him and routed him once more, then
forced the Bithynians into an alliance, laid siege to Chalce-
don, and took Selymbria, almost literally single-handed.
For, entering the city, at a premature signal, with only fifty
men, he found himself at the mercy of the entire garrison,
— whereupon he coolly ordered his trumpet sounded and
proclamation made that the Selymbrians should not take
arms against the Athenians.   So magnificent was the
audacity that it succeeded, and Selymbria surrendered
without a blow. Greatly to Alcibiades' honor, he, with a
true Greek shrinking from the barbarities sure to accom-
pany a sack by his Thracian auxiliaries, granted excellent
terms to this city and shortly afterward to Byzantium, not
a man of whom, after the capitulation, was slain or even
exiled. Indeed, except that he is said to have been one of
the majority who voted for the extermination of the Melians,
Alcibiades seems to have been exceptionally free not only

from bloodthirstiness, but from that callousness to human suffering which long years of warfare was inducing in a race that formerly prided itself upon its sensitiveness and humanity.

Covered thus with laurels did Alcibiades at last sail into the harbor of Piræus, and all Athens came out, cheering, crowding, laughing, and weeping, to welcome him home. "Those who could press near him crowned him with garlands, and they who could not come up so close yet stayed to behold him afar off, and the old men pointed him out and showed him to the young ones."[1] Nothing could be more tactful than the way in which Alcibiades met his repentant countrymen. Addressing them in full Assembly, with neither reproach nor vainglory, he invited them to put, with him, the past behind them and look forward with hope and courage to the future. Restored to his full rights, his property returned, the curse upon him solemnly revoked, he resolved to wipe out the last remaining taint of impiety by restoring the ancient splendor of the Eleusinian rites which in his reckless youth he had mocked, and which ever since the Spartan occupation of Decelea had been shorn of their proper solemnities. "With great order and profound silence" the priests and celebrants, encompassed on all sides by the victorious army of Alcibiades, made under the very eyes of Agis and his garrison the long omitted march to Eleusis, — "an august and venerable procession" "wherein all who did not envy him said he performed at once the office of a high priest and of a general."[1]

Thus was Alcibiades restored to the very pinnacle of favor with gods and men. Athens worshiped the ground he trod on. His cup was full — too full. His reputation for success was such as no mortal commander could live up to. When, on his return to the coast of Asia Minor, every city did not

[1] Plutarch.

fall into his hands at the first summons, the fault must needs lie in his will, not in his power. When, in his absence and against his orders, his lieutenant engaged the Spartans and lost the battle, all the old tales of his frivolity, his self-indulgence, his wanton neglect of duty ran like wildfire again among the disappointed populace, who showed their displeasure by removing him from his command.

Stung to the quick, Alcibiades would neither go home to defend his integrity nor remain a subordinate in the army he had led so often to victory. In the rocky uplands of the Thracian Chersonese — which the Great War has made familiar to all as Gallipoli — he owned a castle, or fortified country-seat. Thither he retired, shaking the dust of Greece and Grecian affairs from his feet, to live like a Highland chief among his Thracian archers, with whom he hunted now the wild game and now the scarce less wild tribes of the interior. Once, for the last time, Athens gripped his heart. Looking down from his eyrie, his soldier's glance could see the Athenian fleet lying disorderly and unguarded in the wretchedly chosen harbor of Ægospotami, while the men, slack and undisciplined, wandered at pleasure up and down the shore. Swallowing his pride, the deposed general mounted his horse and rode down to warn his incompetent successors, but his advice to remove to Sestos and his warning against a sleepless enemy were alike rejected with insult. A few days later, Lysander fell upon the fleet and destroyed it utterly. The political greatness of Athens was gone forever.

With Sparta all-powerful in Hellas, by sea and land, there was now no safe place within its bounds for Alcibiades. Guided, it would seem, by the example of Themistocles, nursing great dreams of enlisting Artaxerxes himself in his cause and that of Athens, the indefatigable adventurer bent his steps toward Persia. Before he could gain the ear of the

Great King, he must win the safe-conduct and recommendation of Pharnabazus, and to that end he addressed himself to a long course of patient flatteries, while living quietly as a private gentleman in Phrygia. But even as an obscure exile, Alcibiades alive was unendurable to the victors of Greece. To friends and foes alike, to Athens crushed to earth, yet ever whispering of former glories, to Sparta nursing undying sullen resentment over unexpected betrayals and defeats, the name of Alcibiades was too closely associated with miraculous changes and upheavals; while he lived, anything might happen. A word from Lysander to Pharnabazus, and the matter was settled. What happened may best be told in the words of Plutarch: —

Those who were sent to assassinate him had not courage enough to enter the house, but surrounded it first, and set it on fire. Alcibiades, as soon as he perceived it, getting together great quantities of clothes and furniture, threw them upon the fire to choke it, and, having wrapped his cloak about his left arm, and holding his naked sword in his right, he cast himself into the middle of the fire and escaped securely through it before his clothes were burnt. The barbarians, as soon as they saw him, retreated, and none of them durst stay to expect him, or to engage with him, but, standing at a distance, they slew him with their darts and arrows.

So he died, in a corner, obscurely, almost pettily assassinated at his own door in a small Phrygian village, yet with a gallant gesture to the last. One sees the lithe Greek figure outlined against the lurid background which lights up with its ever-mounting flames the ring of skulking barbarians and the flashing sword that holds them all at bay. He died a Greek.

SOCRATES

(Died 399 B.C.)

ONE day in March, 423 B.C., there was performed in Athens a comedy by the poet Aristophanes, in which, as usual, he made great fun of well-known citizens and satirized the manners and morals of the time. The play opens with a dispute between Strepsiades, a crabbed old farmer, and his fashionable spendthrift son, Pheidippides, who has brought him heavily into debt. As a last resort, the father, pointing out a certain wicket gate, says to his son: —

That is the thinking-house of sapient souls.
There dwell the men who teach — aye, who persuade us,
That Heaven is one vast fire-extinguisher
Placed round about us, and that we're the cinders.
Aye, and they'll teach (only they'll want some money)
How one may speak and conquer, right or wrong.
   Pheidippides. Come, tell their names.
   Strepsiades.   Well, I can't quite remember,
But they're deep thinkers and true gentlemen.
   P. Out on the rogues! I know them. Those rank pedants,
Those pale-faced, barefoot vagabonds you mean:
That Socrates, poor wretch, and Chærephon.
   S. Oh! oh! hush! hush! don't use those foolish words;
But if the sorrows of my barley touch you,
Enter their schools and cut the Turf for ever.
   P. I would n't go, so help me Dionysus;
For all Leogaras's breed of Phasians!
   S. Go, I beseech you, dearest, dearest son.
Go and be taught!
   P.   And what would you have me learn?
   S. I'm told they have two Reasons — one the better
(Whatever that may mean), and one the worse;
The worse of these two Reasons, so they say
Puts forward unjust pleas, and always wins.

> Now, if you were to learn this unjust reasoning,
> Of all the debts that I've incurred for you
> I would not pay one creditor a penny.

Pheidippides, however, is too much afraid of losing his complexion to adopt a student's life, so old Strepsiades has to go himself. The door is opened by a pale and sickly student who complains of being interrupted in the midst of an important discussion: —

> 'T was asked by Socrates of Chærephon
> How many of its own feet a flea could jump;
> For one bit Chærephon upon the eyebrow
> And hopped from thence on to the Master's head.

On entering, Strepsiades finds a group of pupils groveling on their faces, while Socrates swings above them on a sort of perch — "I walk on air," he explains, "and contemplate the sun." When the old farmer, desiring to join the class, offers, in the usual form, to swear "by the gods" that he will pay the dues, he learns to his surprise that there are no gods, and that their plans are taken by "divine spheres" and clouds. Summoned by a prayer from Socrates, a chorus of women, representing clouds, appear upon the stage, chanting a very beautiful song, and Socrates explains: —

> It is these whom alone we as deities own: all else is mere fables and
>   lying.
> *Str.* Great Earth! that is odd — and is Zeus not a god? Sure his
>   deity's past the denying.
> *Soc.* Nay, from prating desist — your Zeus does n't exist!
> *Str.*   No Zeus? I can hardly believe it:
> Then perhaps you'll explain what occasions the rain, if it is n't
>   from him we receive it.
> *Soc.* Why, my answer is pat — 't is the Clouds give us that, for
>   it comes when they loom and they gather:
> Were it sent us by Zeus, they'd be no sort of use: he would rain
>   in the clearest of weather.

The old man, half pleased and half frightened, enters the school, but proves so dull-witted that he is ignominiously

turned out by Socrates, who offers, however, to accept his
son in his place. Pheidippides therefore is obliged after all
to become a pupil, but before he begins his lessons, the
Worse and Better Reasons have a great dispute as to which
shall be his tutor, and this gives Aristophanes a chance to
air his views about the education of boys, which, he believes,
has departed sadly from the good old ways. Says the Better
Reason,

Now first you must know, in the days long ago, how we brought
    up our youngsters and schooled them;
When to argument just 't was the fashion to trust, and when
    virtue and modesty ruled them.
Little boys, 't was averred, must be seen and not heard, and to
    school they must all go together,
Unprotected by coats, or by wraps for the throats, in the coldest
    and snowiest weather.
Where they learned to repeat, in a posture discreet, all the ancient
    respectable ditties,
Such as "Sound of the war that is borne from afar," or "Pallas
    the sacker of cities";
And to render with care the traditional air without any new-
    fangled vagary:
If you played the buffoon, or the simple old tune if you tried to
    embellish or vary,
And to show off your skill in a shake or a trill, or in modern fan-
    tastical ruses,
All you got by your trick was a touch of the stick, for the outrage
    you did to the Muses.

The Worse Reason is very scornful of this old-fashioned
stuff, but the Better insists that

            ... these are the precepts which taught
The heroes of old to be hardy and bold, and the men who at
    Marathon fought.

She goes on, —

You, therefore, young man, choose me while you can, cast in with
    my method your lot,

    ·   ·   ·   ·   ·   ·   ·   ·   ·   ·   ·   ·

And rise from your chair if an elder be there, and respectfully give
    him your place,
And with love and with fear your parents revere, and shrink from
    the brand of disgrace.

"He'll be known as a 'mother's boy,'" throws in the
Worse Reason, but the Better goes on: —

But then you'll excel in the games you love well, all blooming,
    athletic, and fair.
Not learning to prate as your idlers debate with marvellous
    prickly dispute,
Nor dragged into court day by day to make sport in some small
    disagreeable suit:
But you will below to the Academe go, and under the olives contend
With your chaplet of reed, in a contest of speed with some excellent
    rival and friend:
All fragrant with woodbine and peaceful content, and the leaf
    which the lime-blossoms fling
When the plane whispers love to the elm in the grove in the
    beautiful season of spring.

But the Worse Reason wins the day, and Pheidippides
when he reappears is fully instructed how to baffle all the
creditors. Unluckily, he is quite willing to turn his new
weapons against his father as well, and poor Strepsiades,
very woebegone, has to relate how, when he asked the boy
to sing at supper some good old favorite from Simonides,
he got for an answer, "You're quite behind the times!
It's not the thing to sing at meals, like maids grinding corn."
Moreover, he had turned up his nose not only at Simonides
but at the great Æschylus himself, calling him "A mere
bombastic blusterer replete with sound and fury," and when
asked to give something in the new fashion, had reeled off
a story from Euripides which so shocked his father that
the old man could not contain himself, and the wrangle
ended in the son giving the father a thrashing. Pheidippides,
not a bit ashamed of himself, now undertakes to prove by

the new logic that father-beating is perfectly reasonable and
correct: —

"When I was young did you to me administer correction?"
"Of course I did — it showed my care and natural affection."
"Well, 't is in just the self-same way that I by you am dealing —
I beat you just to show my love and proper filial feeling!
I'm sure it can't be just or right your floggings should be fewer
Than those that I received from you: I'm quite as free as you were.
Then, if you say to beat a child is merely human nature —
An aged man's a child again, of rather larger stature:
And all the more he needs the rod, for when you catch him trip-
    ping,
He has not the excuse of youth to save him from a whipping."
"But everywhere 't is held a crime — by no tradition backed
    't is!"
"Well, 't was a man in days of old who penalized the practice,
Just a mere man like you or me, his fellows who persuaded,
And if I make another law, I simply do what they did.
If they passed bills for beating sons, then surely I should gather
That I've a right to pass a bill for sons to beat their father."

He goes on, moreover, to prove that he is equally entitled
to beat his mother, and this is the last straw. Strepsiades,
desperate with rage at the new teaching which has created
such a monster, leads an attack upon the "Thinking-
house" and burns it to the ground. At the close of the play
we hear the outcries of Socrates and his favorite pupil: —

> *Soc.* O, I shall suffocate! O dear! O dear!
> *Chœrephon.* And I, poor devil, shall be burnt to death!
> *Str.* For with what aim did ye insult the gods
> And pry around the dwellings of the moon?
> Strike, smite them, spare them not, for many reasons,
> But most, because they have blasphemed the gods!

Popular as Aristophanes was, *The Clouds* fell rather flat,
coming out third in the competition. Socrates, at whom it
was chiefly aimed, was then a well-known middle-aged citizen of good repute, eccentric, doubtless, but a great favorite
with many men of wealth and high standing. The Sophists

(traveling professors of rhetoric, ethics, and science), with whom he is in this play confused, were also at the height of their popularity, sought by all the young men of fashion and making large fortunes from their fees. It was just this fad, of course, that Aristophanes was attacking, but the time was not yet ripe for his satire to raise more than a passing laugh from the crowd and a sympathetic wag of the head from the old fogies. The play, however, was not dead; its author, indeed, was particularly fond of it and later published a revised version. Twenty-four years after, Socrates, on trial for his life, spoke of it as really underlying the complaint against him: "'Socrates is guilty of crime in that he busies himself with prying into things under the earth and in the heavens, and making the worse appear the better reason, and teaching the same to others.' This is the kind of charge, and this is what you yourselves have seen in the comedy of Aristophanes, where a certain Socrates appears wandering around, asserting that he walks the air, and babbling many other follies, about which I confess that I understand absolutely nothing at all." "Nor is the report true," he goes on to say, "which you may have heard, that I undertake to teach men and charge fees for my instruction; there is not a word of truth in it."

What, then, was the truth about Socrates? The facts of his life are very few and simple. He was born in 469, the son of Sophroniscus, a statuary, or artisan-sculptor, and nominally followed his father's calling, but apparently paid very little attention to it, for his habits were so extremely frugal and hardy that he needed only the bare necessities of life, and his whole delight was in social conversation and in friendships, to which in democratic Athens poverty was no bar. He did not marry, moreover, until late in life, when his unbusinesslike habits were quite fixed, and his friends are said to have come to the rescue of his family. Originally, he seems to have possessed a little property and a house in Athens — though his *deme* was a suburban one — and belonged therefore to the middle class, or Zeugitæ, who served as hoplites in the militia.

His youth was passed in the great days of the Periclean Age, but we hear of no special interest on his part in politics, art, or literature. What did attract him from the first were the new subjects which were just beginning to be taught and discussed. For, with all her rapid progress in democracy, art, and commerce, Athens had remained in other ways one of the most conservative cities in all Hellas, holding fast to the old unquestioning faith in the gods and in the sacredness of the state itself. Now, however, the advance of natural science could no longer be checked; "wise men," mostly from Ionia, brought in their revolutionary theories as to what the universe really was. Anaxagoras, the close friend of Pericles, even taught that the sun was no god but a ball of molten, red-hot stone, revolving around the earth. To the multitude, of course, such ideas were rank blasphemy; Anaxagoras was driven from Athens. But the result of such teaching was a new division, running right across the old ones of birth and wealth: alongside of the ignorant, believing many stood the skeptical, enlightened few. These latter were in just the frame of mind to receive with joy the next set of newcomers, the "Sophists," who professed to teach the art of persuasion and included in that a whole philosophy of life. Some of these were men of high character and much learning; the bad meaning which clings to our word "sophistry" comes from the fact that their teaching might become so dangerous. "Man is the measure of all things," was their typical saying: that is, "there's nothing good or bad but thinking makes it so." There is no absolute truth or duty, for constitutions, laws, and moral customs have all been created by men at one time or another and may therefore be made over by them. There is something to be said on both sides of every question; one of these arguments may be weaker, to begin with, than the other, but a clever student of rhetoric will know how to turn a situation to his advantage by making it prevail. (This is, of course, the ground for the common charge against the Sophists of "making the worse appear the better reason.") For a clever, "enlightened" young man who had already lost his belief that his city government, just as it stood, was under the special favor and protection of the gods, this new teaching opened up wonderful opportunities for advancement. Crowds of pupils flocked to these teachers, whose fees only the rich could pay, and many of them later used the skill they learned in attempts to overturn the democracies in their states and seat themselves in power.

That the learning of the "wise men" early attracted Socrates we have plenty of evidence. He himself became well versed in mathematics, physiology and other branches, but he found them all unsatisfying. What was the use, he felt, of knowing that the world was or was not made thus or so, unless one knew *why* it was made and what was the meaning of it all? He turned then to the Sophists — according to one report, a friend paid his fees for a course of lectures by Prodicus — but was repelled by their shallowness. They took money for their teaching, and yet they had no truth to teach, — indeed, confessed that they had none. Where, then, was real truth, real wisdom, to be found? It was apparently at about this stage of his thought that a very curious incident took place. His intimate friend Chærephon — the same whom Aristophanes included in his satire — visiting Delphi, inquired of the oracle who was wiser than Socrates, and received the answer that there was no one. Now, Socrates, with all his scientific education, kept all his life his inherited respect for oracles; at the same

time, he had far too much humor and common sense to
take himself solemnly as the wisest of men. The interpre-
tation that he came to put upon the saying was that the
world was full of sham knowledge and self deception, and
that his own sole claim to wisdom lay in his frank acknowl-
edgment of his own ignorance. To prove Apollo right, as
he quaintly put it, was henceforth the main business of his
life; in other words, he became wholly absorbed in investi-
gating and testing the common opinions and judgments of
men, and showing where they were confused or unfounded.
The method he used, which has been called "Socratic"
after him, he had doubtless learned from his own early
teacher, the philosopher Zeno. It consisted of a sort of
quiz, or series of questions calling for brief, direct answers,
almost as in a game of "Yes or No." Armed with this
weapon, Socrates passed his whole time in the streets, the
market-place, the gymnasiums, — wherever there were men
to be met and questioned. No figure in all Athens can have
been more familiar than this sturdy, middle-aged citizen,
already developing a large stomach (which he tried to keep
down, to the great mirth of his friends, by taking dancing-
lessons), dressed always in a single rough woollen garment,
striding along, barefoot, in all weathers, and gazing rapidly
in every direction with large eyes set prominently in a
broad, flat-nosed, satyr-like face of quite peculiar ugliness.

Socrates is a man impossible to describe without contra-
dictions. Among the beauty-loving Greeks his ugliness was
proverbial, yet it seemed to exert a positive fascination over
the young men who swarmed about him. Nothing more ir-
ritating than the process of being proved a fool, before an
applauding audience, by his cross-questioning, can be imagined, but statesmen, poets, craftsmen alike submitted to
it for a whole generation. The secret must have lain in his
geniality. No wise man has ever been more human, more

sympathetic, more eager for companionship and affection. He could live as sparely as a hermit and yet make one at an all-night supper with the zest and jollity of a booncompanion. Much of his recorded teaching is as hardheaded and practical as Benjamin Franklin's; on the other hand, he was subject to odd spiritual experiences, such as his famous "voice" or "dæmon" — a presentiment which all his life warned him what *not* to do — and the fits of absorption, if not positive trances, which were so common with him that his friends would give up waiting for him when one came on, and simply leave him standing in the street till he woke up and followed them. The most remarkable of these instances is told by Alcibiades in Plato's story of *The Banquet*, very probably as Plato himself heard it from the speaker: —

One morning [during the siege of Potidæa] he was thinking about something which he could not resolve; he would not give up, but continued thinking from early dawn until noon — there he stood fixed in thought; and at noon attention was drawn to him, and the rumor ran through the wondering crowd that Socrates had been standing and thinking about something ever since the break of day. At last, in the evening after supper, some Ionians out of curiosity (I should explain that this was not in winter but in summer) brought out their mats and slept in the open air that they might watch him and see whether he would stand all night. There he stood all night as well as all day and the following morning, and with the return of light he offered up a prayer to the sun and went his way.

Socrates, it will be noticed, is here described as a soldier. He himself speaks of three campaigns in which he served, those of Potidæa, Amphipolis, and Delium, and of his endurance and his contempt of danger in two of these campaigns Alcibiades also gives examples.

At Potidæa [he says] we messed together, and I had the opportunity of observing his extraordinary power of sustaining fatigue and going without food when our supplies were interrupted at any place. . . . His endurance of cold was also surprising. There was a severe frost, for the winter in that region was really tremendous, and everybody else either remained indoors, or if they went out, had on no end of clothing and were well shod and had their feet swathed in felts and fleeces; in the midst of this, Socrates, with his bare feet on the ice, and in his ordinary dress, marched better than any of the other soldiers who had their shoes on, and they looked daggers at him because he seemed to despise them.

And during the disastrous retreat from Delium: —

You might see him, Aristophanes, as you describe, just as he is in the streets of Athens, stalking like a pelican and rolling his eyes, calmly contemplating enemies as well as friends, and making very intelligible to anybody, even from a distance, that whoever attacks him will be likely to meet a stout resistance.

It is from the same speaker that we get the most eloquent account of that personal charm which gathered so many followers about this poor, homely, unflattering and un-compromising man. These were, of course, of many sorts and affected by many motives. There were lifelong friends of about his own age, like Crito and Chærephon; youthful, devoted pupils, like Plato and Xenophon, who sat at his feet during his latest years and became his interpreters to future ages; clever, self-seeking young men such as Critias and Alcibiades, who hung around the group to amuse them-selves with the clever fooling and pick up arguments and methods that might prove useful to themselves. These latter usually dropped off after a while, but over Alcibiades himself, though the most reckless and unprincipled of them all, the master exercised a positive fascination, a hold upon all that was best in that complex nature, which the young man could describe only by declaring himself in love with him. Taking up the praise of Socrates at this same banquet, he compares him to the masks of Silenus, the old satyr, "which may be seen sitting in the statuaries' shops, having pipes and flutes in their mouths, and they are made to open in the middle, and there are images of gods inside them."

This, he says, is an allegory not only of the man but of his words, which "are ridiculous when you first hear them; he clothes himself in language that is as the skin of the wanton satyr — for his talk is of pack-asses and smiths and cobblers and curriers, and he is always repeating the same things in the same words, so that an ignorant man who did not know him might feel disposed to laugh at him; but he who pierces the mask and sees what is within will find that they are the only words which have a meaning in them, and also the most divine, abounding in fair examples of virtue and of the largest discourse, or rather extending to the whole duty of a good and honorable man." But most of all is he like the satyr Marsyas, who charmed the souls of men with his flute-playing, "but you, Socrates, produce the same effect with the voice only. . . . When we hear any other speaker, even a very good one, his words produce absolutely no effect upon us in comparison, whereas the very fragments of you and your words, even at second hand and however imperfectly repeated, amaze and possess the souls of every man, woman, and child who comes within hearing of them. . . . For my heart leaps within me more than that of any Corybantian reveler, and my eyes rain tears when I hear them. . . . I have heard Pericles and other great orators, but though I thought that they spoke well, I never had any similar feeling; my soul was not stirred by them, nor was I angry at the thought of my own slavish state. But this Marsyas has often brought me to such a pass that I have felt as if I could hardly endure the life which I am leading . . . and I am conscious that if I did not shut my ears against him and fly from the voice of the siren, he would detain me until I grew old sitting at his feet. For he makes me confess that I ought not to live as I do. . . . And he is the only person who ever made me ashamed, which you might think not to be in my nature."

Such was the man whom the conservative poet already, during the prosperous and confident period known as that of the Peace of Nicias, picked out for attack as the chief underminer of the old order in Athens. During the next twenty years events moved fast and tragically. The Sicilian disaster, the treachery of Alcibiades, the enemy's occupation of Decelea, the short-lived oligarchic revolution of the Four Hundred, the crushing defeat at Ægospotami, the heart-breaking surrender to Sparta, the deep mortification of the pulling down of the Long Walls, the hateful tyranny of the Thirty, the restoration at last of the democracy — at the end of such an experience a city impoverished, humiliated, betrayed by its "best" citizens, shorn of its empire and almost of its independence, might well, looking back to the days of its splendor and its pride, seek for the underlying reasons of its downfall and cast about for victims on whom to wreak its bitterness. No wonder that with guides like Aristophanes to point the way men began to put the blame on the new education which had borne such poisonous fruit. In the good old days, they said, men had learned enough when they knew how to worship the gods, obey the laws, and serve the state; then Athens was invincible; she it was who beat back the Persian and saved Hellas, who built up a vast and mighty empire, and withstood the shock of the whole Peloponnesus leagued against her; her misfortunes began when mockers and reprobates like Alcibiades insulted the gods and went over to the national enemy, when cruel and selfish aristocrats like Critias conspired to overthrow the Constitution and to tyrannize over the free people of Athens. And who had been the teacher of these men but that same old vagabond stone-cutter whom Aristophanes had shown up so deservedly, long ago? The other Sophists[1]

[1] The persistent confusion of Socrates with the Sophists whom he particularly criticized is very like that of Socialists and Anarchists now — although their views are diametrically opposed.

had come and gone like evil birds of passage, but he at least was still within reach, still tramping the streets in his silly old cloak and badgering better men than himself. True, his talk was ever of such things as wisdom and virtue, temperance and justice, but when had he ever shown willingness to serve the state as an active citizen should? Once, just once, in his long life, had he offered himself for the lot and served his term in the Council — and what use had he made of the position? On the day when it was his turn to preside over the Assembly he had deliberately thwarted the will of the sovereign people by refusing, on a mere point of order, to put to the vote a proposal to execute those admirals who had abandoned their drowning sailors at Arginusæ. When, indeed, had he ever spoken with respect of the people or the constitution? Was he not forever holding up to ridicule that safeguard of pure democracy, election by lot, and pointing out that no one would venture to choose his cook or his tailor as he chose his senators and magistrates? True, he did refuse to obey the Thirty when they ordered him to help arrest an innocent citizen — let that stand to his credit — but did he leave Athens with the real, unquestioned democrats, with even his own bosom friend, Chærephon? Not he! He stayed on, evidently under the protection of his former pupil, the unspeakable Critias, until better patriots than he drove out the tyrants. And now that our afflicted, beloved city is herself again, though sad and poor, now that she must set herself to the long task of rebuilding her ancient state, must we let this bad citizen, this corrupter of youth, continue to ply his old trade in our streets and teach still another generation to despise the religion and the laws which were good enough for Aristides and the men of Marathon?

Such, roughly enough, were the ideas of many perfectly well-meaning, if not very intelligent men in the year 399, and of these a very fair example was a certain Anytus, a well-to-do, highly respectable citizen, devoted to the cause of the restored democracy, who, together with two less prominent persons, a third-rate tragic poet named Meletus, and Lycon, a minor politician, brought against Socrates a formal charge of corrupting the youth by his teaching and professing disbelief in the national gods. The trial, since it concerned a religious offense, took place in the court of the "king-archon," and the case was argued before five hundred and one citizen jurors, chosen, of course, by lot, as well as in the presence of a crowd of interested spectators. Socrates, appearing in court for the first time, whether as plaintiff or defendant, in all his seventy years, pleaded his own case, as coolly and cheerfully as if he were carrying on one of his favorite conversations in the market-place. The account of this famous trial which Plato gives in his "Apology" and which doubtless reports faithfully the spirit and manner if not the actual words of his beloved master, should be read in full by every one who wants to know Socrates. A few extracts can only suggest the shrewd humor, the entire composure, and the deep underlying seriousness of the fearless old philosopher.

Almost his first words show that he realizes the central difficulty of the situation, the fact that what he actually has to meet is not the formal accusation, which is so absurd as to be hardly worth refuting, but the mass of prejudice which has been gradually built up against him in the course of many years and by many and nameless accusers — "unless some one among them happens to be a comic poet."

Declaring, then, as we have already seen, the picture of himself in *The Clouds* absolutely untrue, he goes on to sketch his life as it has really been, telling of the strange oracle and of his efforts to find out its meaning by examining all classes of men. Next, taking up the immediate charge against him, he proceeds to cross-examine Meletus, in whose name the indictment was brought — a hawk-nosed young man, we are elsewhere told, with long, straggling hair.

Come hither, Meletus, and tell me this. Have you not very much at heart that the young should be as good as possible?

Mel. Certainly I have.

Soc. Well, then, tell the court who it is that makes them better. This of course you must know; it is your business, for it is you who have discovered me, you say, to be their corrupter, and have brought me here, and accused me before this tribunal. Speak up, then, and tell us who it is that improves them. Do you not see, Meletus, that you are silent, and have nothing to say? And yet is not this silence shameful, and a sufficient proof, moreover, of just what I say, that you have never given a thought to these things? But tell us, my good friend, who does improve the young?

Mel. The laws.

Soc. But, my excellent sir, what I asked was not this, but who the man is; and he of course, to begin with, must know these very laws of which you speak.

Mel. These judges here, Socrates.

Soc. What do you mean, Meletus? Are they able to train up the young, and do they improve them?

Mel. Certainly.

Soc. All of them, or only some and not others?

Mel. All.

Soc. You bring us welcome news, by Hera, of a great harvest of benefactors. And who besides? Do these bystanders improve them, or not?

Mel. Yes, they also.

Soc. And the senators?

Mel. The senators as well.

Soc. But is it possible, Meletus, that those who sit in the public assembly corrupt the young, or do not they all too improve them?

Mel. They too improve them.

Soc. It seems, then, that all Athenians, except myself, make the young good and virtuous, and that I alone corrupt them. Is this what you assert?

Mel. I assert it most emphatically.

Soc. You are laying a great misfortune at my door!

.   .   .   .

But really, Athenian citizens, as I said before, it is clear enough that Meletus has never cared either much or little about these matters. Tell us, however, Meletus, in what way do you say that I corrupt the young? Is it . . . by teaching them not to believe in the gods in whom the city believes, but in other new divinities? Is this the teaching by which you say I corrupt them?

Mel. Most emphatically I say it is this.

Soc. Then, Meletus, in the name of these very gods of whom we are now speaking, tell me and these others here still more plainly what you mean. For I cannot make out whether it is that I teach men to believe in certain gods — in which case I myself also must believe, and so do not offend by being an utter atheist . . . or whether you charge me with not believing in any gods at all, and teaching the same to others.

Mel. That is what I say, that you do not believe in any gods at all.

Soc. To what end, O wonderful Meletus, do you say this? Do I not then hold, with the rest of mankind, that the sun and moon are gods?

Mel. No, by Zeus, judges, he does not, for he says that the sun is stone, and the moon earth.

Soc. Do you forget, friend Meletus, and imagine that it is Anaxagoras you are accusing; or do you hold these persons here present to be so stupid and unversed in letters as not to know that the doctrines which you ascribe to me belong to Anaxagoras of Clazomenæ, whose books are loaded with them? And the young men learn them *from me*, forsooth, when they can often hear them at the theatre, for the sum of a drachma at most, and can then laugh Socrates to scorn if he pretends that they are his own, — such singular doctrines too as these are! But tell me, in the name of Zeus, do you really think that I believe there is no God?

Mel. By Zeus I swear that you believe there is no God at all.

Soc. Nobody will believe that, Meletus, and I doubt whether you do yourself.

After a little more badgering of the unlucky Meletus, whom one can imagine stepping down very red and perspiring, Socrates becomes more serious as he meets the real charge, his unpopularity: —

"But," some one perhaps may say, "are you not ashamed, Socrates, of having followed a pursuit on account of which you are now in danger of being put to death?" To such an one I might with good reason reply: "You say not well, my friend, if you think that a man who is good for anything at all ought to take into account the chances of living or dying, and not rather, when undertaking anything, to consider only whether it be right or wrong, and whether the work of a good or of a bad man. Why, according to your opinion, all the heroes who fell at Troy would be but sorry fellows. . . ." It would be a strange act indeed on my part, O men of Athens, after my remaining in whatever post I was stationed by the leaders whom you had appointed over me, at Potidæa, Amphipolis, and Delium, and facing death like any other man, if, now that I am, as I think and believe, under orders of the God to pass my life in the pursuit of wisdom and in examining myself and others, — if now, I say, through fear of death or any other evil, I were to desert my post! That would be strange conduct indeed, and then might I in truth be justly arraigned in court for not believing in the existence of gods; for then I should be disobeying the oracle, and fearing death, and thinking myself wise when I was not. For to fear death, citizens, is nothing at all but to think you are wise when you are not wise, — to think you know what you do not know. For no one knows what death is, or whether it may not be the greatest of all goods to men; yet do they fear it, as if they knew it to be the greatest of evils; and what is this but the same old ignorance? . . . So that, if you were now to acquit me, in despite of Anytus, who has urged that . . . I ought not by any possibility to escape death, and who has moreover, assured you that, if I am let off now, your sons will all be utterly ruined . . . and if, in acquitting me, you should say: "We will not put faith this time, O Socrates, in Anytus, but will let you go, on the condition, however, that you no longer spend your time in this search nor in the pursuit of wisdom, . . ." I should say to you, "Athenians, I love and cherish you, but I shall obey the God rather than you; and as long as I draw breath and have the strength, I shall never cease to follow philosophy, and to exhort and persuade any one of you whom I happen to meet, saying as is my wont: 'How is it, friend, that you, an Athenian, of the city greatest and of most repute for wisdom and power, are not ashamed to be taking thought for glory and honor, and for your possessions that they may become as great as possible, while you take neither thought nor heed for wisdom and truth, and for your soul that it may become as good as possible?'" . . . Do not interrupt, Athenians, but keep that promise which I asked of you, — not to interrupt, no matter what I say, but to listen; for I think that you will gain by listening. I am now going to tell you other things at which you will very likely raise a clamor; but do not do so, I beg of you. You may be very sure that if you put to death such an one as I have just said I am, you will not injure me more than your own selves. Neither Meletus nor Anytus could injure me in the least: they have not the power; for it is not, I think, in the nature of things that a bad man should injure one better than himself. . . . Wherefore, O men of Athens, I am far from defending myself for my own sake, as might be expected; but for your sake I do it, lest in condemning me you err, by rejecting the gift which God offers you. For if you kill me, you will not readily find another man who will be (if I may make so ridiculous a comparison) fastened upon the state as I am by God. For the state is exactly like a powerful high-bred steed, which is sluggish by reason of its very size, and so needs a gadfly to wake him up. And as such a gadfly does God seem to have fastened me upon the state; wherefore, besetting you everywhere the whole day long, I arouse and stir up and reproach each one of you. Such a man, citizens, you will not easily find again, and if you take my advice you will spare me.

Finally, after telling why he has, obeying his "voice," kept aloof from politics, arguing that if he had really injured the morals of his pupils, their relatives would be present to testify against him, and explaining that he does not consider it manly or dignified to bring into court, as was customary, his own family to appeal by their grief to the mercy of the judges, he leaves his case to their consciences. After a brief interval the jury, having retired to vote, return with a verdict against Socrates by a rather small majority. The penalty of death is then proposed by Meletus, and it is the turn of Socrates, according to custom, to suggest a counter-penalty. Already he had had a good chance of escaping (indeed, Meletus, who probably would have preferred not to bear the responsibility of his death, seems to have been quite irritated with him for staying to stand trial); the close vote of the jury showed that he had many friends upon it, and a proposal of exile or even a considerable fine would almost certainly have been accepted. Socrates, however, had no mind to be let off. At first, indeed, be provoked his judges by what must have struck them as a supreme piece of insolence, declaring that if they really wanted to give him his deserts, they would vote him a pension for life as a public benefactor. After this piece of mischief he condescended to explain why he would not offer or even accept exile, since no other city would be even so likely as Athens to put up with his manner of life, and nothing would induce him to change that, and he ended by proposing a tiny fine — all he could afford — which the entreaties of Plato and other friends who were only too eager to pay for him finally induced him to raise to a more reasonable sum. It is not strange that after all this defiance the jury voted, much more heavily than before, against the defendant. Socrates bade them farewell in words so grave and beautiful that it is hard to cut them short. Death, he says, must be one of two things, either a dreamless sleep, such as all men find sweet, or a transition to another world where live the souls of all the departed heroes:

I, at least, would gladly die many times, if this be true; for to my thinking that state of being would be wonderful indeed, if in it I might have the chance of meeting with Palamedes and Ajax, the son of Telamon, and other heroes of the olden time who died through unrighteous judgment. To compare my own suffering with theirs were, methinks, no unpleasing task; but best of all would it be to examine and question there, as I have done here, and discover who is really wise, and who thinks himself so but is not. What, O judges, would a man not give to question him who led the great army against Troy, or Ulysses or Sisyphus or the thousand others, both men and women, whom one might mention? To dwell and converse with them and to question them would indeed be happiness unspeakable! . . . But you too, O judges, it behooves to be of good hope about death, and to believe that this at least is true, — there can no evil befall a good man, whether he

be alive or dead, nor are his affairs uncared for by the gods. . . .
But now it is time for us to go away, I to die, you to live. Which
of us is going to the better fate, is unknown to all save God.

As it happened, the sentence of death which Socrates was
so ready to meet was not carried out for a month, since the
sacred ship, bearing the fourteen youths and maidens in
annual commemoration of Theseus' victory over the Min-
otaur, had but just sailed for Delos, and until its return
no person could be put to death in Athens. This month the
old man spent in prison, comfortably enough and very cheerfully, conversing every day with his disciples, who were
allowed free access to him. Again he had a chance to save
his life, for his friends would have been only too thankful to
arrange for his escape by bribing his guards and smuggling
him over the frontier. Socrates, however, very gently and
affectionately, but firmly, pointed out that whatever they
had found to be true and right in happier days was no less
so now; that the one great misfortune, as they had long
agreed, was to do wrong, and that the greatest wrong a man
could do to his state was to break its laws. Since in Athens
he was born and in Athens, with all its faults, he had freely
chosen to spend all his life, the decision of Athens, when it
went against him, he was bound to accept. And to this
decision his friends sadly submitted.

At last came a morning when the little group of faithful
disciples stood outside the prison, waiting for the last sight
of their beloved master — for the ship had come in. When
the doors were opened, they found him with Xanthippe —
who has come down to tradition as a shrew, but who seems
rather to have been a fussy but devoted mother and an
affectionate wife — sitting beside him with her youngest
child in her arms. Already overwrought, she burst into
tears at sight of the visitors, and Socrates asked Crito, the
old family friend, to send one of his servants home with her.

He then turned composedly to his guests and began talking with them, gravely but not uncheerfully, on death and immortality. How far his arguments in the *Phædo* represent his own ideas and how far those of his great follower, Plato, who gives them to us, we can never know, but the little details of the scene — such as the interruption of the jailer, who warns his prisoner that if he overheats himself with talking he may have to take two or three doses of the poison, and the picture of Socrates sitting on his couch and gently stroking the fair locks of the youthful Phædo, who sits on a low stool beside him — are evidently true to life. After a while he and Crito went into an inner room where he spent a long time with his family, giving his last instructions to them all. It was nearly sunset when he came back and sat down again with his friends, "but he did not speak much after this." The jailer, coming to bid him farewell, burst into tears, and Socrates, gently refusing Crito's plea to wait till the sun had actually dropped behind the hills, sent for the hemlock and "took it right cheerfully, without tremor, or change of color or countenance, and, looking at the man from under his brows with that intent gaze peculiar to himself, said, 'What say you to pouring a libation from this cup to one of the gods? Is it allowed or not?' 'We prepare, Socrates,' answered he, 'only just so much as we think is the right quantity to drink.' 'I understand,' said he, 'but prayer to the gods is surely allowed, and must be made, that it may fare well with me on my journey yonder. For this then I pray, and so be it!' Thus speaking, he put the cup to his lips and right easily and blithely drank it off. Now most of us had until then been able to keep back our tears, but when we saw him drinking . . . we could do so no longer."

On the master's asking them, however, to let him die in stillness, they forced back their sobs, and after walking about the room a little, Socrates lay down upon the couch, while a gradual numbness crept over him. Just before it reached his heart, he uncovered his face and said to his oldest friend of all, "Crito, we owe a cock to Æsculapius. Pay the debt and do not neglect it." "It shall be done, Socrates," said he, "but think if you have nothing more to say." "There was no answer to this question. . . . Such was the end of our friend, a man whom we may well call, of all men known to us of our day, the best, and besides the wisest and the most just."

AGESILAUS

(Died 360 B.C.)

SPARTA was not, and did not wish to be, a nursery of great men. Her ideals were utter subordination of the individual to the state, and absolute equality of condition and uniformity of education among citizens; even for the kings the exceptions were trifling. Striking individualities were so thoroughly discouraged rather than fostered that it is no wonder we find few in her history. Of those few one or two, like Brasidas and Callicratidas, stand out as men of an un-Spartan humanity and breadth of vision, while others, such as Pausanias I and Lysander, surpass the average Lacedæmonian in genius and resourcefulness as much as they do in cruelty, deceit, and overweening ambition. There is one prominent figure, however, who may fairly be called the normal Spartan — abler than the mass, of course, but just about the person "whom every [Spartan] man-at-arms would wish to be." This is Agesilaus, who in 398 B.C. became king under unusual circumstances.

For some six years Sparta had held, unresisted, a dominion unique in history. A privileged caste supplying fewer than two thousand men of fighting age was holding down not only a great mass of inferiors at home but three or four millions abroad. Athens at her height, with seventeen times as many citizens, had controlled only half as much of the Greek world. And the control was absolute, as is shown by the degrading awe in which even a private member of this terrible ruling caste was held, especially among the Ionian Greeks. "All the cities," says Xenophon, "then obeyed whatever order they might receive from a Lacedæmonian *citizen.*" Nothing, of course, could have been worse for the citizen so obeyed, or more fatal to the old Spartan ideals of frugality, simplicity, and subordination. The Spartan who went out as harmost, or as mere traveler, returned laden with ill-gotten wealth and flattered with an outrageous pride. It was impossible to keep up the old law against gold and silver. An exception was legally made on behalf of the state itself; illegally, the rule was constantly evaded by individuals. Gross inequalities became evident; while some families grew rich, others sank below the threshold of ability to pay their scot to the common tables, and lost their citizen rights. Thus a constantly shrinking caste, itself demoralized by new vices, was dominating an ever-increasing mass of misery and discontent. Outwardly and inwardly, Sparta was attempting the impossible; new wine was pouring into her old bottles, and the result, however delayed, was inevitable.

There was a group of high-minded statesmen, of whom King Pausanias II was one, who hoped to meet the difficulty by strengthening the bottles. In imperial affairs, they opposed Lysander's brutal and perfidious policies, refused to restore the iniquitous Thirty in Athens, allowed many cities to throw over their decarchies — though not their harmosts — and generally stood for conciliation rather than oppression. At home, they would restore the pure Lycurgan discipline, put a stern check on the influx of foreign luxuries and manners, re-divide all property equally among full Spartiates, and strengthen the authority of the Kings and the Senate, as over against the Assembly and its annually elected representatives, the Ephors.

Lysander's policy was just the opposite and, while much less honorable in motive, showed probably a truer grasp of the situation. Realizing, on the one hand, that a world-dominion so unnatural as that of Sparta could be maintained only by a policy of "frightfulness," he saw at the same time that the system of checks and balances by which the executive power of the state was divided between one set of officials (the Kings), ruling by accident of birth, and another (the Ephors), by will of the people, was unequal to the greater tasks set by Sparta's new rôle, and therefore, on his recall from Athens, plotted a change in the constitution, by which the kingship should be made elective — for life — from the whole body of Spartiates. As the great admiral, the winner of Sparta's crowning victories, he might well hope to be the first king thus chosen; resting on the choice of the citizens, he need fear no check from the Ephors who represented the same electorate and who would, rather, become his ministers; thus concentrating in himself all the power of the state, confident of his own genius and un-Spartan adaptability to new conditions and new methods, he might well look forward to a dazzling career as tyrant of the Hellenes.

To bring about such a change, however, required an appeal to the superstition, rather than the reason, of the intensely conservative Spartans. Twice his plans were well laid to "work" the oracles, and twice they fell through at the last moment; — his confederates dared not. Giving up the whole plan, he turned quickly to another, which circumstances had just made feasible. King Agis died, leaving a young son, Leotychides, as to whose legitimacy there was some question, and a brother, Agesilaus, a man of about forty, of excellent reputation, especially for the hearty good will with which from childhood he had always met the severest requirements of the Lycurgan discipline. Lysander, who had known him well when they were boys, thought Agesilaus exactly the person he wanted for his tool, — a proof, says Grote, of how the Spartan education repressed all evidence of individual character, — and threw all his influence in favor of the rejection of Leotychides and choice of Agesilaus. This time he had to controvert, instead of inspiring, an oracle, for his candidate was lame of one leg, and an ancient prophecy bade Sparta beware of a lame reign. He was equal to the occasion, however, and explained that it would be Leotychides, as not a true descendant of Heracles, who, if he ruled, would make Sparta halt on one foot. Agesilaus was therefore chosen.

The outstanding fact about the new King was his pleasantness. Small, insignificant, and lame, in a community which set especial store by physical perfection, he had from childhood taken away all the sting of his deformity by being the first to make a joke of it and (like Walter Scott) refusing to let it keep him out of any exploit whether in sport or war. Moreover, as Plutarch says, "the goodness of his humor and his constant cheerfulness and playfulness of temper, always free from anything of moroseness or haughtiness, made him more attractive even to his old age than the most beautiful and youthful men of the nation."

His personal popularity was increased by the generosity with which, on succeeding to his father's estate — poor Leotychides being wholly thrown out of the family — he at once handed over half of it to his mother's kindred, who were among those whom the changing conditions had reduced to extreme poverty. But what sealed it was his complete departure from the usual attitude of lofty social superiority and jealous suspicion maintained by the Kings toward the Ephors. He went, indeed, to the other extreme, in regard to both them and the senate: "Instead of contending with them he courted them; in all proceedings he commenced by taking their advice, was always ready to go, nay almost run, when they called him; if he were upon his royal seat, hearing causes, and the Ephors came in, he rose to them; whenever any man was elected into the Council of

Elders, he presented him with a gown and an ox." In all this he was, of course, in entire harmony with the policy of Lysander, which aimed at government by a popular strong man, and it is very possible that he was acting by the king-maker's advice.

In the first event of the new reign, the discovery and prompt suppression of the ominous conspiracy of Cinadon, Agesilaus seems to have taken no prominent part. His opportunity came in the threatening attitude taken up by Persia. The real danger to Spartan empire lay in the great fleet which Persia was assembling in alliance with Evagoras of Cyprus, under the leadership of Sparta's ablest and bitterest foe, the exiled Conon of Athens. Dercyllidas, the Spartan general in Asia Minor, with an army stiffened by a large remnant of the Ten Thousand, was quite competent to deal with the feeble and cowardly Persian commanders, and Sparta should have put all her fresh energies into the defense of her sea power. But she miscalculated. The sea was never her element, and a land campaign in Asia offered great temptations. Lysander was anxious to restore and strengthen his own creatures, the tottering decarchies in the Ionian cities, but, more than this, the campaign of the Ten Thousand had left on all Greece such an impression of the hollowness of the Persian empire and the imbecility of its officials that the idea of an actual invasion and conquest of the East began, sixty years before Alexander made it a fact, to dance before the eyes of ambitious Greeks as a dazzling possibility.

Agesilaus, for all the unassuming simplicity of his manners, was a man of strong ambitions, and he became fascinated by this vision. It even turned his head for a moment, and we see the man all the rest of whose career was marked by hard-headed common sense and absolute lack of display making himself ridiculous by attempting, in the guise of a new Agamemnon setting out for a new Troy, to sacrifice at Aulis before the departure of the fleet — and being ignominiously ordered out of the temple precincts by the local magistrates.

By Lysander's influence, he had received a year's appointment in command of the forces in Asia, to reinforce which he took with him two thousand freed Helots, six thousand allied troops, and a war council of thirty Spartans, including Lysander himself. On his arrival the wily satrap, Tissaphernes, played his old familiar game of asking for a truce. This gave Agesilaus time to get his army into shape and also to find out how the land lay, politically. A very unwelcome fact soon forced itself upon his notice: among the Asiatic Greeks Lysander was "the whole thing." The military prowess which he had so lately shown, the thoroughness with which he had rewarded his friends and punished his enemies, the terror of his rule, and — not least in that orientalized environment — his haughty and high-tempered bearing caused him to be received in every city like a conquering king, while his quiet, courteous little commander was practically ignored. Grateful as Agesilaus had cause to be to the man who had got him both his kingship and his immediate command, and thoroughly in accord as he seems always to have been with his policies, he had not the least intention of playing the part of his puppet. Instead of protesting or entering into any sort of rivalry, he at once adopted the very effective course of ignoring not only his advice, but, what was more vital, his personal influence. Applications for any sort of favor made through Lysander or backed by him were sure to be rejected: thus he struck at the very root of Lysander's position among the Ionians, and so humiliated him that he was reduced to asking an appointment for himself and was promptly sent to the Hellespont. Henceforth Agesilaus need fear no rival.

Thanks to Lysander's teachings and his own shrewdness
and decision, he had attained at the very beginning of his
reign a power greater than any Spartan king had held for
a hundred years.

Meanwhile, Tissaphernes had found it convenient to
break the truce, and Agesilaus received the news with cheerfulness, sending word to the satrap that "he was under great
obligations to him, as he had, by perjuring himself, rendered
the gods his enemies and . . . favorable to the Greeks." The
strategy of his campaigns against Tissaphernes seems to
have consisted chiefly in surprising that cunning trickster,
but cowardly and incapable general, by always appearing
where he was least expected and then quickly withdrawing
before the huge but unwieldy Persian forces could overtake
him. Thus, when the satrap made ready for him in his
home province of Caria, Agesilaus suddenly moved north,
invading the satrapy of Pharnabazus, reduced town after
town, gathered in a vast amount of booty, and returned to
the coast, having received no worse check than one un-
favorable cavalry skirmish which taught him the necessity
of raising an efficient mounted force. This he did by means
of requisitions upon the rich men of all the Greek cities, and
in the spring of the next year assembled his whole army —
now about twenty thousand — at Ephesus and brought it
to a high degree of efficiency by constant drills stimulated
by competitions and prizes. Xenophon, who was one of his
officers, has left us a vivid picture of the scene. "In consequence, a person might have seen all the gymnasia full of
men at their exercises, the horse-courses full of riders, and
the javelin-men and archers improving themselves in their
duties. He indeed made the whole city in which he was
quartered worthy of being seen, for the market-place was
crowded with horses and arms of all kinds for sale; and the
braziers, carpenters, smiths, curriers, and decorators were

all engaged in preparing equipments for the field; so that a
person might really have thought the city to be a workshop
of war. Every spectator, too, would have felt encouraged
at seeing Agesilaus walking in front, and his men following
him with chaplets on their heads, as they went away from
the places of exercise, and proceeded to offer their chaplets
to Diana; for where men reverence the gods, cultivate martial exercises, and are careful to obey their superiors, how
can everything be otherwise than full of the best hopes?"

Renewed in his command for another year, and supported
by a fresh group of Spartan councilors, Agesilaus now
threatened to invade Lydia and attack Sardis itself.
Tissaphernes, however, persuaded that this open announcement was only a blind, determined once more to await him
in his own country, so that the Greeks, marching straight
upon Sardis, got three days' start of any opposition at all.
Moreover, when attacked by the Persian cavalry, Agesilaus
reaped the fruit of his winter's preparation and after a
sharp battle completely defeated the enemy and took his
camp with more than seventy talents' worth of booty —
including camels, which, Xenophon takes pains to tell us,
the army took back to Greece.

The imbecility of Tissaphernes had now got beyond the
patience of even the not much more warlike Artaxerxes,
and Tithraustes was sent to succeed, and, incidentally,
behead him. The new commander, however, showed himself no whit more anxious to come to close grips with
Agesilaus, and actually paid him thirty talents to evacuate
Lydia and invade instead the territory of his brother satrap, Pharnabazus. Nothing loath, the Greeks set forth on
another lucrative campaign in the rich fields of Phrygia.
At the suggestion, moreover, of Spithridates, a Persian
sub-satrap whom Lysander had induced to revolt against
his government, Agesilaus made an alliance with the King

of Paphlagonia, who gave him a considerable force of cavalry and peltasts. A quarrel over spoils, however, following an attack on the camp of Pharnabazus, lost the Greeks both their new allies, much to the mortification of Agesilaus.

An extremely picturesque incident of this campaign was the personal meeting between the Greek and Persian commanders, which was brought about by a mutual guest-friend. The satrap, arriving in state and about to seat himself upon one of the rich carpets spread out by his attendants, caught sight of the plain little Spartan lying under a tree and immediately flung himself down "without regard for his delicate and richly dyed clothing" upon the grass beside him. Pharnabazus was a man of very different metal from his fellow-satraps, and the talk between him and Agesilaus has a right manly ring. The Persian began by recalling the faithful assistance which he, unlike Tissaphernes, had always given to Sparta during the Peloponnesian War. "In recompense," he went on, "I receive such treatment from you that I cannot get even a meal in my own province, unless I gather up, like the beasts, a portion of what you may have left; while I see the beautiful houses, and the parks stocked with timber and cattle, which my father left me, and in which I delighted, cut down and burnt." He left it to the Spartans present, he concluded, to say whether such behavior was just. The officers hung their heads, and Agesilaus himself was nonplussed for some minutes. Gathering his wits together, he replied, reasonably enough, that so long as the Spartans were at war with Persia and Pharnabazus was an officer of the Great King, they were obliged to treat him and his property as belonging to the enemy, but that nothing would delight them more than to have him renounce his allegiance to an unworthy master and make alliance with them. The proposal may have been tempting to Pharnabazas, who knew how slippery a seat was a satrap's throne, but he answered like. an honest man that so long as his king trusted him he would be faithful to his trust. In case, however, Artaxerxes threw him over as he had Tissaphernes, he was ready, rather than share that governor's fate, to come over to the Spartans. With that they shook hands and parted, Agesilaus saying as he rose, "How much rather had I have so brave a man my friend than my enemy!" A pretty sequel to this interview was the running back of the son of Pharnabazus, a handsome lad, to present Agesilaus with a beautiful lance, saying, with a smile, "I make you my guest-friend." The King, much pleased, gave him some fine horse-trappings in return, and years later, when the young man, driven out of his own country, took refuge in Sparta, remembered him and showed him every kindness.

Besides such dramatic incidents, Xenophon, who took part in all these campaigns of Agesilaus, leaves us many details which throw valuable light upon the customs of ancient warfare as well as on the humanity of his hero — for Xenophon adored his general. The plunder of private property was then as generally recognized a part of war on land as it still is of war at sea, and frightful must have been the sufferings of the harmless populations through whom an invading army made its way, not only "living upon the country," but gathering up every article of value, and multitudes of wretched human beings as well, to be sold at auction for the benefit of the host. Even besides all this there was often sheer wanton destruction, burning of towns, and severe oppression of conquered populations. Against these excesses Agesilaus took a firm stand, and won the pitiful gratitude of the cities which he spared. Organized plunder he authorized as a matter of course, and did not scruple, indeed, to throw particularly tempting lots in the way of his personal friends, but he gave strict orders that the

herds of captives kept for the slave-market should be
treated like human beings, that the aged and decrepit
whom even the raiders had left behind as worthless should
be gathered up and placed in safety "from wolves and dogs"
—a ghastly detail—and that in their charge should be put
the even more pitiful flotsam left in the wake of the tide
of invasion, the little children who, sold to slave-traders by
their starving parents, had been left to die on the roads as
not worth the expense of feeding and transporting. One
act of cruelty Agesilaus did commit, doubtless quite uncon-
sciously. In his first campaign, to inspire his soldiers with
contempt for the vastly more numerous enemy they were
to meet and to steel them against the temptations of eastern
luxury, he exhibited a band of prisoners at the slave-auction
naked, that the Greeks might compare their white skins,
plump figures, and flabby muscles with their own lean
brown bodies, tough as wire with daily exercise. To strip
for the public games was for a Greek, even of the highest
rank, a matter of course, and the Spartan could never have
dreamed of the agony of humiliation he was causing his
Persian captives, who were as unaccustomed as we are to
being seen unclothed.

Agesilaus was now at the very height of power and success. Every campaign had been victorious and profitable,
his fame redounded throughout the Persian empire, and his
adherence, under circumstances which had turned the heads
of other Spartan generals, to the strict rules of his upbring-
ing delighted the Greeks, who "were much pleased to see
the great lords and governors of Persia, with all the pride,
cruelty, and luxury in which they lived, trembling and
bowing before a man in a poor threadbare cloak, and at one
laconic word out of his mouth, obsequiously deferring and
changing their wishes and purposes." Sparta, moreover,
had honored him above any former general by granting him

command of the fleet as well as the army, and he had taken
measures to increase the number of ships gathered to check
the rapidly increasing menace of Conon's fleet at Rhodes.
Unluckily, yielding to his chief weakness, he had appointed
to the command for reasons of personal friendship his
brother-in-law, Pisander, although there were abler and
more experienced admirals at hand. The disastrous result,
however, was not yet evident, and Agesilaus, in the full
flush of his success, was dreaming great dreams of an invasion of Persia proper and the overthrow of Artaxerxes from
his very throne, when a message from Sparta brought all his
castles tumbling about his ears.

While Agesilaus was carrying all before him in Asia, war
had broken out in Greece. Argos and Corinth, Thebes and
Athens, bitterly restless under the hateful Spartan domination, and encouraged by money and promises sent by
Tithraustes, had formed a league against the oppressor.
Lysander, invading Bœotia from the north, had been defeated and slain outside the walls of Haliartus, and Pausanias, coming up from the south a day too late, had found it
wisest to beg a burial truce and withdraw without a fight.
Thus at one blow Sparta lost both her generals, for her
wrath against Pausanias was so great that he dared not
for his life return within her bounds. Faced by a strong
coalition, with her ablest commanders gone and her prestige
seriously shaken, there was nothing for it but to recall
Agesilaus. With a heavy heart he obeyed the summons,
leaving four thousand men to guard the Greek cities, and
assuring them that he would come back as soon as he could.
With the flower of his army, including of course Xenophon's
comrades of the Ten Thousand, he repaired in all haste to
Greece, following the route which no general since Xerxes
had taken, through Thrace and Macedonia.

Meanwhile the Allies had assembled at Corinth, in such

high hopes that it was even proposed to attack Sparta itself and "burn out the wasps in their nest." When it came to battle, however, the Lacedæmonians were victorious, and the good news reached Agesilaus at Amphipolis, who immediately dispatched the bringer of it to spread it among the cities of Asia. It is to his honor, and shows, perhaps, the broadening effect of foreign service, that while taking due advantage of the victory, he was grief-stricken at the losses it involved, seeming to realize, in a passing flash of insight, the suicidal policy upon which all Hellas had entered. "O Greece!" he sighed, "how many brave men hast thou destroyed, who if they had been preserved to so good a use, had sufficed to conquer all Persia!" He then advanced through Thessaly, beating off attacks of hostile cavalry as he went, but in a few days a partial eclipse of the sun gave omen of bad news indeed.

Pharnabazus, true to his determination to support Persia's cause with all his energy, had joined Conon at Rhodes. The combined fleets, far outnumbering that of Pisander, had inflicted upon it a crushing defeat at Cnidus, and the rash but valiant admiral, deserted by his allies, had fought his own ship to his death. Realizing the importance of this disaster, Agesilaus saw that the first necessity was to conceal it from his army and to hurry on a battle before it became known. Pretending, therefore, to have received good tidings, he pushed forward, picking up troops as he went, to where the army of the Confederates awaited him on the field of Coronea.

Of the battle which followed Xenophon, who says it was the hardest fought he ever saw, has left us a vivid account. Agesilaus himself commanded on the right wing, opposite the Argives; the Asiatic troops, stiffened by Xenophon's, held the center, while the recently joined Orchomenians on the left faced the Thebans. Slowly and in dead silence the armies advanced until they were within an eighth of a mile of each other, when the Thebans raised the war-cry and the whole Confederate army went forward at a run. The troops of Agesilaus rushed forward to meet them, his right and center carrying all before them. Just as some enthusiastic officers were offering the victor's crown to their general, came word that the Thebans, on the other hand, had equally overwhelmed their opponents. Thereupon, Agesilaus wheeled round to meet them, and the real battle began with such a crash as Greek warfare had never known. Shield to shield, body to body, the hoplites struggled and slew and died, without a shout — only the low, furious murmur of the *mêlée*. Agesilaus himself, fighting in the front rank, fell, covered with wounds, and was only saved from being trodden to death by the devoted courage of his Spartan bodyguard. At last the remnant of the Thebans pushed through and joined their fugitive allies on the slopes of Mt. Helicon. The wounded king, carried about the field by his soldiers to give the final orders, provided for the safety and honorable escort of eighty Thebans who had taken sanctuary in a neighboring temple, and detailed men to gather up and separate the Spartan and Theban dead, whose bodies, in one wild welter of friends and foes, pierced bucklers, and shattered spears, covered the bloody field. The next morning he erected a trophy and, after granting the burial truce asked for by the enemy, had himself taken to Delphi, to have his wounds treated and to offer to Apollo the tenth — amounting to one hundred talents — of the booty acquired in his two years in Asia. The army, after some desultory fighting, was dismissed to its several cities, and Agesilaus, as soon as he was well enough to travel, went home by sea.

During the miserable wars of the next thirty years, in which a whole generation of Greeks killed each other off for

the future benefit of Macedonia and Rome, Agesilaus seldom appears as a military commander. Distressed by his
wounds and by a long illness which followed them, he remained for the most part in Sparta, honored by all, including his young and modest colleague Agesipolis, son of the
exiled Pausanias, over whom he soon established a strong
and lasting influence. Occasionally, however, he found it
necessary to take the field. Thus while the war centered
about Corinth in 393–90, he twice led an army to the Isthmus. On the first occasion he succeeded in storming the
"long walls" which connected Corinth with the sea and in
capturing her port, Lechæum. As he was assisted in this by
his extremely popular brother, Teleutias, with a small fleet,
their mother was hailed as a happy woman, whose sons had
won victories by sea and land on the same day. The second
time he went forth was during the Isthmian games. Agesilaus broke up the celebration and proceeded to hold it himself, but as soon as he was gone the Corinthians came back
and celebrated the festival over again, some athletes winning the same events twice! The Spartan, however, had
not gone very far. He was busy taking the Peiræon, the
port by which Corinth communicated with her Bœotian
allies, and a little detail of the business which Xenophon
has preserved shows why he was so beloved a commander.
Bethinking him that a battalion he had sent to occupy some
heights must have been chilled by a passing hailstorm, he
sent ten men with pots of burning charcoal who, scrambling
up the hillside, found the soldiers, in their light summer gar-
ments, shivering in the darkness, too cold to enjoy their
rations; soon large fires were kindled, "and they all anointed
themselves and many took supper a second time."

Soon after this homely scene Xenophon paints us a highly
dramatic one. We see Agesilaus, after taking a Corinthian
fortress, seated by the harborside, overlooking the distribu-

tion of prisoners and spoil and refusing with "a very lofty
air" even to recognize the existence of a group of Theban
envoys who have come to discuss terms of peace. Suddenly
a horseman gallops through the crowd, flings himself from
his foaming steed before Agesilaus, and "with a very sad
countenance" gives him such news that the king jumps
from his seat, snatches up his spear, and, calling upon his
officers to follow, hastens off at such a pace that his heavy-
armed troops can scarcely keep up with him. Dire indeed
was the need, for a full regiment of Spartan hoplites, returning from escort duty, had been set upon, as they passed
with careless confidence under the walls of Corinth, by a
swarm of peltasts, light-armed mercenaries commanded by
the celebrated free lance, Iphicrates, and so harassed, driven,
and demoralized by these inaccessible enemies that they
had at last fairly taken to flight, leaving half their number
dead upon the ground. The blow to Sparta's prestige was
the heaviest since the disaster at Sphacteria, thirty-five
years before, and Agesilaus, gathering up his deeply mortified army, took it home by night marches to avoid the open
exultation of the Arcadians, allies though they were.

The only other campaigns of Agesilaus at this period were
two incursions into Acarnania, of no great importance,
though successful enough. After this, thoroughly broken in
health, he remained for many years at home, exercising a
predominant and not very good influence over Spartan
policy. For Agesilaus, a true Spartan in his virtues, was
equally one in his limitations. He had no power of growth
or of adaptability to changing conditions; gentle and plac-
able in his personal affairs, as a Spartan dealing with other
— and therefore, to him, immeasurably inferior — Greeks,
he would never admit the possibility of concession.

It was no time for so stiff-necked a policy. Sparta's relative position was changing rapidly for the worse. The

crushing victory of Pharnabazus and Conon had deprived
her at a stroke of her Asiatic empire, and, followed up as it
was by the immediate dispatch of the Persian fleet to
Athens, had made it possible for her old rival to raise her
head once more and work her way back into a position of
something like equality. The alliance against her had re-
sulted in confining her domination to the Peloponnesus, and
the spirit in which it was borne there is sufficiently shown
by those night marches of Agesilaus. True, she was still
the strongest single state in Greece, and still looked on as a
sure victor in a pitched battle — but pitched battles were
becoming few and far between. All Greece was worn out;
the war had degenerated into petty banditry and was getting
nowhere. Without the financial help of Persia, Sparta believed that her opponents would be unable to keep the field
at all, and twice she sent her ablest diplomat, Antalcidas,
to persuade the Great King that Sparta, not Athens, would
be his best friend in Greece. The second time he succeeded,
and, backed by the two great despotisms of Persia in the
east and Syracuse in the west, Sparta was able to force upon
an exhausted but mortified Greece a peace by which she
definitely abandoned the Greek cities of the Asiatic mainland to Persia on condition that the autonomy of every
other Greek state should be guaranteed.

This "autonomy" one might almost call Sparta's obses-
sion. It appealed sentimentally to the deepest instinct, the
oldest tradition, of the freedom-loving Hellene, — and at
the same time left all the states helpless before the superior
military power of Sparta, who, without technically interfering with their self-government, could frighten them into
the position of subservient allies. Therefore the fact that
the time had gone by when small powers could long exist
without federation never penetrated her mind, and the
attempts at such federation which, like the union of Corinth

and Argos, were made in several quarters at this period, were instantly recognized as a danger to her own supremacy and sternly suppressed. Even — or, rather, especially — the ancient Bœotian confederacy, which Thebes would have reëstablished by swearing to the King's Peace in the name of all Bœotia, was forbidden to exist, Agesilaus summarily informing the Theban envoys that they might sign for their city alone or be left out.

His especial dislike for Thebes appears again and again and may have influenced his condonation of the treacherous seizure of her citadel by Phœbidas, in full peace. This atrocious act shocked all Greece and called forth strong protests at Sparta itself, but Agesilaus coolly declared that the only thing to be considered was whether the result inured to the benefit of the state; Phœbidas therefore was merely fined for looks' sake, while the Cadmea was kept as a Spartan outpost in the face of all law. One can hardly doubt that the equally outrageous attempt of Sphodrias upon the Piræus would have received the same backing had it been successful. Since the crime turned out to be also a blunder, however, Spartan justice was relentless, and the unlucky tool of her policy escaped the death-penalty only through the accident that his son was a bosom friend of a son of Agesilaus, one of whose amiable weaknesses — from the Spartan point of view — was an excessive fondness for his children.[1]

The same mingling of private with public considerations he had shown in the cases of Mantinea and Phlius, two of the Arcadian allies whom Sparta taught their place. Having an hereditary friendship with the Mantineans, he held back personally from the expedition which was to reduce their flourishing city to its primitive condition of five villages,

[1] This is prettily attested by the story of his being caught by a friend riding hobby-horse with them when they were little, and telling him not to mention it till he was himself a father.

sending the none too well-pleased Agesipolis to do his dirty work. But in the case of Phlius, on the other hand, being personally attached to certain aristocrats whom the Phliasians had banished and who, on being restored under pressure from Sparta, complained that their property was not given back to them, he took active and zealous part in besieging and severely punishing the city, old and faithful ally though it had been to Sparta.

When Thebes, by the daring stratagem of Pelopidas, threw off the Spartan yoke, and Athens made common cause with her, Agesilaus, though nearing sixty, was called upon by the Ephors to lead the army into Bœotia. He did so twice, with much skill and prudence, but was obliged each time to return with little accomplished except a first-rate training of his Theban foes, for it was in these campaigns that they learned the tactics which were in a few years to make them invincible. For the punishment of the tyrant city was drawing on apace, and the state she had most foully injured was to be the instrument of her overthrow. On the fatal field of Leuctra, in 371, Sparta received her death-blow. Four hundred full-blooded Spartans died with their young King Cleombrotus — a loss which could never be made good. The news was borne with superb stoicism; no lamentation was allowed for the heroic dead, and the only sad faces were of those whose relatives had survived defeat. Not till seven years later, when the army, returning from a complete but minor victory in Arcadia, was received by the whole population streaming out, headed by old Agesilaus and the Ephors, with tears of joy and hands uplifted in thankfulness to the gods, was it seen how cruelly the iron of defeat had entered into their souls.

Henceforth the parts of Thebes and Sparta are reversed. Again and again Epaminondas invades the Peloponnesus, till Lacedæmon is fighting for her life at her own gates. And

meanwhile the news of Leuctra had been greeted as the long-
awaited signal for the freedom of Arcadia. In vain Agesilaus
tried both diplomacy and arms; the restoration of Mantinea,
the revolt of Tegea, the founding of Megalopolis were
accomplished facts. Worse yet, the Helots of the western
peninsula rose at the call of the invaders and became men
and Messenians once more. In 370 Epaminondas broke
through into Laconia, the first invader for six hundred
years, and plundered down the banks of Eurotas till Spartan women for the first time in history saw the smoke of
the enemy's fires. In the midst of their cries and lamenta-
tions, of taunts and reproaches, of plots and desertions, and
of his own bitter reflections, Agesilaus kept a cool head and
with iron discipline held his desperate troops at bay within
the strongest quarters of the city, where they looked so
formidable that the Theban dared not attack them and
turned north again.

Year after year, with varying fortunes and shifting alliances, the wretched war dragged on. Sparta would have
accepted almost any terms, but those offered her included
the recognition of Messenian independence, and to that
she would rather die than consent. One great need was
money, and Agesilaus, tireless in his country's service, set
sail in search of it. The Persian empire was breaking up,
and in the scramble there might be a chance to pick up a
bit of profit. Sparta could of course lend no soldiers to the
revolting satraps, but the old man went alone to see what
his name and experience were worth to them and, succeeding
in bringing about a negotiation, came home with pay from
both sides.

His days of military service, however, were not over. Once
more Epaminondas came down on Lacedæmon, and once
more the aged king — now past eighty — took up the desperate defense. This time he threw over his cautious tactics

and with all the fire of youth led out his Spartans, strength-
ened by mercenaries hired with his Asiatic gold. Epaminondas slipped by him and all but took the city, but a Cretan
"under some divine influence," as Xenophon says, brought
word to Agesilaus just in time. Back he hurried to call the
little city guard to arms, and the Theban found the unwalled city bristling with desperate men ready to die in
their narrow streets while the old and the women hurled
down missiles from the housetops. Before such a costly
storm he hesitated, and Archidamus, the king's gallant son,
rushing out with a bare hundred Spartans, fairly put the
enemy to flight.

Before the year was out, Epaminondas had fallen at
Mantinea, and with him the danger from Thebes was over.
But Sparta was left in sorry plight. Decimated, impoverished, robbed of a great part of her property and her servants, she must yet take the field against the Messenians,
who raided her borders day and night. For, though reduced
to her last gasp, she still refused to acknowledge her former
serfs, and Greece made peace without her. In such straits,
there was no help for it but to hire soldiers, and again there
was only Agesilaus to get the money. This time, too, he
must work for it. The best chance seemed to be to hire himself out, as captain of a band of mercenaries, to the Egyptian
Tachos, and this action, which brought upon him the sneering criticism of his fellow Greeks, was perhaps the noblest
and most unselfish of his life. For Agesilaus, says Plutarch,
"valued not other men's discourses; he thought no public
employment dishonorable; the ignoblest thing in his esteem
was for a man to sit idle and useless at home, waiting for his
death to come and take him." To Egypt he went, therefore,
where the great officers, and all the people crowded to see the
famous Spartan king, "but when they found, instead of the
splendid prince whom they looked for, a little old man of

contemptible appearance, without all ceremony lying down upon the grass in coarse and threadbare clothes, they fell into laughter and scorn of him." What yet more astonished the oriental mind was that when all sorts of provisions were brought him, he took only the meat and meal, turning over the sweetmeats and perfumes to his servants.

Finding himself less trusted and honored by Tachos than he had expected, and besought by Nectanabis, who was making rebellion against the rebel, to go over to him, Agesilaus felt no scruples — what was it to him which barbarian he served, so long as he got the money for Sparta? — but changed sides, won his new employer a good victory, and sailed for home with the tidy sum of two hundred and thirty talents (about a quarter of a million dollars). But the old man was not to see again the green fields of his beloved Lacedæmon. Just as his ship put in from a storm at an empty harbor on the African coast, he died, worn out at last.

To few men is given such absolute identification of their lives with their country's as was the lot of Agesilaus. Within the space of his four and eighty years was comprised Sparta's rise to the height of her power and fall to her lowest ebb. His youth saw the whole course of the Peloponnesian war; in his full manhood, at the head of a great and victorious army, he stood on the threshold of the conquest of the Persian Empire; for twenty-five years of Sparta's supremacy in Greece he was the guiding spirit of her counsels — and at eighty-three, a grizzled veteran, he went out in search of the money needed to preserve her from annihilation. When we realize, in addition, that in his own person he shared the faults and furthered the policies which brought about his country's downfall, we must feel that though Agesilaus was not a great man, there is true epic greatness in the tragedy of his career.

DIONYSIUS THE ELDER

(Died 367 B.C.)

FEW men have made a deeper impression upon the minds
of men of their own time than did Dionysius of Syracuse.
The sight of this obscure, middle-class citizen raising himself so suddenly, without the aid of wealth or family, party-
standing or even striking personal gifts, to the absolute
leadership, first of his own city, and then of the whole of
western Hellas, maintaining his despotic empire for nearly
forty years, and handing it on, an unquestioned heritage,
to his eldest son, filled every Greek with a painful mixture
of astonishment and anger, fear and reluctant admiration.
In order to understand how such a career was possible, one
must first see clearly the main features of the Sicilian situation just before this spectacular rise took place. The two
outstanding facts are the Carthaginian peril and the failure
of Syracusan democracy.

It will be remembered that just when the hosts of Persia
seemed about to overrun old Greece, another great barbarian invasion had swept down upon the Greek cities of
Sicily, and that on the very same day, as tradition fondly
had it, of the year 480, the Persians were defeated at
Salamio and the Carthaginians at Himera. For more than
seventy years the one deliverance had seemed as final as
the other. There were still Phœnician cities in Sicily, to be
sure, but they were the old ones in the western corner —
Panormus, Solus, Motya — and no attempt was made to
extend their sway. Now, for the first time within most
living memories, Carthage loomed up as an invader and a

conqueror, bent at once on vengeance for the past and empire for the future. In 409, Hannibal,[1] with over one hundred thousand men, swooped down upon Selinus and on Himera; Selinus and Himera were no more. In 406, he and Himilco led another mighty host against Acragas, the sumptuous queen of the southern coast, wealthiest, most luxurious, and most beautiful of Sicilian towns, "fairest of the cities of men." Syracuse sent help against the common foe, and had her forces been led by the able and energetic commander who not long before had foiled the great Athenian siege, her help might have availed. But the rising tide of democracy in Syracuse had wrecked the career of her best citizen. Suspected of tyrannical ambitions, Hermocrates had tried in vain to earn his recall from exile by patriotic exploits, and finally had met his death in a desperate attempt to win back by force of arms. The extreme democrats now held full sway, but the generals they chose proved incompetent or treacherous, or both, and as soon as the defense of Acragas became difficult, they deserted the sinking ship. The Agrigentines, left alone, were not the stuff that goes down fighting; their lines had been too long cast in pleasant places. In one night, without a blow, they marched away forever, men, women, and children; "they were compelled to leave for the barbarians to pillage, those things which made their lives happy." The ruined temples of Girgenti, looking across in the mute reproach of their desolate beauty to the African coast, bear witness to-day of the sacking of Acragas.

For Syracuse the situation was now extremely serious, and thoughtful men could not but realize how ill-prepared she was to meet it. One of these was Philistos, known to future scholars as the historian of his period, and one of those unusual men who, with a profound and lasting interest

---

[1] Not, of course, the Hannibal of Roman history.

in public affairs, yet prefer always to keep in the background and work through others. He and a few like-minded thinkers picked out, to represent their views in action, a young man whom few in the city can have known by sight. This was Dionysius, by profession a government clerk, in politics a follower of Hermocrates, whose daughter he afterward married. Taking part in his leader's ill-advised attack upon the city, he had been left for dead in the agora — and so obscure was he that no one had challenged his reappearance. Serving in the levy of Syracuse at Acragas, he had, however, borne himself noticeably well, and now he was chosen to express in the public assembly the indignation of those whose valor had been brought to nought by worthless generals. Again and again, in his fiery attack, he overpassed the limits of permitted speech, but each time Philistos stepped forward to pay the fine incurred, and the orator went on. Of course he did not lay the blame for the fiasco on the democracy; on the contrary, he charged the generals, aristocrats by birth, with being no true representatives of the people, who should be led by men of their own stock. His success was complete; the generals were deposed, and a new board chosen, of whom Dionysius himself was one.

The first step in the "despot's progress" had been taken; the next followed rapidly. On his return one day from the neighboring city of Gela, where he had helped to carry through a democratic revolution, Dionysius met his own townsfolk streaming out of the theater at the close of one of the great open-air performances, and seized the chance of making them a fiery speech. His fellow-generals, he said, were taking bribes from the enemy; he himself had been approached by secret Carthaginian envoys; he could not bear to hold for another day an office which laid him open to such suspicion. The people, much excited, met next day in regular assembly and made him "general with full

powers " — dictator, in short — as they had made Gelon
some eighty-five years before.

Only one thing more was needful — an armed force, all
his own. The citizen army was at his orders, but just because it was a citizen army it might take it into its head
to be patriotically disobedient. Remembering, doubtless,
the famous stratagem of Pisistratus, Dionysius employed
a similar one; having gone out with the Syracusan levy to
Leontini, then full of fugitives from all the ravaged towns,
on whose friendship he could count, he suddenly divulged a
perfectly imaginary attempt upon his life, and asked for a
bodyguard. A mixed multitude of soldiers, citizens, and
exiles, calling themselves an Assembly, voted him at once
six hundred men, a number which Dionysius took the
liberty of increasing to one thousand. With this body,
which, chosen for individual merit, highly paid, and splendidly equipped, formed henceforth not merely his personal
guard but the core of his army, Dionysius returned to
Syracuse and took up his residence in the Castle, a full-
fledged tyrant.

However influenced the Syracusans may have been by
fear of the armed forces of Dionysius, — and he quickly
filled the city with mercenaries of every race and speech, —
their main reason for giving him extraordinary powers was
to enable him to put up an energetic defense against the
national foe, and it was high time that he should justify his
election, for Himilco, after a comfortable winter in deserted
Acragas, was bearing down upon Gela. With fifty ironclad
ships and a great mixed army — the Syracusan levy of foot
and horse, an auxiliary force of Italian Greeks volunteered
in the common cause, and many thousands of mercenaries
— Dionysius advanced to meet him. His plan was well laid:
the Italiots, marching by the coast road and supported by
the ships, and the Sicilians, going around north of the city

by the inland road, were at the same moment to attack the
Carthaginian camp to the west of Gela, while he himself
with his mercenaries, going straight through the city, would
engage the main army which was battering at its western gates. Unluckily, the combination did not work out.
The Italiots, though they had the longest march, were
first at the rendezvous and performed their task well, but
the Syracusans were late, and the mercenaries, apparently
caught in the narrow congested streets, never got into the
fight at all, so that the Carthaginian main force, not being
held at the city, was able to turn back and rout the invaders
from their camp. To complete the discouragement and
mounting distrust of the army, Dionysius now decided that
it was hopeless to defend Gela at all. In the darkness of the
night the whole population forsook their homes and, escorted
by the troops, set forth on the unhappy march to Syracuse,
gathering up into the stream of fugitives the men, women,
and children of Camarina, through which they passed. The
tragic sight burned itself into the memory of every Greek
who witnessed it — the roads choked with the aged, the
sick, delicate ladies, young maidens — all torn at a moment's notice from their comfortable, happy, sheltered
homes and fleeing for their lives from a barbarous pursuer
whose tortures, culminating in impalement and crucifixion,
were the certain fate of any who dropped behind.[1]

It is no wonder that in the minds of many the grief and
horror roused by such a spectacle swelled to burning indignation against the leader to whose strange tardiness and
timidity it seemed due. The Italiots, who, of the army, had
done and suffered most, deserted in a body and went home.
The Syracusan horsemen, young nobles, whose dislike of
the upstart dictator had been intensified to hatred by their

[1] To realize the situation, read the published accounts of the sufferings of the Armenians
at the hands of the Turks during the (present) Great War.

bitter mortification, galloped off to Syracuse, hoping to raise
a revolt and meet him on his return with a restored republic.
They showed, however, no political ability, only a frenzied
personal hate, which wreaked itself not merely upon the
tyrant's house and personal belongings, but on his newly
married wife, whom they cruelly did to death. When
Dionysius, coming up in all haste with a chosen troop,
burned down the Achradina gate and burst into the city,
there was no popular uprising to resist him; only the cava-
liers rode forth and fell, cut down like grain by his avenging
mercenaries. A few escaped to Ætna; the fugitives from
Gela and Camarina went to join their fellow-exiles from
Acragas at Leontini; with the rest of his great mixed multitude, Dionysius established himself once more in Syracuse.

His first business was to come to terms with the invader
whom he had been unable to drive out, and Himilco, his
army weakened by disease, was satisfied at present with
what he had accomplished. The conditions agreed upon
are not unlike those of the King's Peace arranged by
Antalcidas a few years later. As Persia, by that pact, was
acknowledged mistress of the Greek cities of Asia, so was
Carthage of all those on the north and south coasts of Sicily,
some of them becoming her out and out possessions and
others her tributaries. The Sicels were declared independent, and so were the new settlers of Leontini. But between
that city on the one side and Camarina on the other the
rule of Dionysius was guaranteed, even as the predominance
of Sparta had been by Persia.

The motives of Dionysius in consenting after scarcely
any resistance to such a humiliating peace have been sharply
debated in modern as in his own times. Was he a traitor?
Did he deliberately, from the first, sacrifice Gela and
Camarina as the price of Carthaginian recognition? The
suspicion of his contemporaries is absolutely natural, yet

when we remember that his rule was founded on the expectation of his becoming the deliverer of Sicily, and that nothing would have done so much to establish and popularize it as a brilliant victory over the national foe, it is hard to believe that he intentionally rejected such a glorious means and preferred the position of a hated and suspected tyrant dependent on foreign support. It is more probable, then, that he honestly failed at Gela and afterwards accepted the best terms he could get, but the people who had raised him to power had hoped so much from him that the disappointment cast a dark shadow over his whole reign.

In his own mind, however, these hopes had never died. Carthage might regard the peace as final, but for Dionysius it was a truce to be used in unceasing preparation for the day when he might once more take up the great task of his life. But since he had not been able to accomplish that task in the character of a popular hero, he must first of all rivet his hold upon a now unwilling people. Taking up his residence in Ortygia, the original island-city, he proceeded not only to build for himself a new castle of extraordinary strength, through whose five gates any visitor coming across the causeway from Achradina must be successively admitted, but to turn the whole island into his personal stronghold, in which only his soldiers and his most trusted adherents were permitted to live. The need of such a fortress was soon shown, for a most formidable revolt of the citizen army led to an actual siege of the tyrant within the city. Between the new Syracusan government — for such it proclaimed itself — on the heights of Epipolæ, and the ships gladly sent by Messana and Rhegium to revenge his apparent betrayal of their troops at Gela by blockading his harbor, Dionysius really thought his hour had come, and his best friend could only bid him die like a king. Another encouraged him at least to cling to his dominion till he was "dragged out by the leg," and the tyrant, gathering courage, set his wits to work. Pretending to yield, he asked only to be allowed to sail away with his own property. The besiegers, confident and deceived, relaxed all vigilance, and were utterly taken by surprise when twelve hundred Campanian mercenaries from the Carthaginian service, summoned by secret messengers, burst upon them from the north and forced a way through to the city. With these and some other reinforcements Dionysius sallied forth upon his disorderly besiegers and put them utterly to rout. The victory won by his arms was sealed by his mercy; the previous revolt of the cavalry had been followed by severest punishment, not to be wondered at considering the cruel personal wrong they had done him, but now he recalled his pursuing soldiery, gave quarter freely, and buried the slain with due funeral rites. On the strength of this generosity he invited back those of his enemies who had made their escape to Ætna, but most of these preferred to keep at a safe distance, and to his boast of having buried the dead replied that they should be glad to do the same by him and only hoped the gods would soon give them the chance.

It is at this point that we first catch a glimpse of the relations between Dionysius and Old Greece, particularly Sparta, which were so interwoven with the story of his life. The account is confused, but it appears that the rebellious Syracusans had sent to the mother city, Corinth, for a "mediator" to help them set up a new government, and that a Spartan envoy managed to betray this Corinthian and his plans into the hands of the tyrant and to lend the latter the full countenance of his city. It was the beginning of that long and sinister alliance against which patriotic Hellenic orators were to thunder in vain.

Now that he was firmly seated in Syracuse, Dionysius' next undertaking was to get control of all eastern Sicily.

There were two populations to be considered, the native Sicels of the interior and the Greeks of the coast cities. The former he managed chiefly by means of a close friendship with the vigorous Sicel tyrant of Agyrium; the Greeks of Catane, Naxos and Leontini he bribed and frightened into complete submission. Leontini he left in the possession of its own inhabitants, while turning it, politically, into a kind of distant suburb of Syracuse, but Catane he handed over to a band of Campanians to live in, while Naxos, sacred in Greek eyes as the oldest Greek settlement in the whole island, he simply wiped off the face of the earth forever. Messana in her corner, now the only free Greek city, made a half-hearted attempt, spurred on by Rhegium, to resist the onward sweep of his power, but hesitated and turned back in time to win his politic pardon. Rhegium, too, he forgave, and would have wooed as an ally, seeking a wife from among her daughters, but the Italiot city, feeling safe on the further side of the straits, allowed herself the luxury of expressing her feelings, and so rejected his overtures with a scorn which she was bitterly to rue.

Dionysius had won his object, but his progress had been a sinister one; as Freeman says, "His power had advanced without victories, and there is something especially terror-striking in the course of the man who achieves great results without proportionate means." Moreover, he had done a supremely hateful thing; he, a Hellene, had destroyed the oldest monuments of Hellenic occupation and had handed over an Hellenic city to barbarians for permanent settlement. Treason to his race could hardly go further, — yet, on the other hand, if his chief duty was to organize resistance to the national foe, he might plead that he was using the only practicable means. Independent cities had shown that they could not, even when allied, resist the invader; only by uniting all Sicily as the single state of Syracuse, could he forge a mighty weapon to be wielded victoriously by one master-hand.

At least, this greater purpose was never out of his mind. The proof of it is the elaborate fortification of Syracuse which he now undertook. With almost incredible speed he carried out "the greatest work of military engineering that the Greek world had yet seen. . . . At a single stroke he made Syracuse the vastest fortified city in Europe" — more than three times as large as Athens and the Piræus together, half again as large as imperial Rome. The long plateau of Epipolæ, to the west of Achradina, from which the Athenians had so seriously threatened the city, was now wholly enveloped by a great wall connecting with the existing fortifications, and at the steep and narrow western tip of the heights was erected the mighty fortress of Euryalus, of which five towers and a whole system of underground works remain to this day. These buildings were evidently not, like the castle and gates of Ortygia, mere strongholds of personal power; they inured to the safety and glory of Syracuse itself, and were enthusiastically supported by the citizens, who turned out to the number of sixty thousand to work with their own hands at the new wall. Every part of the work was done in the very best way that the state of military science made possible: the masonry was of the finest, six thousand yoke of oxen drew the well-cut blocks of stone to the places where they were needed, engineers and master-builders at fixed intervals directed evenly divided bands of workmen, and Dionysius himself, throwing off the suspicious aloofness in which he ordinarily hid himself, was continually on the spot, observing, directing, praising, and rewarding. Under such spur the whole north wall, nearly four miles long, was built in twenty days.

It was not to be expected, of course, that the population of the city would soon, if ever, occupy the huge area now

enclosed, yet it was itself greatly enlarged as well as, in some
ways, immensely democratized, by the measures of Dionysius. In orthodox Hellenic eyes it had indeed ceased to be a
city at all, for there was no longer any body of pure-blooded
original citizens privileged to make laws alike for themselves
and for non-citizens. What with the multitudes of freedmen
and aliens to whom he had given land and citizen rights, the
slaves he had emancipated, the adventurous soldiers from
all over the world who swarmed to his capital seeking service, Syracuse was more like a great modern city than an
ancient Greek one. And upon his popularity with this mixed
multitude Dionysius knew he could, on the whole, rely,
especially as republican forms were in a shadowy way still
observed, assemblies met, if only to register the will of the
actual ruler, and he still bore no title, within the city, but
his original one of commander-in-chief.

It was against private assassination, not popular upris-
ings, that his extreme precautions were taken, and even
that was the less probable as, unlike most tyrants, he gave
little excuse for personal vengeance. His own habits were
decent and domestic; as he pointed out in his famous rebuke
to his son, he made trouble in no man's home. His marriage,
to be sure, was somewhat extraordinary, since he now took to
himself two wives at the same time, one from the Italiot
city of Locri and the other from Syracuse itself. The double
wedding was celebrated with great solemnity, and, incredible as it sounds, Dionysius appears to have lived in perfect
amity with both consorts, taking the greatest pains to show
absolutely equal attention and regard to each.

About seven years of peace had now passed, and Dionysius began to feel strong enough to resume his great national
task. First, however, complete military and naval preparations must be made, on a vaster and more scientific scale than
had ever been attempted. As in the fortification of the city,

his great energy and unusual talent for organization came into full play. From all Hellas and even from Carthaginian provinces the best artisans were called in to supervise the constant manufacture of weapons of every sort, appropriate to the use of soldiers of every nation. Every technical improvement was eagerly welcomed and applied. In a large "artillery park" outside the city a new invention was tried out which was to revolutionize ancient warfare — the catapult, which could hurl either darts or great stones with a force far beyond human strength. At the same time and largely, like the walls, by citizen labor, a fleet was built, huge not only in numbers but in the unprecedented size of the ships, many of them having four and even five banks of rowers instead of the conventional three.

There must have been something wonderfully exhilarating about all this activity, an excitement in taking one's part, with all one's might, in such big work, so well organized, so evidently planned for a great national purpose. Men were even willing to face the tremendous expense which all this "preparedness" meant and which had to be met by every sort of means, regular and irregular. Dionysius stopped at nothing — taxes of every kind, forced loans, confiscation of private property, debasement of the currency, even barefaced seizure of the temple treasures. Athens, it is true, had in time of need borrowed freely from the treasury of Athena, honestly holding that the goddess would be glad to contribute to the defense of her chosen city, but Dionysius followed the example without the excuse, — for he was a notorious freethinker, — and without even the pretence of a loan. Perhaps the coolest of all his performances was to sell a lot of his own belongings at auction, and then take them back from the unlucky purchasers. Yet there was apparently no general discontent. By hook or by crook, the money had to be raised, and it was raised.

Finally, in the spring of 397, with all preparations complete and soldiers enlisted from every part of the world, Dionysius called upon Syracuse to declare war. The declaration was voted with enthusiasm and sent at once to Carthage with the alternative of giving up all the Greek cities in Sicily.

Naturally, the activities of Syracuse had not been unobserved, but Carthage, enfeebled by a plague, had failed to arm herself in time, and until Himilco with a hastily gathered army could reach Sicily, Dionysius was free to carry all before him. As he marched westward, every Greek community rose to hail him as a deliverer, Carthaginian residents were set upon with plunder and outrage, contingents joined the army as it advanced, the Elymian towns came over, and at last, with more than eighty thousand men, supported by two hundred warships and five hundred transports, he passed the border of the original Carthaginian possessions and laid siege to the island fortress of Motya.

This siege, although unusually interesting on account of the novel and ingenious methods of attack and the desperate valor of the defense, can be only briefly outlined here. The first task of Dionysius was to rebuild in broader, stronger form the artificial causeway, connecting the city with the mainland, which the Motyans had destroyed. While the crews of his ships, which were drawn up on the inner shore of the deeply curved harbor, were engaged in this work, the relieving fleet of Himilco bore down upon them, closing the narrow mouth of the port. Dionysius had no mind to engage his vessels where their numbers would have no advantage. Leaving them ashore, he set his slingers, his archers, and, above all, the engineers of his catapults, now used for the first time, to repulse the attacking Carthaginians, while the marines, withdrawn from their labor on the causeway, were set to laying wooden runways across the low and marshy neck of land which separated the harbor from the open sea. Two miles and a half, the ships were dragged across, and, putting to sea, made round to look for Himilco, who, knowing himself outnumbered, sailed away without a battle, leaving Motya to its fate.

That fate was certain, but the population of the old Semitic town held out with a stern and terrible determination such as only their race, when pushed to the last extremity, has shown itself capable of. In vain Dionysius, having finished his mole, brought across it his catapults, battering-rams, and lofty movable towers; from tall masts set on the high housetops the Motyans hurled back flaming tow upon the wooden engines, and even when the rams had actually breached the walls the fight seemed only begun, for every house was a fortress, every street a trench to be carried by assault. Only by a surprise attack at night was the city taken at last, and handed over to a destruction as terrible and complete as those deeds of Carthage which it avenged.

In this first year of the war Dionysius had changed the whole face of affairs in Sicily. Carthage, instead of being the attacking power, was now on the defensive, even as to her most ancient possessions. The second year, however, was much less fruitful. Himilco, with a new and huge armament, sailed round the west of Sicily, keeping well out to sea, landed at Panormus, and proceeded to take back city after city along the coast, while Dionysius remained strangely absorbed in the siege of inland Segesta. As a matter of fact, though urged by his Greeks to meet the enemy in a pitched battle, he believed it unsafe to do so; the difficulties of maintaining his army were growing very great, the Sican natives were unfriendly, and the consequence of defeat would have been utter destruction. Giving up all his recent conquests, therefore, and even part of his own domain, he retreated to Syracuse, Himilco following along the north

coast as far as Messana, which he took by assault and razed
to the ground. Thence advancing southward, the Carthaginian ingratiated himself with the Sicels by founding for
them a hill stronghold, which still, as Taormina, is far-famed
as the loveliest site in Sicily. Further he could not advance
directly, because a recent lava flow from Mount Ætna
barred the shore road; he had to make a long detour around
the mountain. Dionysius came out as far as Catane to meet
him, but the defeat of his fleet by the Punic admiral, Mago,
forced him to hasten back to Syracuse and prepare to stand
a siege. Bitter were the critics, many the faint-spirited and
the traitorous, but the tyrant kept good heart and sent out
a call to all Hellas to come to the rescue of the last free
Hellenic city in Sicily. Soldiers came in from Italy and the
Peloponnesus, and Sparta, faithful to her old ally, sent
thirty triremes under an admiral, who arrived in time to
throw all his weight in support of the despot against a popular movement to overthrow him.

Both sides seemed well prepared for a long and desperate
siege, but as the midsummer heats advanced, a frightful
epidemic broke out in the invading army, encamped in the
marshy valley of the Anapus, and Dionysius took advantage
of its weak and demoralized condition to make a surprise-
attack upon camp and fleet at once, with such success that
Himilco asked only for leave to withdraw his forces. This
Dionysius granted as far as the Carthaginian troops were
concerned, and held back his own while the defeated commander sailed away with forty triremes, leaving as his ransom his mercenaries and his Sicilian allies. So disgraceful
was held this escape that Himilco preferred suicide to the
reproaches of his countrymen, and Carthage, her prestige
sorely diminished, had to spend the next three years in putting down a great insurrection of the native Africans.

These years gave Dionysius a good opportunity to consolidate his victory by winning, rather as allies than as subjects, the Sicels of the interior, and resettling the coast towns, Messana and Leontini, with mercenaries and exiles. A picturesque incident of this time is his attempted storm of the snow-covered heights of Tauromenium, from which he himself came tumbling down with his men, the only one to arrive at the bottom with his breastplate still on.

In the spring of 393 Carthage was ready to try again, and her new commander, Mago, advanced well into the interior of the island, winning over by humane measures some of the native towns. The stalwart despot of Agyrium, however, remained faithful to Dionysius, who joined him with twenty thousand men and, without giving battle, made Mago's position so difficult that negotiations were soon under way and Carthage finally agreed to a very satisfactory peace. She gave up all her conquests, retaining only her old dominion, with the Elymian towns which had always preferred her rule. In five sixths of Sicily Dionysius was left practically supreme, his rule over the Sicels being expressly recognized. The long war, therefore, in spite of its moments of defeat and disappointment, had, on the whole, ended with considerable glory and a very fair approach to the attainment of its original object. That object, in its fullness, Dionysius never abandoned, but it was to be nine years before he again put it in the forefront of his policy.

Those years were to be, for the most part, years of peace, but before they could take that form Dionysius had one long reckoning to pay, one pestilent enemy to clear out of his path for ever. From the time when Rhegium had scorned his proffered friendship and refused him one of her daughters, she had been a persistent thorn in his flesh. Just before Mago's invasion her jealous attacks upon the rebuilding Messana had brought him down to punish her, but the approach of the Carthaginian had forced him to patch up a half-truce. Now he resolved to run the chance of no more back-fires.

To attack Rhegium, however, was no simple matter, for she had recently joined a strong league of Italian-Greek cities. To meet this situation, Dionysius allied himself with the Lucanians (native Italians), who inflicted on the Italiots a crushing defeat which would have ended in complete annihilation had not Leptines, Dionysius's brother and admiral, been unable, as a Greek, to bear the sight of such a barbarian triumph and stood between his victorious allies and his suppliant enemies. It was an act which highly displeased his royal brother, not for its humanity, for Dionysius himself, as he was shortly to prove, could be merciful on occasion, but for its independence and interference with his own plans, and Leptines was promptly displaced in favor of another brother. The good impression, however, which his behavior had made upon the Italiot cities was not lost upon the politic commander, who seized the opportunity of a sweeping victory next year, at the river Elleporus, to outdo him by first requiring an absolute surrender at discretion and then almost stunning the great host of captives, who could not hope, from even Hellenic custom, for a lighter fate than slavery, by letting them all go free, unransomed, every man to his own city.

This act of unparalleled mercy completed his conquest of the Italiots, and Rhegium was left unsupported to meet a very different doom. For her there was no forgiveness, even when she would have made terms. After a desperate resistance of eleven months, during which the rage of Dionysius was yet further exasperated by severe wounds, the city fell. Her population were sold or held to ransom, but her brave commander, whom he had vainly tried to bribe, was subjected to insult and torture and finally drowned with all his kin. The town itself was destroyed and a pleasure garden made upon its ruins. Henceforth the ruler of Sicily held firmly both sides of the strait; the "toe" of Italy was his, and the Italiot cities as well as the Lucanians were his firm allies.

It is from this point in his career that one may fairly begin to speak of the *empire* of Dionysius. By politic alliances, even with such barbarous strangers as the Gauls who had recently sacked young Rome and who henceforth provided some of his most valiant mercenaries, by vigorous and useful operations against the Etruscan pirates who infested the western Mediterranean, and especially by the Greek colonies he founded and supported around the Adriatic, he extended that empire until it filled a truly imposing place on the world map. As an Adriatic power, moreover, he was in a position to play an important part in the affairs of Old Greece, and this he was well pleased to do. Already, even while busy with the siege of Rhegium, he had sent a gorgeous embassy to the Olympian Games, whereat the popular feeling of the Greek world against the tyrant had burst into flame at the eloquence of the Athenian Lysias and wreaked itself upon the Syracusan tents. If anything was needed to confirm the friendship between Dionysius and Sparta, this Athenian indictment of them both as the betrayers and tyrants of Hellas must have done so, and accordingly we find the Syracusan warships and Dionysian mercenaries, including Gauls and Spaniards, appearing again and again to assist the Lacedæmonians in their wars. For some time Athens maintained her attitude of holy horror; at another Olympian festival, in 380, we find Isocrates painting in eloquent words the melancholy picture of a devastated Italy and an enslaved Sicily. After a while, however, her virtue yielded to the temptation to win this tremendous force in the Greek world over to her own side. It is a shabby sight — the city of Pericles and Socrates loading with flatteries and honors the tyrant of Syracuse, granting her citizenship to him and his family, and capping the climax by awarding first prize, after a long succession of failures, to his tragedy, The Ransom of Hector. This bait proved irresistible, and a defensive alliance between Athens and Syracuse was signed in March, 367 — too late.

Meanwhile, what had become of the old ambition of Dionysius, to drive the barbarian out of Sicily? It was still the guiding principle of his life and, on the whole, the one thing which gives it consistency and dignity. Twice more he struggled with the huge task. Of the war waged between him and Carthage during the years from 383 to 378 we have very little account. About all we know is that it was fought in both Sicily and Italy, that Dionysius won a great victory followed by a yet greater defeat, and that in consequence the Carthaginian limits on the south coast of Sicily were actually moved forward to the river Halycus. Ten years later, Dionysius, an old man now, made one more effort to complete his life-work. With army and fleet, as in the great war of thirty years before, he burst into the enemy's territory, took Selinus, Entella, and Eryx, and sat down before Lilybæum, the fortified fort which Carthage had created alongside of deserted Motya. The arrival of Hauno forced him to raise the siege, but neither commander seemed eager for a decisive battle, and before the truce they made was out, Dionysius had died of a brief illness, brought on, tradition said, by a joyous carouse at the news of his success as a tragic poet.

He was sixty-three years old, and for thirty-eight of those years he had been an absolute monarch, the most powerful and significant single figure of his time. When we try to sum up his accomplishment, we see it against the background of one great undeniable fact: the city states of the fourth century, whether in Greece or Asia, Italy or Sicily,

were unable either to maintain their independence or to
form permanent and effective unions. As a result, it was
simply a question of time as to when some barbarian power
would swallow them up. Persia did gather in the Asiatic
Greeks, and only because she was herself falling to pieces
left those of the old country to become the prey of Macedonia. The great Semitic empire of Carthage — not, like the
Persian, tottering to its end, but with two hundred years of
power yet before it — had overrun most of Sicily and would
undoubtedly, if unchecked, have established itself in Italy,
probably to such effect that Rome would have been choked
in its cradle. When we see, then, that Dionysius, by creat-
ing, single-handed, one great, unified, powerful Hellenic
state, prevented this alien civilization from spreading beyond
one small corner of the Hellenic world, all of us who believe
that Greece and Rome have been more precious and indispensable to the life we know than any Asiatic-African empire could ever have been, must realize the debt we owe to
the tyrant of Syracuse.

Yet it is hard to feel any enthusiasm for the man or even
for his deed. For one thing, the price paid was appalling.
Unlike Rome, he invented no way of preserving local self-
government along with a strong central authority; every
community that passed under his sway lost its liberty.
Likewise his own great capital, though decrees and treaties
ran in its name, and the beautiful golden coins which delight
the sight-seer to-day bear "Syracusa," not "Dionysius,"
upon their face, was made up of subjects, not citizens. And
just because his rule rested upon no principle of willing
loyalty, because

> The same arts that did gain
> A power, must it maintain, —

the despot had to fill Sicily with hired soldiers of every race
and tongue, men without a fatherland or a tradition, upon

whose purely selfish support he could alone rely, and whose
fidelity must be rewarded by lavish gifts of land. Thus the
arch-defender of Hellas against the barbarian was himself
the greatest introducer of barbarian stocks in an Hellenic
land.

Moreover, he exhausted his empire by a really terrible
taxation. The tremendous growth of Syracuse was at the
expense of the absolute ruin of many cities and their commerce, while the Syracusans themselves finally had to pay
him twenty per cent of their capital. It is true that the
wealth thus forced into his coffers was all spent on political
and military objects, not on himself. Never was a tyrant
less luxurious or less given to personal excesses of any sort.
Untiring in industry, he boasted that he did not know what
a leisure hour meant. His was no splendid and delightful
court like that of Pisistratus, the favorite haunt of poets
and philosophers. Although his one weakness was a craving
for literary fame, he could not get on with literary men, and
the plain speaking of Plato, the only genius of the first rank
who visited his capital, brought a quick and dangerous dismissal.

On the other hand, if he was no genial and gorgeous
despot, neither was he one of the ogreish variety. In only
one or two cases do we hear of unusual severity to individuals, and for the most part his treatment of vanquished
enemies was one of rather unusual clemency, though calculation of effect and need of ransom-money may have played
more part than humanity. Above all, the price he paid for
his dazzling success and power was an utter loneliness,
bred of never-dying suspicion. Even his brothers and long-
tried friends fell sooner or later under the ban; Philistus
himself, who had "made" him and been for half a lifetime
his most trusted counselor, ended his days in honorable
banishment. Cold, shrewd, and intensely practical, without

a scruple or an illusion, valiant on occasion but by nature more the schemer than the warrior, Dionysius seems in temperament much like Louis XI of France, who also had the task, more useful to future ages than popular at the time, of erecting a centralized power on the ruins of local independence.

EPAMINONDAS

(Died 362 b.c.)

EPAMINONDAS was born in Thebes, at least as early as 415 B.C., of a very old family — so ancient, indeed, as to be one of those fabled to have sprung from the dragon's teeth sown by Cadmus. He was nevertheless poor and remained so, with serene satisfaction, all his life, dying, the greatest general and statesman in Greece, without enough money to pay his funeral expenses. Wealth, indeed, meant nothing to him; he was unmarried, had no dependents, devoted the first forty years or so of his life to the pleasures of a student and the remaining fifteen to unremitting public service. In almost every respect, except personal valor, he was what the biologists call a "sport" from the Bœotian stock; indeed, with the exception of the poet Pindar, he was the only man of genius that stock ever produced. Strong bodies and thick heads, rude manners and narrow, selfish views, — such were the characteristics which the word "Bœotian" implied throughout Hellas. Epaminondas branched off, however, even in the gymnasium, where he practiced wrestling and running, rather than the pugilism and feats of sheer strength in which his fellows delighted; in music he was as adept with the Athenian lyre as with the much ridiculed Theban flute; but what did more than anything to raise and train his mind for the great tasks awaiting him was his study under Lysis, a Pythagorean from Croton, "to whom he was so devoted that, young as he was, he preferred that grave and rigid old gentleman before those of the same age as himself, in his familiarity." By nature, indeed, he seems to have been much more interested in

scholarly pursuits than in politics, and to have led, under
the Spartan domination of his native land, the same sort of
detached, meditative, and undisturbed life which satisfied
Germans like Goethe in the days of Napoleon. He had a
dear friend, however, younger than he and much more
active and impulsive, through whom he was eventually
drawn into the *mêlée*. Pelopidas was, indeed, an irresistibly
attractive character. Valiant, impulsive, generous, and affectionate, as disinterested as Epaminondas if less scru-
pulous, he seemed born, first to prepare the way for his
adored elder, and then to act as his most trusted lieutenant.

When, in 382, the state of subordination to Sparta which
Thebes had reluctantly shared for twenty years with the
rest of Greece was exchanged, through the dastardly seizure
of the Cadmea by Phœbidas, for one of actual slavery to
her garrison, her harmosts, and her partisans (a small gang
of Theban oligarchs), Pelopidas, though but a young man,
was sufficiently prominent, through his wealth, his activity,
and his pronounced anti-Spartan sentiments, to be driven
into exile along with other democratic leaders, all of whom
found asylum at Athens. Epaminondas, evidently considered a poor student not worth persecuting, stayed at home
unmolested, though it was his habit to speak freely of public
affairs and to stir up the youths he knew to rivalry, at the
games, with their Spartan governors. After three or four
years the more fiery spirits among the patriots resolved to
put an end to the tyranny or die in the attempt. The dramatic story of the successful plot of which Pelopidas was
the life and soul is told in every history of Greece. That
it involved the assassination of the drunken oppressors did
not at all shock the Greek conscience, brought up as it was
on the praises, in song and story and statue, of similar deeds
in the past. Rather was it unusual that Epaminondas, then
as always averse to civil violence, did scruple to take part

in any attempt which would stain his hands with the blood of fellow-citizens. He was quite willing, however, to accept and applaud the result, and, presenting Pelopidas and his band to the assembled people, exhorted them to fight for their country and their gods.

During the next seven or eight years Thebes was absorbed in two tasks: resistance to the Spartan armies which tried to punish and reduce her, and the consolidation of Bœotia. From very early days the Bœotian cities had been united in a league, of which Thebes was the president, providing two, and later four, of the eleven Bœotarchs, or federal magistrates, who were also generals of the federal army. It was the ideal of the democratic leaders who now controlled Thebes, not merely to revive this league, which Sparta had dissolved, but to convert it into a real state. In local matters the cities were to retain self-government, but the affairs of Bœotia as a whole were to be voted on by general councils and carried out by Bœotarchs, reduced to seven in number and elected no longer from separate towns, but at large. At the same time, the franchise was to be extended from the hoplite-class — about three sevenths of the whole — to all adult citizens. Thebes was to be the capital, but, as an individual city, was to have no more rights than the others. This scheme was agreed to by most of the cities, though Orchomenus held aloof and Platæa was first forcibly enrolled and then, on suspicion of treason, seized and depopulated.

Meanwhile, the Spartan invasions had been successfully checked, and the rather desultory fighting had been of good service in training the Theban soldiery. During these campaigns, particularly, was developed the famous Sacred Band of three hundred chosen warriors, fighting every man beside his best friend. With this company and a handful of horsemen Pelopidas won the most significant and decisive engagement of the war. On the road between Orchomenus and Tegyra he came suddenly upon two Spartan regiments, advancing through the pass. "We are fallen into our enemy's hands!" cried one of his men. "And why not they into ours?" he cheerfully replied, and, after sending out his horse to clear the way, charged headlong with the full impact of his band, in close formation. The Spartans, who had never met anything like it, first divided, like water before the prow of a ship, then fairly broke and fled. It was but a small affair, a passing skirmish, so far as numbers went, but its effect was great in encouraging the Thebans and shaking the prestige of the terrible Spartan infantry which had never before, in a set battle, been defeated by an equal, much less by an inferior, force; in its tactics it foreshadowed Leuctra.

Just what part Epaminondas took in all these affairs we do not know. Plutarch tells of a battle — which cannot possibly have been where and when he places it — in which the friendship between him and Pelopidas was cemented by his heroic rescue of the latter, covered with wounds on a heap of slain. All we can be sure of is that both in war and in politics the former student and philosopher was winning the confidence and respect of his fellow-citizens, for in the year 371 he suddenly emerges into full view as Bœotarch.

Representing his people, he attended the congress at Sparta, at which that city and Athens, both thoroughly tired of a long and meaningless war, agreed to a peace, known as that of Callias, on the same basis as that of the famous King's Peace of 387 — namely, that every Hellenic city should be independent and all confederacies, so far as in any way compulsory, should be dissolved. Sparta was to withdraw her harmosts and garrisons, all the states were to call back any troops they had in the field, and the punishment of any state which broke the peace was to be left to purely voluntary enterprise. To these terms all the envoys agreed, but after the signatures had been affixed, it appeared that those of Epaminondas and his colleagues were set down as for Thebes only, implying that Bœotia, like the Peloponnesus, was not a state but a league, now automatically dissolved. To admit this would have been to forego the whole work of the last eight years, and Epaminondas was not the man to submit to such defeat. Maintaining, alone among the delegates, an attitude of dignified equality with the famous old Spartan king who presided over the respectful assembly, he made a ringing speech, setting forth before all Greece the overbearing nature of Spartan policy and demanding not a nominal autonomy but a real equality as the only basis of a lasting peace. With a sneer Agesilaus asked him whether he did not think that in the name of this precious equality the Bœotian towns should enjoy their independence. The instant reply was a question the daring of which must have sent a shiver through all present, for it challenged the unquestioned dominion of seven hundred years: " Do *you* not think equality demands the freedom of Laconia? " The old king started from his chair. "Will you," he shouted, "leave each of the Bœotian towns independent?" "Will you," retorted the imperturbable Theban, "leave each of the Laconian towns independent?" Agesilaus struck out the name of Thebes from the treaty, the envoys went home, and Greece was proclaimed at peace.

The feelings of Bœotia when her envoys returned must have been a strange mixture of pride and anxiety. She had proclaimed her nationality, held up her head with the best, but she was an outlaw. Athens had thrown her over. Every Greek state, at peace with every other, was her potential enemy. It remained possible, however, that none of them would actually undertake the task of forcing her into the general agreement. Sparta alone, in war-weary Greece, had any interest in such police-work, and under the terms

of the peace just signed she was bound to withdraw the
Peloponnesian army, which was at the time, under King
Cleombrotus, stationed in Phocis, send home the contingents to their various cities, and only then, if she chose,
invite voluntary assistance for a campaign against Thebes.
This was the line of action which one honorable citizen,
named Prothous, urged upon the Spartan assembly, but in
vain, for it seemed, says Xenophon in the light of the result,
as if an evil spirit were leading them on. The spirit, we can
hardly doubt, spoke through the mouth of Agesilaus, whose
lifelong hatred of Thebes had been fanned to flame by
the unheard-of insolence of her envoy. Word was sent to
Cleombrotus not to disband, but to demand once more the
autonomy of the Bœotian cities and, if it were refused, to
march at once across the border. With a heavy heart — for
he was a conscientious man and a leader of the anti-imperial-
ist party — Cleombrotus perforce obeyed. As he marched
toward Thebes he found himself blocked at Coronea, but
going around the enemy by a difficult mountain road, he
seized the port of Creusis with twelve Theban ships and,
having thus secured his rear, started again, this time in a
northerly direction, for the offending city.

On a range of low hills overlooking the plain of Leuctra,
which was crossed by the road to Thebes, the Bœotian army
awaited the invader. There on the little intervale, some
half a mile broad, the fate of Thebes must be decided. As to
what it would be, there could be little doubt. Not only was
the Peloponnesian army nearly twice as large as the Bœotian
(roughly, eleven thousand to six thousand), but Sparta's
reputation as a conqueror was such that all Greece looked
for her overwhelming victory and the wiping out of Thebes
from the map. For that city it was indeed a battle for sheer
existence, even more than that of Marathon had been for
Athens, and, as at Marathon, there were divided counsels

among the generals. Three Bœotarchs were for withdrawing behind the city walls and taking the chances of a siege. But now the weight of Epaminondas's personality and the contagious effect of his courage and confidence made themselves felt. Heartily seconded, no doubt, by the valiant Pelopidas, he succeeded in winning a decision for a battle where they stood, and was granted the disposition of it.

That the fight was to be a desperate one he did not attempt to disguise; indeed, he boldly declared that none but desperate men were wanted to wage it. Almost in the words of Gideon, "He that is fearful and faint-hearted among you, let him go back," he made proclamation, and the men of Thespiæ took him at his word. With the remaining thousands who that day devoted themselves to victory or death, he formed his line of battle.

Leuctra (August 5, 371) is one of the decisive battles in Greek history, not only for its immediate political effect, but also because it marks a revolution in military method. For centuries Sparta had set the fashion in tactics, according to which each army, drawn up in a long shallow line with its best troops on the right wing, pressed forward with a strong tendency to the right, seeking to get round the enemy's left and roll up his line. The frequent result, of course, was that *both* right wings were victorious, leaving the battle practically indecisive, unless, as happened at Coronea (394),[1] they advanced so far as to meet each other and begin all over again. For several years, however, such pitched battles had been rare, as the increased use of hired javelin-men led to a new system of warfare, in which the object was to avoid serious conflict and by clever manœuvres harass and wear out the enemy. Epaminondas now returned to the pitched battle, but absolutely reversed its tactics. While retaining a strong right wing, he put his main reli-

[1] See pp. 115–116.

ance on his left, ranged in a column forty shields deep and
headed by the Sacred Band under Pelopidas. The excellent
Bœotian cavalry was to open battle and clear the field; the
right wing, from which the enemy expected the attack, was
to hold back, while the left struck with all its force at the
enemy's advancing right. The advancing line, therefore,
was a slanting one, the attacking end getting far ahead of
the other; so this order came to be known as the *oblique.*

Cleombrotus, posted on the opposite hills, had of course
no idea of what was coming. With his own line drawn out
as usual in a long shallow array, the four Lacedæmonian
regiments (twelve men deep and one hundred and ninety-
two front) massed at the right, he could have no doubt of
success in outflanking and surrounding the Theban army,
which presented a front of only half his width. But before
his offensive was fairly started came the terrific shock of
the Theban phalanx, led by the irresistible fury of the
Sacred Band. This time there was no break or flight; the
Spartan troops resisted desperately till Cleombrotus himself
— the first king to die in battle since Leonidas — fell mor-
tally wounded among a thousand Lacedæmonians, of whom
four hundred, more than half of all such engaged, were full-
blooded Spartans. The left wing, puzzled by the delay of
the Bœotian right, had hesitated, then advanced, and been
carried down in the defeat. Truly, it was Sparta's Flodden:

> Then might their loss the foemen know, —
> Their king, their lords, their mightiest, low,
> They melted from the field.

The remnants of the beaten army, withdrawn to their
trench-guarded camp, debated stormily whether to renew
the battle. The Spartans, desperate with the shame of defeat, would have returned to die upon the field, but the
allies could not be trusted, and the bitter resolution to ask

the burial truce had to be taken. Not venturing to storm
the camp, the Bœotians granted the request and erected a
stone trophy, the ruins of which mark to this day the grave
of Spartan power.

Thus Bœotia, in just three weeks from the day when she
was turned out with contumely from the Greek family,
raised herself to the headship of it. It was a sufficiently
dizzying experience. Tremendous as the reversal was, however, it would be a mistake to suppose that it made Thebes
the altogether dominant power that Sparta had once been.
She never ruled over all continental Greece, much less the
islands, but for the next eight years she was recognized as
the strongest single power and a dominant influence in all
Greek affairs. To establish and extend this influence was
the absorbing interest of Epaminondas for the rest of his
days.

He began at home. Within the next eighteen months
Thebes became, without serious opposition, supreme in
Central Greece, with the exception, of course, of Athens,
who looked on with growing suspicion and unfriendliness.
The only real danger, which loomed from Thessaly, was
suddenly removed by the assassination, at the hands of his
own subjects, of Jason, the overshadowing despot of Pheræ,
and Thebes was free to reap the fruits of her victory. As
for Bœotia, the pro-Spartans were turned out of Thespiæ,
and Orchomenus, the proud and obstinate old rival of
Thebes, was forced into alliance, but not — by the advice
of Epaminondas — into the unified state. This alliance
spread until it included the Phocians, Malians, both sets of
Locrians, and even several cities of Eubœa and Acarnania.
Nominally it was, like that which Athens had been forming,
a defensive agreement only, but practically each association
tended to become a hard and fast league, swung by its
leading state.

The ambition of Epaminondas for his city, however, was by no means bounded by the limits of Central Greece, and indeed the effects of his victory had been even more complete and startling in the Peloponnesus. The news of Spartan defeat ran like wildfire through the long-subject states, and was the signal for revolt upon revolt and revolution after revolution. For a while the removal of the strong hand seemed to mean simple anarchy. Out of the chaos, however, began to emerge a new Arcadia. The two principal towns of that backward but sturdy and valiant race, Mantinea and Tegea, united for the first time in all their history and formed a Pan-Arcadian union, a federal state with a new capital, built for the purpose and dubbed Megalopolis, the Great City. This new Arcadia was supported by its eastern and western neighbors, Argos and Elis, but the cities in the north of the Peloponnesus still held to Sparta, which of course was bitterly hostile, and it seemed advisable to seek a stronger ally. As Athens held aloof, the invitation went to Thebes, and was welcomed with alacrity by Epaminondas, as offering just the opportunity he was looking for.

In the early winter of 370–69, Epaminondas and Pelopidas, at the head of a great allied army, came down into Arcadia, gathering reinforcements at every step. The Spartan forces had been already withdrawn, and a winter campaign was contrary to all custom, but the Arcadians could not bear to lose such a chance of dealing a death blow to their enemy. Epaminondas, in no awe either of precedent or of the prestige of a country never invaded since the Spartans themselves took possession of it, led his army across the mountains in four divisions, reunited them, and poured down the valley of the Eurotas. The border outposts were overpowered, the villages of the Periœci fell off from their allegiance, the Helots rose — it seemed all over with Sparta. Agesilaus, however, put up so bold a front in the unwalled

city that Epaminondas did not venture to cross the river
under the eyes of the garrison, but forded it a little farther
down and began to lay waste the country. On the third or
fourth day, his scouting parties suffered a defeat which
greatly encouraged the defense. His real weakness then
became apparent: most of his army, made up from a dozen
different states, was undisciplined and intent only on
looting. Meanwhile, reinforcements from the north were
reaching Sparta by sea and a mountain road over Parnon,
and the Theban general, no longer sure of the result of a
battle fought under such desperate conditions, turned back,
after ravaging southern Laconia, to Arcadia.

His campaign, though not complete, had been fruitful
enough, in all conscience. In two months and a half he had
accomplished more than any other general in weary years.
For what Leuctra had done for Spartan leadership, the invasion of Laconia did for Sparta herself. Not only were all
the Periœcan border towns permanently lost to her, but the
Helots of the Messenian plain rose, as at the earthquake of
464, and this time not to be put down. Amid what wild rejoicings, what prayers and tears, can be imagined, the despised and abused serfs of three hundred years were proclaimed once more citizens of a free state; a city, bearing the
long-proscribed name of Messene, was founded by Epaminondas on the slopes of that Mount Ithome which had seen
the last heroic struggle, and word went out to the exiles of the
race throughout all Hellas, to return to their liberated home.
No deed of Epaminondas so gratified Greek idealism as the
restoration of Messenia, for the sight of a purely Greek
population held in virtual slavery had long been an anomaly
and an offense to the most deep-seated of Hellenic feelings.
To Sparta the loss, material as well as moral, was irrepara-
ble. One of the two fertile plains upon the produce of which,
raised by servile labor, the Spartan families and the Spartan

communal discipline were supported, was gone forever, and
the other was henceforth perpetually subject to raids by
day and by night from the bitterest of all enemies.[1]

In February, 369, Epaminondas returned to Thebes, none
too soon, for his allies were breaking up and he himself had
long overstayed the period of his command. In his absence,
however, he had been reëlected Bœotarch, and the next
summer saw him again in the Peloponnesus. / For Sparta
was gathering allies against this new power that threatened
to step into her shoes. Athens, whose recent friendship
with Thebes was but a thin crust over an age-long enmity,
now entered into a definite alliance with her no longer
dreaded Peloponnesian rival, and lent her not only troops
but Chabrias, the best authority on fortifications of his day;
thanks to him, an elaborate system of palisades and trenches,
backed by an allied army of twenty thousand, barred the
Isthmus. Epaminondas, with a much smaller force, got
through by a surprise attack, but was able to accomplish
little and, after leaving a thousand men to guard the build-
ers of Megalopolis, returned without coming to grips with
the twenty shiploads of Celtic and Iberian mercenaries
whom Sparta's old ally, Dionysius of Syracuse, had sent to
her aid, and who, having no awe of the victors of Leuctra,
were likely to prove ugly customers.

Naturally his return from so futile a campaign met with
a cool welcome at Thebes. Besides the popular disappointment, there were real differences of purpose between him
and the leaders of the democratic majority. For one thing,
Epaminondas, however modest and disinterested as an
individual, had his mind set, as a Theban, on the same ever-
vanishing goal which had tempted on the Athenian Alcibiades and the Spartan Lysander — domination over the

---

[1] The situation may be partly suggested by supposing that Germany should have succeeded
in detaching Ireland from Great Britain and setting her up as a separate nation, armed and
financed by the Teutonic Allies and reinforced by large numbers of returning Irish emigrants.

Greek world. Before that could be won, Sparta must be not only checked, as she had been, but completely eliminated as a power. All his policies, therefore, were shaped to this end. Thebans, on the other hand, were accustomed to take near views: world-power was a new idea to them; Sparta, shut up in the Peloponnesus, seemed no longer worth bothering about; but Athens, the old hostile neighbor just across the line, must always be narrowly watched, and her efforts to hem in Bœotia by extending her possessions in Eubœa and on the Macedonian coast nipped in the bud. For this purpose Pelopidas had been sent north during Epaminondas' second Peloponnesian campaign, to establish Theban influence in Thessaly and Macedonia. With the exception, however, of this hostility to Athens, the Theban democracy was pacific. War, which to the Athenian sailors and artisans was always attractive, as likely to increase their profits and influence, meant to the Bœotian farmers heavy burdens and small rewards; prosperity at home was much more attractive to them than the empire abroad for which their great Bœotarch was scheming. Again, between them and what was left of the old oligarchical party in every city of Bœotia there ran a bitter feud, breaking out more than once in ruthless executions of such aristocratic leaders as they were able to lay hands on. Against such treatment Epaminondas, not only personally humane, but in his innermost nature far more sympathetic with his political opponents than with his political associates, always protested, and he sometimes succeeded in balking Demos of his prey, as when he admitted to ransom as prisoners of war, instead of holding for trial as traitors, a whole band of Theban exiles taken in one of the Peloponnesian battles.

All these smoldering causes of discontent burst out after his inglorious return, and the demagogue Menekleidas even brought the two great captains to trial, — for Pelopidas, though much more characteristically Theban and personally popular than his friend, was far too loyal not to share his bad as well as his good fortunes. The conduct of the trial is obscure, but the result, of course, as far as punishment was concerned, was certain — whether or not Epaminondas actually made the court break up in laughter, as Nepos asserts, by asking to have written on his tomb that he was put to death by the Thebans for having forced them to beat the Spartans at Leuctra. Although acquitted, however, he and Pelopidas both failed of reëlection as Bœotarchs, and in 368 there was no Theban invasion of the Peloponnesus.

Instead, Pelopidas was sent north again to try what diplomacy could do to check the alarming increase of Athenian influence at the disreputable court of Macedon. On his return from making a satisfactory arrangement with the regent, Ptolemy, he and his colleague Ismenias were seized, in defiance of the most sacred of all international laws, by the raging tyrant, Alexander of Pheræ. Even the pacifists of Thebes realized that such a man must be dealt with by force, and an army was sent into Thessaly. But the new democratic generals were not up to their work, and the whole force, outmanœuvered, would have been lost had not the troops mutinied and unanimously elected Epaminondas, who was serving as a private in the ranks, to the command. His skill extricated them from a very dangerous position and brought them safely home. Thebes had learned her lesson; she fined the incompetent generals and promptly reëlected Epaminondas as Bœotarch. With a new levy he hurried to the rescue of Pelopidas, which had to be effected with great dexterity, since Alexander, who seems to have been a regular story-book ogre, would, if driven to desperation, have wreaked his wrath on his prisoners. Thebes got back her unlucky diplomats and freed the city of Pharsalus from the tyrant, but otherwise left him to go on massacring his countrymen at pleasure. A strong and united Thessaly without need of Theban aid was no part of her policy.

Of the general war, meanwhile, every one was getting tired, and after an abortive congress had been held at Delphi, the chief states took the step of sending representatives all the way to Susa, to ask each the authority of the Great King for such settlement as she desired. Pelopidas, as envoy for Thebes, made much the best impression; his own attractive and manly bearing, the prestige of his country's recent victories, and the anything but glorious fact that Thebes had never in her history fought against Persia, all combined to win just the decision he was sent to seek: Sparta must recognize the independence of Messenia, but Thebes need not dissolve the federal state of Bœotia; Athens should recall her fleet, relinquishing her attempt to regain Amphipolis; even on a matter regarding which Persia could have no interest or knowledge, a border quarrel between Elis and Arcadia, Thebes got a decision for the side she favored, which, significantly, was not the Arcadian.

For Arcadia was "feeling her oats." The largest, most vigorous state in southern Greece, proud alike of her descent, alone among the Peloponnesians, from the original inhabitants, and of her recent achievements, she felt quite confident of her power to take care of herself even against Sparta, of whose armies in the past, she was well aware, she had herself supplied the best troops next to the Lacedæmonians themselves. Thebes had been a kind friend and would always be a welcome ally, but Arcadia saw no reason why she should exchange one domination for another and take orders, even from the victors of Leuctra. One cannot help sympathizing with this attitude and feeling that Epaminondas and the war party in Thebes made a great mistake in following the same old road which Sparta had trodden to her destruction.

There was no excuse as yet for actual conflict with Arcadia, but in 367 Epaminondas invaded the Peloponnesus for the third time, to secure the adhesion of the Achæan cities along the northern coast, on which he suspected the Arcadian League of having its eye. This object was easily obtained, but, contrary to the policy of Epaminondas, the democratic party at Thebes insisted on setting up democratic constitutions in these cities and expelling the ruling oligarchies on the charge of being pro-Spartan. The result was to make them so; the exiles, banded together, won back the cities, drove out the Theban harmosts, and attached Achaia firmly to the Spartan side. Thus, though by no fault of his own, this campaign of Epaminondas was without result, except that of straining yet further the relations between Thebes and Arcadia.

For the next four years Thebes let the Peloponnesus alone, realizing more and more that her essential rivalry was with Athens. As a part of this rivalry it was important to secure supremacy in Thessaly, and Pelopidas, burning with desire to avenge his mistreatment, was so eager to lead an army, at the request of Thessalian exiles, against the tyrant of Pheræ, that when an eclipse led to the disbanding of the national levy, he started off with three hundred volunteers and a band of mercenaries. In a fierce battle at Cynoscephalæ, he was the life and soul of his little army, turned defeat into victory, but, carried away by a passion of rage at sight of his hated adversary, rushed blindly after him, shouting out challenges to single combat, and fell, pierced by a hundred darts. Profound as was the grief of the army, which passed the night in fasting and darkness as if the victory had been a defeat, it was outdone, at least in clamor, by that of the Thessalian cities, who felt that they had lost their only friend and protector against the wild beast of Pheræ. The next year, however, a Theban army avenged the hero and reduced Alexander to the government of his own city. At the same time, a conspiracy against the democracy, engineered by Theban exiles living in Orchomenus, led to a bloody revenge on Thebes' old Bœotian rival. The ancient town was razed to the ground, its men were slain for resisting the decree, and the rest of the population sold into slavery. This cruel deed, which horrified all Greece, showed what the Theban democracy really was, when not held in check by its one great man.

For Epaminondas was far away at the time. The rapid spread of the new maritime empire of Athens had alarmed him for the supremacy and even the safety of Thebes, since, if Athens were allowed to recover Eubœa, Bœotia would be completely shut in on the northeast and constantly threatened. Characteristically, he had not contented himself with a defensive policy, but had conceived the ambitious idea of meeting and outdoing Athens on her own element and making Thebes what Athens had been a century before, the mistress of the sea. In his own rather showy phrase, he would "transplant the Propylæa from the Acropolis and set it up on the Cadmea." It may be seriously questioned whether this policy of Epaminondas's was not a grave error of judgment. Some resistance to the threat of encirclement was doubtless called for, but there was nothing in the character and circumstances of the Bœotians, a thoroughly agricultural people with hardly any commerce, to fit them for sea power. The assembly, however, was persuaded to try the new venture, a Locrian port was annexed for the purpose, and Epaminondas, with a hundred triremes hastily built and manned, sailed for the Propontis in 364.

The first naval campaign of Thebes — and she was never to undertake another — was successful enough. Epaminon-

das and the Athenian admiral, Timocrates, kept carefully
out of each other's way, and there was no fighting to speak
of, but many discontented members of the new Athenian
league seized the opportunity to revolt, the Eubœan cities
made definite alliance with Thebes, and Epaminondas was
able, unopposed, to visit the Bosphorus and make a treaty
with Byzantium, thus threatening Athens in her most vital
nerve, the grain supply from the Black Sea.

On his return, he found that Peloponnesian affairs were
once more in the foreground. The Arcadian League, left to
itself and no longer held together by pressing danger, was
showing a natural tendency to fall apart. War with Elis
had led to the scandal of a battle among the very temples
of Olympia, in the midst of the festival itself, and need of
money to pay the federal army, to the yet greater scandal
of laying hands on the sacred treasury. Mantinea, already
disaffected, had taken the opportunity to withdraw on high
moral grounds from the League and was sure sooner or later
to drift into the Spartan alliance. Thebes felt it time to
take a hand, and, by what seems to have been a plan approved at headquarters, the commander of her garrison at
Tegea seized the moment when peace with Elis was being
celebrated with general rejoicings to imprison the leaders
of the anti-Theban party from the various cities. He missed
the Mantineans, however, who were his chief object, and
was easily frightened into giving up the rest. It shows the
difference between public and private morality that Epaminondas, when complaint was made at Thebes, approved the
arrest and condemned the release. Arcadia, moreover, he
declared, having asked the help of Thebes against Elis, had
had no right to make peace without her consent. In short,
Thebes, under the leadership of her great Bœotarch, had
determined to be obeyed in the Peloponnesus or know the
reason why. In the summer of 362, Epaminondas, at the

head of a great army, representing nearly all the states of Central Greece, marched southward for the fourth and last time.

The Peloponnesian allies of the Thebans were Argos, Messenia, and the democratic members — Tegea, Megalopolis, and many smaller towns — of the disrupted Arcadian League. The others, who, led by Mantinea, also claimed to be "the League," were assisted by Elis, Achaia, and, above all, Sparta, and expected help from Athens. Megara and Corinth remained neutral. Thus not only were nearly all the states of Greece involved, but they were arranged in layers, so to speak. Sparta was separated by an almost continuous line of Messenians, southern Arcadians, and Argives from her north-Peloponnesian allies, and they again from Athens by the neutral cities of the Isthmus. Likewise, Epaminondas, in order to make connections, through the Isthmus and Argos, with his southern friends, must pass a hostile Athens on his flank and leave a row of enemies behind.

His first decision was to settle with the Athenians by themselves, if possible, by holding Nemea, which blocked the only road from Athens to Mantinea. The Athenians balked him, however, by deciding to go by sea to Laconia, and he therefore went on to Tegea, the citadel of the whole Peloponnesus and meeting-place of all its chief roads, by which supplies of men and provisions poured in from all sides, while he, firmly planted on the direct, though not the only, road from Sparta to Mantinea, waited for the much-desired decisive battle.

One detachment of Spartans had already gone north during the Theban halt at Nemea. A second, under old Agesilaus himself, started out to join it and the Arcadians at Mantinea, avoiding Tegea by taking the circuitous route. Epaminondas, well served by his spies, heard by noon of the movement and resolved on a surprise. His army, contrary to precedent, was encamped inside the town and could be quickly and secretly mobilized. After an afternoon spent in apparent preparations for an attack on the Arcadian position, he marched at twilight in the opposite direction, hoping to fall on a Sparta as helpless as "a nest of young birds." This was no mere mischievous raid; Sparta's constitution was such that the fall of the city would mean the fall of her whole government — the keystone would be knocked out of the arch of the hostile alliance. The plan failed, however. Agesilaus, getting word of the direction of the Theban march, turned back on his steps, sending a runner ahead to call the city guard to arms. He and Epaminondas had a race for it — thirty-five miles, up and down hill, in the clear cool summer night — and, not having to cross the Eurotas, he got into the city first. It was about eight in the morning when the Theban attacked, but one assault convinced him that his plan had failed; without the loss of a moment he formed another. Drawing back his weary troops across the river, he gave them an afternoon's rest and at nightfall started north again, leaving his watch-fires burning and a few cavalry to make familiar sounds. The main army from Mantinea, he knew, would be by this time well on its way to the support of Agesilaus; if he could reach that city the next morning, he would find it undefended. Immediately, therefore, on reaching Tegea, he sent forward the cavalry, without a moment's rest, to fall upon the unsuspecting town, whose laborers were gathering in the harvest in the open fields around. This raid, too, was dictated by high policy, for Mantinea was the chief stronghold of the enemy and, taken, would complete the girdle around Sparta. This time it did seem that nothing short of a miracle could thwart his plan — but the miracle was to happen. The Athenians, having once more changed their minds, had started south by land, and an advance-detachment of cavalry had just that moment reached Mantinea and were taking up quarters in the city. When the alarm was sounded the gallant six hundred threw themselves on their tired horses and without a moment's hesitation charged the more numerous but equally weary and utterly surprised Bœotians and drove them headlong back.

It is an extraordinary proof of the influence of Epaminondas that such fatigues and disappointments do not seem to have shaken the morale of his army in the least. After a few days' rest, during which the enemy troops which had gone to Sparta returned to their position at Mantinea, he made ready for the pitched battle which had now become inevitable. In order to understand this battle, which in tactics and in the number of men and cities involved was the greatest so far fought in Greece, it is necessary to have a clear picture of the country in which it was fought.

The plain of Mantinea, in which the city of that name stood at the northern end and that of Tegea at the southern, is about eighteen miles long and averages about five miles wide, but near the middle two precipitous mountains jutting out, Kapnistra on the east and Mytika on the west, from the ranges that enclose the whole valley, narrow it to a pass of hardly more than a mile in width; the whole, therefore, has something the shape of an hourglass. In this pass the shrewd old campaigner, Agesilaus, placed his twenty thousand men to great advantage. His chief danger, that of being outflanked by the superior numbers of the enemy, was obviated by the cliffs on either hand, for his line, drawn up at ordinary depth, just sufficed to hold the pass from side to side. Behind him two roads ran back to his base at Mantinea through a thick wood which provided a shady camp, much needed in the broiling midsummer days. From the heights above, moreover, his watchmen could observe every movement in the southern plain.

The task of Epaminondas was thus very difficult, for it was not merely to defeat the enemy and drive him back upon his base; what was wanted was a decision, which could only be obtained by capturing that base and destroying or breaking up the army. The eyes of the born general saw his only chance; if he could get possession of the road which ran through the right wing of the enemy, close under Mytika, he might from there break through that right wing, get between it and Mantinea, and drive the whole army into the roadless mountains to the northeast. To do this, the "oblique" tactics of Leuctra, the division of his army into an attacking wing in which all its energies were collected, and a defensive one, to be kept back, if possible, until it could be used to defeat a broken enemy, were obviously necessary, and geographical reasons determined that again the attack should be made from the left. For its full effect, however, this attack must be a surprise, and here the genius of Epaminondas shows most clearly.

On July 5, 362, lining up, about five miles from the enemy, at the customary depth of fourteen files, he made as if to advance directly upon him, but soon began to wheel to the left and approach a low, gently sloping hill a little south of Mytika. The enemy, fully expecting an attack, was in his best order: the Mantineans, being on the home grounds, held the right wing, the post of honor, with the Spartans next to them; the Athenians were on the left, and the lesser contingents of the other allies filled up the center. Watching with surprise the side-stepping of the Theban troops, and seeing them make for the hill, they concluded that the confused looking movements on the easy slope were those of encampment and that there would be no fight that day; relaxing discipline, therefore, they broke ranks, and many fell back into the grateful shelter of the wood. Meanwhile Epaminondas by these misunderstood movements was massing his six thousand Bœotian hoplites into one phalanx, led by a front line composed entirely of officers, with whom he took his own place. Yet farther to the left, a similar deep column of cavalry was to charge the enemy's horse. There was no need to tell his right wing to keep back, since from the nature of the ground and direction of the march it was about a mile farther from the foe. Against the only possible danger, a flank attack by the unopposed Athenians on his advancing left, he provided by sending a detachment across the plain to hold a spur of Kapnistra which threatened their own flank. Thus by the simple means of the oblique march Epaminondas had attained all his objects at once — position, deception of the enemy, and time to rest and reform. Every single movement had had its purpose and its effect.

Then came the charge. In feverish haste the astonished foemen leaped to their horses and their arms. Even under such a shock Agesilaus did not lose his head, but, as his right hastily formed to meet the attack, pushed his Spartans in front of the Mantineans, to thicken the resistance and bear the first brunt. The strife was tremendous and heroic; in the *mêlée* Epaminondas himself went down. Carried from the field with a spear-head in his breast, he faintly asked for his two best captains, and when told that they too were slain, he murmured, "Then make peace," and drawing out the spear, fell back dead.

Never was news so literally paralyzing. All had gone well, the enemy's horse were in full retreat, the hard-fighting right was shattered, the left had been held in check, nothing remained but to close in and complete the victory. Instead, the hoplites stood as if turned to stone, and the pursuing cavalry actually halted and fled back as if themselves pursued. Only a few peltasts, perhaps out of reach of the tidings, pushed their way across to the Athenians and were slain. Each side erected a trophy, each side removed its own dead; what was within a moment of being one of the greatest victories in history stands as a drawn battle. And with Epaminondas fell at the same time the hopes and pretensions of Thebes in the Greek world; peace was made on the basis of the *status quo ante*, and the great army went home.

It has seemed worth while to give so much space to the military operations of Epaminondas because it is upon them that his greatness really rests. As a statesman he was commonplace and built nothing permanent, but as a commander he is the direct teacher of Philip and Alexander, the forerunner of Cæsar and Frederick the Great and Napoleon. The secret of all these was *concentration*, striking with one's whole force at a chosen spot in the enemy's position, and, with them all, the means to this end was superior *mobility* — extraordinarily rapid and unexpected marches. To put it in another way, Epaminondas was the first to treat an army as an organism. Before him it had been an aggregate of thousands of warriors, acting as a unit in delivering the attack but fighting thereafter thousands of little individual battles; under him, every division had its own specific task, acted as a member of the whole body. The great lesson of specialization, which has revolutionized our mechanical and business life, was first applied by Epaminondas to the art of war.

DEMOSTHENES

(Died 322 B.C.)

In the middle of the fourth century before Christ, Athens, although in reality no longer a great power, was still the chief city of Greece and incomparably the most delightful. The glorious works of the Periclean age no longer stood out, as they had done a century before, against a background of low and huddled houses, among which no stranger could have picked out by its size or ornament the residence of a Themistocles, a Cimon, or a Nicias, but private luxury was catching up with public magnificence, and stately mansions and beautiful gardens proclaimed the right of the rich to enjoy their own. Business was extremely good; in both trade and manufactures Athens easily maintained her lead. The boast which Pericles had made when he called her the school of Hellas was now literally fulfilled, for strangers from every corner of the world flocked to her, as we should to a combination of Rome, Paris, and the German universities, for their artistic and scholarly education. The year-round succession of stately and elaborate festivals, on which the wealth of the state and of individuals was ungrudgingly spent, and, above all, the superb representation of the greatest tragedies were of themselves a rare attraction and discipline to all seekers after culture, as well as an endless entertainment to the Athenian populace, whose theater money was provided from the Theoric Fund. Equally dramatic in a cheaper, but still, by our standards, an amazingly artistic fashion were the debates at the weekly meetings of the Assembly and the ingenious and often highly rhetorical arguments made before the great citizen juries. Serious students, meanwhile, came for the unrivaled opportunity of listening to Plato's lectures on philosophy in the grounds of the Academy or working under Isocrates, the world-famous professor of rhetoric, who, like Jowett of Balliol, exerted a lasting influence over not only the style but the thought of the ablest young men of his day.

One of the marked features of Athenian life of this time is that it was essentially peaceful. Technically, to be sure, Athens was at war most of the time, but the hostilities, brought on chiefly by her "far-flung" commercial and imperial interests, were waged for the most part at a distance and by hired troops. In nearly two generations the militia, which, indeed, had shrunk to less than half its former numbers, had been hardly ever called out, the required military drill had fallen into disuse, and party-leaders were no longer generals but pure civilians. This division of functions had the advantage that successful politicians were no longer feared and ostracized as possible tyrants, but the great practical disadvantage that measures involving serious military operations might be urged and carried by men who had no experience in such matters and no responsibility for putting them into effect. It is very significant that the single exception to this rule, Phocion, being a practical and efficient soldier, was the chief "pacifist" of Athens, since he knew better than any one else how little his countrymen could be relied on to follow up their words with deeds. For Athens, the ancient champion of Hellas, had undeniably grown "soft." There was a marked tendency, as in our own day, among the finer spirits, to withdraw from politics altogether, as from a confused and dirty game, and give themselves up to the satisfactions of a retired and cultivated life. The well-to-do, dreading the burdens of war-taxation and looking with a cynical eye upon the volatile and pleasure-loving multitude, preferred a moderate, defensive policy that should be good for business, and the multitude itself, while rejoicing in a good deal of national swagger and always pleased to hear of themselves as the true sons of the heroes of Marathon, were not at all anxious, when it came to the point, to exchange their agreeable and easy life for the hardships of daily drill and campaign fare.

The statesman who represented most accurately the ideas of the wealthy, conservative class, while keeping, by his splendid expenditure of the Theoric (Festival) Fund, the good will of the people, was Eubulus, a thoroughly able and respectable man and an excellent financier, who for several years directed the policy of Athens on a strictly realistic basis. In this he was strongly supported by the unflattering but absolutely trusted Phocion, and by a group of younger men, of whom Æschines is the best known, "practical politicians" in a much lower sense. Such was the Athens and such the easy-going, disillusioned society in which there came to the front a new statesman, one to whom dreams were the only realities and the city of Themistocles and Aristides was the only true Athens, worth living and dying for.

This was Demosthenes, son of a well-to-do manufacturer of the same name, who died leaving two young children to the care of guardians whom he had taken all pains to attach to their interests. The boy grew up sickly and unattractive, and the over-anxiety of his mother, holding him back from the athletic sports which meant so much to Greek youth, intensified the unsociable temper which kept him through life a man apart; he never learned to be a "good fellow." Otherwise, his education was the usual one, and we know of his boyhood only his early and absorbing interest in oratory. He would beg his tutor to take him to hear the famous speakers of the day, and hang fascinated on their words, dreaming of the time when he too should sway great audiences and move them to tears and laughter.

The first rude shock to his dreams was the discovery when, at sixteen, he should have received his estate, that his trustees had made away with most of it. With the help of Isæus, the best lawyer of the day, Demosthenes made a long and spirited fight in the courts, but, though he won his cases, he succeeded in recovering hardly more than one twelfth of the property and found it advisable to increase his income by his own exertions. The profession most congenial to his tastes was that of advocate, to which he devoted himself for several years. Theoretically, an Athenian was still expected to plead his own case, and professional lawyers were in somewhat the same anomalous position as college "coaches" to-day. But in practice most men found them quite necessary, and the business flourished, the "logograph" (advocate) either supplying the speech for his client to read, or himself appearing in court after a few words of introduction by the latter. As a writer of speeches the young Demosthenes soon excelled, his "private orations" showing not only effective rhetoric but considerable dramatic imagination, shaping his style to fit the various characters and circumstances of his clients.

When it came to pleading in court, however, he found himself at a mortifying disadvantage. In his solitary and sedentary youth he had grown up awkward and short-breathed, his enunciation was extremely poor, and he was even subject to fits of nervous stammering. The real character of the man first appears in the extraordinary energy and persistency with which he applied himself to overcome these defects. He gave himself a thorough gymnastic training, he studied gesture and pose with an actor friend, he conquered his faults of breathing and enunciation by various quaint expedients, such as declaiming while running or climbing, and with his mouth full of pebbles, — most of all by incessant practice in recitation as well as in phrasing, making not only every speech he heard, but every casual conversation, a text for criticism and re-wording. It was doubtless due to the recollection of his early failures and the stories that got about regarding his peculiar efforts that he whom posterity has held the greatest of all orators was considered by his contemporaries a most excellent speaker, indeed, but one whose orations "smelt of the lamp" in comparison with the spontaneous outbursts of more naturally gifted men.

While oratory had thus fascinated Demosthenes from his childhood, it had been by no means his only study. He was a great reader of history, especially that of Thucydides, and from his reading he imbibed that idea of the glorious mission and responsibility of Athens which became the guide, for good or ill, of his political career. It appears even in the semi-political speeches, otherwise not remarkable, which he delivered before the law courts in 354: —

"Never to this day," he breaks out, "has this People been eager for the acquisition of money; but for honor it has been eager as for nothing else in the world. It is a sign of this that when Athens had money in greater abundance than any other Hellenic people, she spent it all in the cause of honor; her citizens contributed from their private resources, and she never shrank from danger when glory was to be won. Therefore she has those eternal and abiding possessions — the memory of her actions, and the beauty of the offerings dedicated in honor of them — the Porticoes which you see, the Parthenon, the Colonnades, the Dockyards."

With such views Demosthenes, now thirty years old, first addressed the Assembly. The situation of Athens at the moment must be briefly summarized. The so-called Social War, caused by the revolt of her maritime allies, had recently ended (355 B.C.) with the permanent secession of Byzantium and the principal islands and the loss by death or disgrace of all her best commanders. The financial strain had been great, and it was about this time that Eubulus, who believed a peace policy absolutely necessary for recuperation, seems to have procured, as a safeguard against any rash enterprise, the passage of a law applying all surpluses to the Theoric Fund. Only after the specific repeal of this law by the special court created for such business, would it be possible to vote any unusual sum for war purposes.

Eubulus was not without reason for his anxiety. Great preparations in Persia, really directed against Egypt, aroused alarm in Greece and led some hot-heads to propose attacking the huge Asiatic empire. A year later, the cities Epaminondas had founded in the Peloponnesus, Megalopolis and Messene, fearing aggression from Sparta, asked the aid of Athens as well as Thebes, and again, in 351, there was a call to assist the exiled democrats of Rhodes against the Queen of Caria. On each of these occasions Demosthenes spoke, and these orations, though by no means equal to his later efforts, are interesting as witnesses to his early grasp of the principles by which he was to guide his whole political life. Although in the first he opposed, and in the other two advocated, active intervention, his appeal in all was to the sense of national and individual obligation — the duty of Athens to live up to the generous ideals of her past as the champion abroad, as well as at home, of liberty and democracy, and the corresponding duty — much less palatable — of every citizen to make the personal sacrifices necessary to the carrying out of such a policy. It is this insistence, from the beginning to the end of his career, upon the full realization by the people that the price of glory is hard work and sacrifice, which lifts Demosthenes, even at his most unreasonable and inflammatory moments, far above the ordinary "jingo" agitator.

That he could be very unreasonable is evident when we

observe that the speeches for the Megalopolitans and the
Rhodians, in which he urged Athens to scatter her forces
by expeditions into the Peloponnesus and oversea, were
made at the very time when all Greece, and Athens, through
her indispensable grain route, more than any other state,
was threatened by the miraculously sudden rise of an overwhelming power on the north. Within eight years a great
military and political genius had transformed Macedonia
from a negligible inland state of wild highlanders and primitive peasants into a great kingdom, possessing a coast line
stretching, interrupted only by the towns of the Olynthian
Confederacy, from the Propontis to Thermopylæ, a treasure
in the gold mines of Mount Pangæus, greater than any
other state west of Persia could command, and, alone among
Hellenic powers, a *national standing army*, completely organized in all branches of the service, and ready for use at all
seasons and under all conditions. This army, moreover,
had two rare advantages: it was recruited from a fresh, warlike race, which, like our Teutonic ancestors, lived by hunting, fighting, and drinking, — a man was not held fit to take
his place among his fellows at the feast till he had slain an
enemy and a wild boar, — and it was wielded by one supreme command, responsible to no interfering politicians
or shifting popular will. When it is added that Philip was as
crafty as he was valiant, and past master of all the arts of
bribery, intrigue, and secret service, it will be seen that
before such a foe the Greece of the fourth century, divided,
individualist, sophisticated, and essentially civilian, was absolutely fated to go down.

Yet it could hardly be expected to realize that fact, and
Demosthenes never realized it. The rise of Philip had been
simply too rapid to keep up with. As, one after another, the
allies of Athens along the north coast of the Ægean had
fallen into his hands, she had waked to the danger always

just too late. Only in 352, when Philip, now master of the Thessalians, who had rashly invited him to their aid against the Phocians in the wretched "Sacred War," was actually advancing upon Thermopylæ, had the allies of Phocis — Athens, Sparta, and Achaias — suddenly roused themselves, and Eubulus in particular, for all his pacifism, had shown himself most patriotically active in sending out a force of citizen volunteers to hold the pass in such strength that Philip had prudently retired. It was only, however, to strike in another place and one alarmingly near the exposed nerve of Athens. His siege of a Thracian fortress close to the precious Chersonese aroused great excitement, and the constant depredations of his fleet upon Athenian commerce became too much to be borne with any patience. In 351, Demosthenes, finding no older man ready to propose a definite measure to the exasperated but vague Assembly, came forward with the first of his really great orations, known as the First Philippic. Never, perhaps, does he show to more real advantage than in this early speech, in which he not only appeals generally, as before, to the patriotism and sense of responsibility of his fellow-citizens, but presents to them a well thought-out and practicable plan. This was, briefly, to maintain two permanent forces — one, wholly of citizens, for home service, ready to repel instantly any attack upon Greece itself; the other, of which at least one fourth should also be of citizens, to be quartered, summer and winter, among the islands of the north Ægean and thence conduct an aggressive warfare upon Philip's own coast. With such a force, wielded by a steady, consistent policy, capable of taking the initiative against the enemy instead of, as the orator described it, running up and down after him like an unskillful boxer swinging his arms to guard whatever spot has been already struck, Athens might, considering the command she still had of the sea, have seri-

ously interfered with Philip's plans; at all events, the policy
of Demosthenes was the only sensible alternative to peace
with Macedon. For neither alternative, however, was the
people ready. It could not bring itself to make the effort
necessary for the one; it was not willing to yield its long
claim to Amphipolis, now in the hands of Philip, by adopting the other. So the war dragged ineffectually on.

By 349, Philip was ready to perfect his coast line by
absorbing Olynthus and the lesser cities of the Chalcidian
peninsula. The appeals of Olynthus for aid, seconded by
three mighty speeches from Demosthenes, did bring some
action on the part of Athens, but it was inadequate and
delayed, so that the whole of Chalcidice fell into the hands
of the Macedonian, who sold as slaves the inhabitants
of Olynthus, including many Athenian citizens, and wiped
out of existence thirty-two towns. Athens had moved too
late, but she was beginning to wake up and to pay some
attention to the grave and stirring admonitions of the
young orator who never ceased from warning her of the
peril from the north and of the effort necessary to save her
from it. For the first time, in one of these "Olynthiacs,"
Demosthenes ventured to point out the step which must be
taken before Athens could really exert her full force — the
repeal of the law concerning the Theoric Fund; and though
the suggestion was not followed at the time, the seed of the
idea had been sown. For the rest, the most notable points
in these speeches are the dangerous kind of idealism which
led the speaker to underestimate the ability and character
of Philip in his confidence that power won by such evil
means must be doomed to defeat, and the moral courage
and frankness with which he insisted on the necessity of
universal service in one form or another and the refusal of
public funds to those who shirked: "It has been no part
of my proposal," he said, "that we should assign the due of

those who act to those who do nothing; that we should be idle ourselves and enjoy our leisure helplessly, listening to tales of victories won by somebody else's mercenaries."

One reason why Athens had been unable to do more for Olynthus was her unwise interference in local quarrels in Eubœa, stirred up for that very purpose by Philip's agents. We note that Demosthenes, though opposed to this campaign, served in it as a hoplite, but returned soon — soldiering was never his forte — to act as choregus (patron or producer of a tragedy) at the Dionysiac festival and, incidentally, to be assaulted thereat by a bitter personal enemy. The Eubœan affair turned out an expensive failure, and it became more and more evident, however unpalatable, that a general peace must be made.

For this Philip was quite ready. Now, as always, he had much rather have Athens as a friend — though, of course, a closely bound and practically subordinate friend — than as a foe. Ambitions and dreams apart, there was no real conflict between their interests. Moreover, Philip had a great admiration, almost touching in its way, for Greek culture and for Athens as its chief representative. He had set his heart on being acknowledged, not as a barbarian conqueror of Greece, but as the commander-in-chief of Greece against all barbarians, and there were high-minded men, like the aged Isocrates, who saw in that dream the best hope for the future of Hellas. But it would be a future in which the *old* ideal of Hellenic freedom — the right of every state to the absolute control of its own affairs, foreign and domestic — must be lost forever, and patriots like Demosthenes, their eyes fixed upon the glories of a bygone age, had rather Greece should go down fighting than surrender those ancient and precious rights.

For the moment, however, even Demosthenes saw that some arrangement must be made and the "Sacred War"

brought to an end before the Amphictyonic Council again
called Philip down to Greece. He made one, indeed, and
the youngest, of the ten ambassadors sent to treat with the
King, a colleague being Æschines, an able orator-politician
of the opposite party. As it happens, we have detailed
accounts of all that took place during the negotiations of
this and the following year, from the pens of these notable
participants, — but unluckily, they contradict each other
at almost every point! As far as can be gathered, however,
the two lifelong opponents were by no means so far apart
in policy at the time as they later said and very likely
thought they had been. Neither seems to have shone particularly at the interview with Philip; in the presence of the
man of deeds, the men of words were reduced, Æschines to
windy rhetoric and Demosthenes to positive stage fright.
Philip, very agreeable, hospitable, and condescending, imbued most of the envoys with the idea that he had none
but the most merciful intentions toward the Phocians — to
punish whose sacrilege the war had been nominally waged —
and the friendliest sentiments for Athens herself. So the
embassy went home very cheerful and were soon followed
by Philip's representatives offering peace and alliance.
After some scruples about the abandonment of Phocis, the
Assembly compromised on an agreement by which that
inconvenient and discreditable ally was tacitly but not ex-
plicitly excluded from the new combination, and the same
ten started northward again to get the King's signature.

On the second return of the embassy, Philip and his army
followed close behind, and the sight of them at Thermopylæ again aroused the qualms of the people, by no means
easy in their conscience. Soothed, however, by the glowing
assurances of Æschines, and in spite of solemn warnings by
Demosthenes, they finally accepted the treaty, yet held
back from the mark of friendship Philip called for, the send-

ing of a contingent to join his army. In a moment he was through the pass, dictating terms to Central Greece. The Phocians, abandoned by all, gave up their cities, became defenseless villagers and yielded to Philip their votes in the Amphictyonic Council, which he henceforth dominated. Thebes, their bitterest enemy, had gained her point but lost her relative position; Athens, though soon relieved, by friendly overtures from Philip, of the panic which had seized her at his approach, was left humiliated, sore, and considerably ashamed of the inglorious part she had played. In later days Æschines and Demosthenes bandied back and forth the reproach of having betrayed the Phocians, but in reality they were past saving, and Demosthenes had already set his mind on a future alliance with Thebes as the only possible bulwark against Macedon. For the present, however grudgingly, Athens must acknowledge Philip's position as an Amphictyonic — that is, a truly Greek — power, but she consoled herself by turning the pro-Macedonian party out of office, and from this time on the influence of Demosthenes became predominant.

The peace which goes by the name of Philocrates lasted nominally for six years (346–40), but to Demosthenes it was never anything but a truce, to be used in awakening Athens and, if possible, the rest of Greece to the dangers which beset them, as well as, after the first year or two, in provoking Philip to throw off what the Athenian persisted in believing the hypocritical mask of friendship and appear in his true light as a hungry tyrant bent on world power. The patience of Philip under this treatment was really remarkable. He was busy consolidating his home-kingdom, establishing his position in Thessaly, creeping eastward in Thrace and westward in Epirus; Greece could wait — not but that, as Demosthenes was always pointing out, his secret service was ever busy there, favoring the pro-Macedonian party which developed in almost every state, for everywhere the "oligarchical," or property-holding class was turning to him, as it had formerly turned to Sparta, for support. It was this underlying, permanent opposition between Philip and democracy which Demosthenes grasped early and firmly and used as the lever of his strongest appeals to Athenian pride: as the champion not only of autonomy, but of democracy was Athens bound to stand forth against the arch-enemy of both.

Gradually, year by year, his insistent eloquence got complete control over the minds of his fellow-citizens. His charge against Æschines, of corrupt betrayal of his duties as ambassador, though urged with brilliant sophistry, failed of its object; yet, in spite of Æschines' acquittal, Demosthenes maintained his influence and kept Athens in an attitude of suspicion that refused to be propitiated by the most flattering advances or concessions on the part of Philip. To tell the truth, Demosthenes, firmly convinced that the conquest of his city was the Macedonian's ultimate object, was anxious to bring on war before he should grow yet stronger, but in face of the inconvenient fact that neither Philip nor the Athenian people wanted to begin hostilities, this was rather difficult. The advance of Philip toward the Chersonesus, however, made the situation more acute, and Demosthenes was able to defend the really piratical behavior of the Athenian commander there against the strong protests of Philip, on the ground that he was maintaining, however illegally, the interests of his country. As to the argument that refusal to hand over the offender would bring on war, he declared that, if Athens could only see it, Philip was already making war on her. His greatest speech yet, however, the Third Philippic, was delivered two or three months later, when war, though more imminent than ever, was still not declared. In this he put his finger on one of the

causes of the disunion and indifference among the Greeks —
the prevalence of political corruption and the cynical amuse-
ment with which it was taken for granted: —

What is the cause of these things? For as it was not without
reason ... that the Hellenes in old days were so prompt for freedom, so it is not without reason or cause that they are now so
prompt to be slaves. There was a spirit, men of Athens, a spirit
in the minds of the People in those days which is absent to-day
— the spirit which vanquished the wealth of Persia, which led
Hellas in the path of freedom, and never gave way in face of battle
by sea or land; a spirit whose extinction to-day has brought universal ruin and turned Hellas upside down. What was this spirit?
It was nothing subtle or clever. It meant that those who took
money from those who aimed at dominion or at the ruin of Hellas
were execrated by all. . . . Where are such sentiments now? They
have been sold in the market and are gone.

By such burning words Demosthenes had at last attained
his object: Athens was ready not only to cheer his policy
but to adopt it, with all that it implied. Given *carte blanche*
as an ambassador, he exerted all his diplomatic powers and
in a few months raised Athens from a position of all but
isolation to that of the center of a fairly formidable alliance, including, above all, Byzantium, a success which, as
he later very pardonably boasted, secured a completely ade-
quate supply of food throughout the war. Another great
achievement was the reform of the trierarchy, which he carried over the strongest resistance of the wealthy men, who
under the old law had been able to shirk their responsibility
for outfitting the fleet. In future every citizen rich enough
to be assessed for this service at all was assessed in proportion to his property, and this system proved not only fair to
all but highly profitable to the state.

By this time the patience even of Philip had been exhausted — he had seized the Athenian merchant fleet at the
Bosphorus, and Athens had replied by a declaration of war.

She had also assisted Byzantium, which he had now reached the point of besieging, so effectively that he dropped the undertaking for the time and disappeared inland to refresh his Macedonians with a little old-fashioned fighting and cattle-driving in the highlands of what is now Bulgaria.

Athens, highly elated at this auspicious beginning of the war, had no idea of the terrible danger she had actually incurred in provoking to war, without a single first-class ally or first-class general, the greatest military genius, backed by the greatest resources, of the Greek world. Demosthenes, to be sure, had still a card to play. The best army south of Macedonia was decidedly the Theban, and an alliance between Thebes and Athens might check the invasion of even a Philip. The long-standing and bitter feud between the two cities made such an alliance most difficult to bring about; every approach to it must be carefully veiled, on account of the extreme unpopularity of the idea. But it must never be forgotten that this was the cardinal point of Demosthenes' policy, to which almost anything else must be sacrificed — quite rightly, if Athens was to resist Philip at all; it was her only chance.

This explains the otherwise incomprehensible attitude he took in the Amphictyonic quarrel which just then suddenly flared up. Though the place of Athens would naturally have been at the head of the forces called out to punish Amphissa for a sacrilege which the Athenian Æschines had been the one to denounce, she as well as Thebes, the friend of the Amphissan Locrians, held back and thus gave occasion for the calling in of Philip to do their work. Demosthenes, who was responsible for this refusal and its consequences, has been severely blamed; his idea, of course, was that, the conflict with Macedon being inevitable, to postpone it would be to lose the best chance of a Theban alliance.

Philip seized his opportunity, pushed through the mountains, and planted himself at Elatea, commanding the high-road to Thebes and Athens. The latter he now openly proclaimed as his object, while from the former he asked assistance or, at the very least, benevolent neutrality. Demosthenes himself has left us a vivid account of the excitement in Athens when the men arrived — the rushing out of the Prytanes from their supper to bid the generals summon an Assembly, the clearing of the market-place and burning of the booths, the crowded town-meeting at early dawn, the long wait for the Senate and the formal opening exercises, the call of the herald, "Who wishes to speak?" repeated again and yet again. After a long silence Demosthenes himself arose and exhorted the people, forgetting all old grudges and suspicions, to throw themselves unreservedly into the arms of Thebes. There was nothing else to do, and by a unanimous vote he was sent with nine others to the rival city to seek the new alliance. It was indeed an undertaking, by his mere eloquence to overcome at once the arguments of the Macedonian envoys backed by a great army a few miles off, and the long-standing enmity of Thebes for Athens, but he accomplished it, though naturally at a high price, and nothing could be juster than the indignation with which he later met the reproach of having made a bad bargain. Did not Athens, he said, in the great days of old, provide two hundred out of the three hundred ships at Artemisium, and did she think herself abused? "No! men saw her rendering thanks to Heaven, because when a common peril beset the Hellenes, she had provided double as much as all the rest to secure the deliverance of all."

It was indeed with old-time self-abnegation that Athens entered into the alliance, not only meeting two thirds of the expenses but granting Thebes the command on land, an equal share of that at sea, and undisputed sway in Bœotia. At the same time she threw herself at last, with all her might, into the military task before her, calling out, for the first time in twenty-five years, her entire citizen levy, stopping all needless expenditures, and devoting, as Demosthenes had so long vainly urged, the Theoric surplus to the national defense. A number of the lesser Peloponnesian states — unluckily, none of the larger — sent troops to join the new allies, and even Philip hesitated to attack so strong a combination; he offered terms, and there were many in both cities, including the experienced and pessimistic Phocion, who would have accepted them, but Demosthenes, knowing well that so favorable a combination was very unlikely to develop again, resisted furiously and successfully, threatening to drag to prison by the hair of his head any one who talked of peace.

For some months the campaign dragged; early minor engagements were even favorable to the allies; at last, in August, 338, the two armies faced each other in the narrow plain of Chæronea. In numbers the opponents were about equal — some thirty-odd thousand apiece; in valor the Thebans, at least, were unsurpassed; the superiority of Philip lay in his vastly superior generalship. Using the tactics he had learned from Epaminondas, with a more serious use of his heavy cavalry, he launched his left wing, horse and foot, commanded by the boy Alexander, upon the stubborn Theban phalanx, while, holding back his right, he lured the Athenians, rushing forward "On to Macedon!" into a disadvantageous position and then fell on them from all sides. Leaving a thousand slain and another thousand prisoner, the remainder, including Demosthenes, broke and ran, together with the allies of the center; only the Sacred Band of Thebes died where they stood, friend beside friend, to the last man.

Terrible as was the blow, the Athenian leaders did not lose their heads — or their influence. Proposals were made

to call in all the rural population, set the old men to guard
the walls, and offer citizenship to metics and freedom to
slaves who would join in the defense. Charidemos, Philip's
bitterest personal foe, was put in command, and Demosthenes, with the office of corn-commissioner, set sail for
food and money.

When he got back it was to a situation totally changed.
Philip, after one wild outburst of barbaric, drunken triumph,
had become again the patient, politic statesman and pan-
Hellene. To Thebes, which had proved a faithless ally, he
was severe, but not savage, while to Athens he was positively
conciliatory. This frightful despot who had been held up
to them by Demosthenes as devoting all his energies, year
in and year out, to their destruction, the amazed Athenians
now saw offering the friendliest alliance with every outward
token of respect, — the bones of the slain restored with honors and the prisoners set free, — and no material loss except
the Chersonese. That loss, of course, left her permanently
in Philip's power, and there could be no question that henceforth her position, however prettily disguised, would be that
of a subject rather than an equal, but the terms were so
beyond all hope that they were accepted with enthusiasm.

The surprising thing is not that in this revulsion of feeling
the pro-Macedonians — Æschines, Demades, and the rest —
gained much influence, but that Demosthenes retained any.
Yet he seems to have done so; though constantly brought to
trial on frivolous indictments, he was as regularly acquitted;
as commissioner of fortifications, he oversaw and generously
aided from his own pocket the systematic strengthening of
the city defenses; and to him was assigned the solemn duty
of pronouncing the funeral oration over those fallen in the
war. It was at this very time, moreover, that his friend
Ctesiphon proposed, and the Council voted, that a golden
crown should be awarded him before the multitude assem-

bled from all Greece at the Dionysiac festival, in recognition
of his patriotic services. But when the measure came before
the Assembly, Æschines blocked it by indicting Ctesiphon
for a technical violation of law.

In the same year an event occurred which seemed likely
to change the whole situation. Philip, in a position at last
to carry out his great dream of a pan-Hellenic invasion of
Persia, had called for contingents from all the Greek cities,
and all but Sparta had agreed to send them. At the height
of his triumph, as he was celebrating the wedding of his
daughter, he fell dead by the dagger of one of his own bodyguard.

That Demosthenes should have felt an immense relief
and even elation at the news was only natural, though his
open exultation was in the worst of taste. Neither he nor
any Greek could have reasonably expected that a greater
than Philip was to succeed him. Within three months the
youthful Alexander had seized the reins of government,
executed all rival claimants to the throne, and marched with
lightning-like rapidity upon Greece. In Athens, as in every
state where the stirrings of revolt had shown themselves,
there was haste to apologize and submit. Demosthenes,
even, was very untactfully put on the delegation sent out
to meet and propitiate the terrible young man, but wisely
thought better of it and came back. Having graciously
visited Athens and called a congress at Corinth to recognize
him, in succession to his father, as general of the Hellenic
forces, Alexander departed northward and soon plunged
into barbaric regions, whence reports of his death aroused
new hopes among the restless Greeks.

It is at this point that Persia begins to take a hand in the
game. Seriously threatened by the Macedonian, she naturally attempted to hamper him by raising revolts in his
rear. Only by Sparta, however, were her envoys openly

received, and the best they could do at Athens was to leave three hundred talents with Demosthenes, to be used "for the good of the service." The part which he, whose words and thoughts were perpetually exalting the glorious achievements of Athens in the war against Persia, henceforth played as the confidential agent of that very power, receiving and handling vast sums from her treasury and scrupling not to invoke her aid against what was nominally, at least, a pan-Hellenic union, can certainly be made to bear an ugly aspect, and the shadow of it falls across all his later career. Yet there is no reason to suppose that he was not sincerely patriotic in his belief that Persia, as the less dangerous and more distant foe, could be safely played off against the immediate and overpowering and, to his mind, no less foreign one, and that, if she could be so played, she ought to be.

Some of this Persian money Demosthenes seems to have sent to Thebes in default of the martial aid which he could not persuade his countrymen to give to her ill-starred revolt in 335. Well for Athens that she held back! Before Alexander was known to be alive again, he had crossed the mountains and fallen like a thunderbolt on the offending city. Only one house, traditionally that of the poet Pindar, stood intact among the ruins of what was Thebes. A paroxysm of horror shook all Greece. It was, as a contemporary said, as if Zeus had torn the moon out of the sky; the sun (Athens) still shone — but for how long? No wonder she was terrified and sent Demades to placate — even to congratulate — the conqueror. It is almost more surprising that she kept courage enough to receive the Theban fugitives and refuse Alexander's demand for their surrender. He asked nothing else except the persons of the anti-Macedonian leaders. It was a dangerous moment for Demosthenes, and he and his comrades showed no such spirit as that with which the burghers

of Calais went out to meet the vengeance of Edward III.
Rather did he beg the Athenians not to surrender their
sheep dogs to the wolf. Phocion, on the other hand, declared that it was madness to refuse the demand and that
any true patriot would be willing to sacrifice himself for
his country. The people compromised by sending Demades
again, to pacify the victor, with such success that he asked,
and obtained, no more than the banishment of the merce-
nary general, Charidemos.

The next twelve years, during which Alexander was pursuing his marvelous career of conquest in Asia, were for
Athens a longer period of complete peace than she had
known for many generations, and for Demosthenes, inevitably, a period of comparative eclipse. From time to time,
at the various crises in the victor's progress, he would lift
his head in hope of some news that would give a chance for
revolt against the Macedonian overlordship. But without
such news even his optimism could not see any chance of
success, and he even held back the more eager spirits, whom
he himself had trained, from a suicidal alliance with Sparta,
which under the heroic Agis was making one last desperate
stand for freedom.

It was at this time, when the anti-Macedonian party
seemed at its lowest ebb, that Æschines revived his accusation against Ctesiphon and so brought on one of the most
famous trials of antiquity. Spectators flocked from all
Hellas to witness the oratorical duel — for every one knew
that Ctesiphon, after a formal opening of his defense, would
make way for his advocate, the real object of the indictment.
The orations "On the Crown" of Æschines and Demosthenes are the masterpieces, respectively, of a great talent
and a great genius. Technically, Æschines had an excellent
case and argued it convincingly. Ctesiphon had illegally
proposed conferring the crown upon Demosthenes while

the latter was in the public service, before his accounts had
been passed upon by the proper authorities; he had proposed, moreover, to have it proclaimed in the Theater, before the great concourse of strangers, instead of, according
to the proper procedure, in the Assembly. Having proved
these charges, Æschines launched into his third, that the
services of Demosthenes had not deserved reward, but quite
the contrary. Here, of course, was the accused patriot's
great opportunity, and on the defense of his record he
poured out all his consummate powers. The best answer he
could make — and it did not amount to much — to the
legal charges, he tucked away in the middle of his oration,
where it not only escaped special attention but made a
needed break in what might have seemed too long and continuous a history of his political life. It was on that history,
marred, to be sure, by some outbursts of unworthy personal
abuse, but set forth, for the most part, with a grave, noble,
and touching eloquence, that he relied, and rightly, for his
acquittal. The verdict was so overwhelming that Æschines,
unable to pay the fine he had incurred by his failure to win
even one sixth of the votes, went into exile, passing the rest
of his days as a teacher of oratory and using as a text the
very speech that had undone him. "Ah!" he would say to
his scholars when they admired it, "you should have heard
the beast himself!"

Happy would it have been for Demosthenes if this great
triumph had at once crowned and closed his life. But there
was to be yet another episode in his long career, and one
which turned against him at last the followers whose fidelity
no fear or failure had shaken. When Harpalos, the abscond-
ing governor of Babylon, fleeing from the wrath of his
master, Alexander, appeared at Athens with his stolen
treasure and troops, the younger and rasher members of
the patriotic party would have welcomed the chance for

revolt, but Demosthenes, who had learned prudence, joined
Phocion in refusing admission to the soldiers. Harpalos
himself came in as a suppliant, and his surrender was sternly
demanded by the Macedonian general, Philoxenus. Athens
was in a delicate position, but, by Demosthenes' advice,
saved her dignity by offering to arrest Harpalos herself and
hold him and his treasure in safe-keeping for Alexander. The
money was given in charge to a commission including
Demosthenes and by them deposited the next day in the
Acropolis. Soon strange rumors arose of the sum being
much smaller than what Harpalos had handed over. He
had escaped, but his account book was found, and it
appeared that he had given up seven hundred talents, of
which only three hundred were in the treasury. In face of
the scandal, Demosthenes demanded an inquiry, but proceedings were delayed by the excitement over Alexander's
demands that the Greek cities should recognize his divinity
and recall all their political exiles. In spite of deep resentment, all finally submitted, even Demosthenes bending so
far as to say, "Let him be son of Zeus if he prefers it, or son
of Poseidon for all I care." Unluckily, his hard-learned
prudence had lost him the support of those radical enthusi-
asts whom no experience could teach and who in their disappointment began to suspect his loyalty and to join his
old enemies in the accusation of having embezzled the
Harpalos treasure. It was impossible for Demosthenes to
clear himself of having taken some of the money; indeed,
he practically admitted the fact, but said he took it for the
Theoric Fund. Naturally, there was no record of it in the
Theoric accounts, but it is probably true that he did put it
by for a reserve fund, and that if war had broken out the
state would have used it without question. Some such
consciousness seems to have been in the minds of his judges,
for though the crime was very serious — since Athens must

account to Alexander for the missing funds — the penalty inflicted was comparatively light. Since the fine was, however, more than he could pay, he had to go to prison, whence, finding confinement insupportable, he escaped, evidently by the connivance of his jailers. He could not bear to go beyond sight of Athens, so spent his exile in Ægina and Trœzen, "with tears in his eyes, looking across to the country of Attica."

One happy day was yet in store for him. In 323 came the news of Alexander's death, and all Athens rose to its feet and breathed again. In vain did Phocion remind them: "If Alexander is dead to-day, he will be dead to-morrow and next day — plenty of time to make plans," and meet the impatient question of Hyperides, "When will you ever advise the Athenians to fight?" with the cool reply: "When I see the young men ready to do their duty, and the rich to pay taxes, and the politicians to abstain from stealing public money." The Assembly was in no mood to listen to such croakers; it resolved to equip two hundred and forty ships, put all citizens under forty in the field, and try for a general rising throughout Greece. Now was Demosthenes not only summoned home, but met at the Piræus by the whole population, which escorted him in triumph while he raised his hands to heaven, blessing the day.

Within a year all these bright hopes had withered: the allied Greeks had failed and fallen apart before the advance of the Macedonian Antipater, and Athens, obliged to surrender at discretion, had been condemned to revise her constitution, receive a garrison, and deliver up the chiefs of the patriot party. Once more Demosthenes fled, taking sanctuary in the temple of Poseidon on the island of Calauria. Here he was pursued by Archias, an ex-actor, now an officer of Antipater's, who tried to lure the old man out by fair words. But he "sate still in the same position

and, looking up steadfastly upon him, 'O Archias,' said he,
'I am as little affected by your promises now as I used formerly to be by your acting.' Archias at this beginning to
grow angry and to threaten him, 'Now,' said Demosthenes,
'you speak like the genuine Macedonian oracle; before,
you were but acting a part. Therefore forbear only a little,
while I write a word or two home to my family.' Having
thus spoken, he withdrew into the temple and taking a
scroll as if he meant to write, he put the reed into his mouth,
and biting it, as he was wont to do when he was thoughtful
or writing, he held it there for some time." When the poison
he had thus absorbed began to take effect, he staggered
to the door, not to pollute the sacred place, and fell down
dead.

It is by his public career, entirely, that Demosthenes
must be judged. Private life he seems to have had practically none, nor are his personal characteristics such as to
impress or attract us. Lacking in geniality, a bitter enemy,
below rather than above the average in physical courage,
and unscrupulous, though not corrupt, in money matters,
he was not a man to win love or veneration. As an orator,
he has always ranked as one of the greatest, perhaps the
very greatest that ever lived, but the ordinary reader,
especially if limited to translations, can never begin to
appreciate the subtleties of style, the musical combinations
of words, the triumphs of art, in short, which delighted the
critical ears of the Athenians. But even oratory became to
him but a secondary consideration, a means to the great
end to which his whole life was devoted. By his choice
of that end and his refusal ever to be turned from it or to
despair of reaching it, his reputation stands or falls. To
those critics who, from Phocion to Professors Beloch and
Bury, have maintained that he misunderstood the meaning of his time and wasted the force of Athens in futile

opposition to the inevitable, the best answer is in his own imperishable words: —

Even if what was to come had been plain to all beforehand . . . even then, I say, it would not have been right for the city to abandon her course. . . . As it is, she is thought, no doubt, to have failed to secure her object, — as happens to all alike, whenever God wills it; but then, by abandoning her claim to take the lead of others, she must have incurred the blame of having betrayed them all. . . . But this was not, it appears, the tradition of the Athenians; it was not tolerable; it was not in their nature. From the beginning of time no one had ever yet succeeded in persuading the city to throw in her lot with those who were strong but unrighteous in their dealings, and to enjoy the security of servitude. Throughout all time she has maintained her perilous struggle for preëminence, power, and glory. . . .

. . . It cannot, it cannot be that you were wrong, men of Athens, when you took upon you the struggle for freedom and deliverance. No! by those who at Marathon bore the brunt of the peril — our forefathers. No! by those who at Platæa drew up their battle line, by those at Salamis, by those who off Artemisium fought the fight at sea, by the many who lie in the sepulchers where the People laid them — brave men, all alike deemed worthy by their country of the same honor and the same obsequies — not the successful or the victorious alone!

ALEXANDER THE GREAT

(Died 323 B.C.)

ONE day in the year 356 B.C. Philip of Macedon, then in only the fourth year of his reign, received three pieces of good news: his general, Parmenio, had beaten the Illyrians, his race horse had won at Olympia, and a son had been born to him. The boy's mother was Olympias, an Albanian princess whose wild young beauty Philip had fallen in love with as he saw her dancing in the religious rites of her own country. Years of marriage and queenship in an at least half-civilized realm never succeeded in taming Olympias; — passionate, vindictive, enthusiastic, darkly superstitious, whether we see her as a Bacchante, leading the mystic dance she loved, with great tame serpents coiled about her upraised staff and ivy-chaplet, or a Medea, brooding in vengeful jealousy the murder of false husband and hated rival, she is always the barbarian, always a tremendous elemental force. From her Alexander inherited his passionate, frank nature, equally prone to vehement, generous attachments, savage anger, and heart-broken repentance; from her, too, came the strain of religious mysticism which ran through his character. Though he had plenty of occasion to regret and to restrain her actions, and though after he started for Asia they never saw each other again, the strong bond between mother and son was never loosened; he wrote to her constantly, sent her the finest of the spoil, and could not bear to cross her as she deserved: "One tear of a mother," he would say when his regent in Macedon, the sorely-tried Antipater, wrote complaining of the Queen's perpetual meddling, "outweighs a thousand such letters as these."

If by temperament Alexander was his mother's son, by intellect he was no less his father's, rightfully inheriting the remarkable talent for organization, the versatility and resourcefulness, as well as the steadfast, tireless energy and ambition which in so few years raised Philip from a Highland chief to the greatest power in Hellas. On neither side, it is well to remember, was he Greek, in the sense that the word had come to stand for in his time. The Macedonians, it is true, claimed to be Hellenes, and the royal family, at all events, had long been acknowledged and admitted to the great festivals as such, but the characteristics of their civilization were those of the Greeks of nearly a thousand years before — the Greeks of Homer. When an Athenian boy of the fourth century studied the Iliad, the characters, the manners, the forms of speech were to him what those of the Bible are to us, but when Alexander took it with him as a bedside companion on his Asiatic campaigns, its details were to him, as an Americanized Syrian has recently said of the Scriptures, "like a letter from home." Although Homer was an important part of his education, as of that of every Greek lad, it was no excellence of teaching that made the story of the Trojan war take such a lasting hold on his imagination, no mere fancy that led him to identify himself with the valiant, glory-loving, passionate, open-hearted Achilles.

Though the busy Philip had little time to be with his son, he early saw that the child was worth the best education he could give him, and he spared no pains. After six years with a nurse whom he loved next to his mother, he was put under the charge of no ordinary slave-pedagogue, but a tutor of good family and very strict ideas of discipline, who brought him up with truly Spartan frugality and put him through a course of physical training which enabled him to perform and endure, as his later exploits showed, almost superhuman feats of agility and endurance, while — another sign of his un-Greek point of view — he grew up with little interest in athletics for their own sake and considered it trivial and undignified to take part in the public games. At twelve years old he was a well-grown boy, mature and thoughtful for his age, as he showed by the practical questions with which he surprised the Persian ambassadors he received in his father's absence; courageous, high-spirited, and willful, as appears in the famous taming of Bucephalus, the horse which none but he could mount. His father, proud and anxious, saw that the lad had out-grown his teachers and must be henceforth less controlled than guided, through the development of his highest facul-ties; for this he summoned Aristotle of Stagira, the greatest intellect in Greece, and set him up in a school for high-born youths — a school where his chair and the paved walks among the trees where he paced with his pupils were pointed out to sight-seers five hundred years later. There Alexander spent the next four years, studying literature, philosophy, and natural science. He never was strong on the æsthetic side — again, un-Greek — and as an imperial art-critic lived to be severely snubbed by the painter Apelles, nor did the study of oratory attract him, but religion, ethics, and science, especially medicine, were subjects that always inter-ested him; he had a great fancy for doctoring his friends, and in the depths of Asia he ordered zoölogical and botan-ical collections made at great expense and sent to Aristotle, with whom he long kept up a correspondence.

At sixteen, when his father, going to Byzantium, left him, well seconded by the able Antipater, in charge of the king-dom, Alexander's formal education was over, and his re-sponsible life began. His first military task was to put down the revolt of a hill-tribe up in the northeast, and a year or so later he commanded the right wing of the army, to

Philip's great satisfaction, in the latter's crowning victory at Chæronea. The relations between father and son, however, hitherto so satisfactory, now underwent a strain which almost severed them. Philip, already estranged from his moody and jealous wife, repudiated her to marry Cleopatra, a Macedonian maiden of high rank, much to the satisfaction of his nobles, who hated the "foreign woman." It is a strange glimpse we have of the old, primitive, hard-drinking Macedon — that riotous wedding-feast where the bride's uncle drank to the prospect of a lawful — i.e., a purely Macedonian — heir to the throne, and the naturally infuriated Alexander hurled a cup at his head; where Philip, staggering with drawn sword to strike his son, slipped and fell headlong, and the young man laughed aloud at the king who was moving heaven and earth to march from Europe into Asia, yet could not walk from one seat to another. Proud and sore, the insulted prince took his injured mother back to her Albanian home, to brood in deadly rage till she should be revenged. His own anger, never lasting, was mollified by his father's advances, and he was coaxed back to court, but an uncomfortable doubt hung about the succession, and Philip, to pacify and unite all parties, arranged a marriage between his daughter and the princely brother of his divorced wife. In the midst of the festivities he fell dead by the dagger of one of his guards, and while the immediate motive was revenge for a private injury, there is little doubt that the baleful figure of Olympias stood behind the assassin's hand.

Thus, at twenty, Alexander succeeded to a kingdom which seemed absolutely fated to collapse. On all sides were pretenders to the throne — cousins, one of an elder branch than his own, and his baby half-brother, backed by Attalus and the Old Macedonian Party; Greece was ready to revolt, and Persia stirring. Without paying the least attention to the advice of his friends to concentrate on rebuilding the home government, he suddenly appeared at the head of his army in a Greece quite unprepared to do anything but hasten to recognize him. It was, doubtless, this proud independence, always characteristic of Alexander, which made him salute a kindred spirit in the philosopher Diogenes, who, alone among the cringing Greeks at Corinth, had nothing to ask of him but that he would stand out of the sunlight in which he was basking. "If I were not myself," he told his sneering courtiers, "this is the man whom I would choose to be." At Corinth he was elected to his father's place at the head of the Pan-Hellenic crusade which he was burning to lead against Asia, but before he could start there was some business to attend to. Of his adult rivals he had made a "clean sweep," in traditional Macedonian fashion, by ordering their summary execution, and Olympias, much to his displeasure, had completed the job by murdering the poor baby prince and his mother. But there were still rude warlike tribes on the north and west who must be made to know their master before he could safely turn his back upon them, and so five months out of his first year the new king spent in the depths of the mountains, climbing, fording, trapping, fighting, with all the zest of a huntsman and the skill of a born soldier. Of a hundred incidents none is more picturesque or more characteristic of Alexander's "gumption" than his taking of that defile of the Balkans famous in modern warfare as the Shipka Pass. The "independent Thracians" — poor fellows! — had blockaded the pass with their wagons, which they prepared to roll down upon the advancing phalanx as it climbed the narrow way, but the ingenious Macedonian bade his men, when they could not separate to let the wagons through, lie down and lock their shields together, forming a roof over which the massive wheels rolled harmlessly. Thus,

with all his father's resourcefulness, he made his victorious
way, and was deep in Epirus, one hundred and fifty miles
from his capital and three hundred from Thebes, when news
reached him that that city, believing him dead, had thrown
off the Macedonian yoke, and all Greece was on the point
of doing the same. Down through the mountain wilder-
nesses he came, headlong, unheralded; in thirteen days he
was encamped before the walls of Thebes; in two more, the
city of Cadmus was razed to the ground, six thousand of its
inhabitants were slain, and the thirty thousand survivors
in the slave-market. This act of calculated "frightfulness"
had the desired effect, yet not on Greece only did the utter
destruction of so famous and ancient a city leave a painful
impression; Alexander himself found it a distressing memory, and with the curious mysticism of his nature laid more
than one tragedy of his later career to the vengeance of
Dionysius, the guardian god of Thebes.

At any rate, there was no more to fear from Greece, and
in the early spring of 334 he was ready to set forth on the
great adventure, the dream of his father's life and of his
own, the conquest, with no fleet to speak of and an army of
thirty-five thousand, of an empire fifty times as large,
twenty-five times as populous, and incalculably many times
as wealthy as his own. That army, however, was for the
times a practically perfect instrument, complete in all arms
of the service, from the compact phalanx with its wall of
protruding spears, and the resistless "Companion" cavalry
with which Alexander himself was wont to charge at the
head of his peers, to all the varieties of light-armed auxiliaries and the latest devices in siege-artillery. Composed
partly of Macedonians, partly of detachments from the
most warlike regions of Greece, thoroughly disciplined, and
wielded by the greatest military genius in the world, it was
an army which was never to know defeat, but to march to

the uttermost confines of the known world, toppling over kingdoms and recasting nations "like gallant boys at play." Its adored leader was now twenty-two, in the full glory of his young manhood, like David "ruddy and of a fair countenance," with a lion's mane of tawny hair tossing about the prominent brow which overhung his large and deep-set eyes. A northern type, unquestionably, and one cannot read of Alexander in those early years without thinking of the northern heroes of legend and history. Time, even the short time vouchsafed to him, and the inevitable influence of the vast and ancient East were to work changes in him, but the romantic youth who visited the site of Troy to garland the tomb of Achilles and offer sacrifice to the offended shade of Priam, the generous sovereign who before starting on his wild enterprise portioned out all the royal property among his friends, keeping, as he said, only his hopes for himself, the chivalrous victor who would not even intrude upon the grief of the royal ladies who fell into his hands after the battle of Issus, but maintained them in all privacy, dignity, and honor — this was no kinsman of Pericles or Themistocles, or even Leonidas, but rather a blood-brother of Siegfried and Cœur de Lion.

From the day that Alexander left the Europe he was never to see again to that of his death at Babylon was a period of less than twelve years, so crowded not only with dramatic and soul-stirring events but with epoch-making conquests and readjustments of the world that its main features are fully impressed upon every student of ancient history. All that can be undertaken in this sketch is to follow the man, Alexander, through the successive phases of his marvelous career, and trace the development of his character and aims as from the knightly leader of a holy war against impious barbarians he grows to the far-sighted ruler, planning and organizing such an amalgamated, cosmopolitan empire as

the world had never seen nor was to see till Rome took up
the scepter dropped from his dying hand.

The events of the first year in Asia, opened and closed
by the two famous battles of the Granicus and Issus, show
that his most outstanding characteristics were still his daring, his self-reliance, and the personal quality of his leadership. With what looks like pure recklessness and pride but
is really a recognition at first glance of the enemy's weak
line-up, we see him rejecting the advice of the experienced
Parmenio and dashing at the head of his crack cavalry
regiment, the white plumes of his helmet waving, like those
of Henry of Navarre, an oriflamme in the forefront of
battle, through the Granicus stream and up the slippery,
clayey bank where men and horses, friend and foe, scramble
and tumble, fight and fall, till the Persian cavalry are put
to rout, and the hired Greek infantry, stupidly posted in the
rear, are left bewildered and defenseless to the simultaneous
attack of Macedonian foot and horse.

Equally unhesitating was his decision, on finding himself
unassisted by the maritime states of Greece, to give up his
fleet altogether and throw himself, like Cortez — though he
disbanded, not burned, his ships — entirely upon the result
of his land victories. And his personal popularity with his
army, already immense, was sealed by the tactful dismissal
to their Macedonian homes, for the winter, of the newly
married among his officers and men. When they rejoined
him with fresh recruits in the spring, he had added the south
coast of Asia Minor to the western fringe of Hellenic cities
which had already come, without much enthusiasm, under his
"liberating" command, and at Gordium, the trysting-place,
he symbolized his intention in regard to the Persian empire
by the famous sword-stroke which cleft the knot whose
unraveler was fated to be ruler of Asia. Meantime, a
plunge, when heated with exercise, in the icy waters of the

Cydnus had all but cut short the conqueror's career, and there is no more charming anecdote of Alexander than that which tells how, warned that his physician, a certain Philip, was about to poison him, he smilingly handed him the accusing letter while he drank the medicine. Another story, enough by itself to show why his men worshiped him, is that of the mountain expedition when, falling behind to encourage the lagging steps of his old tutor, Lysimachus, who had insisted on going with him, he found himself caught for the night with a handful of men in a rocky gully and, casting about how to keep the old man warm, fell single-handed upon a small outpost of hostile mountaineers, slew two with his dagger and returned in triumph with a blazing brand from their watch-fire.

This adventure, however, happened a little later than the battle of Issus, which really closes the first, and opens the second and far more momentous, chapter of his Asiatic career. Thus far his conquests had been chiefly of the already Hellenized outskirts of the Persian empire, nor had he yet tested his enemy's powers of resistance. The famous battle of the Granicus was essentially a skirmish on a grand scale and would not have been fought at all, had not the proud confidence of the Persian nobles overruled the prudent advice of the Greek Memnon, Darius' only able general. While Memnon lived, moreover, and controlled the movements of the Persian fleet, Alexander was never safe from an uprising in Greece and the Ægean which, cleverly led, and maintained by Persian gold, might have cut his communications and left him in a most dangerous situation. The death of this general now put an end to all such schemes, so that henceforth Alexander could leave Greece quite out of his calculations, and threw Darius back upon the policy more natural to a flattered despot in command of countless hosts, the policy of meeting the audacious invader face to face and crushing him by sheer numbers.

That it was with such an overpowering host that the
Great King, too impatient to wait in the lowlands for his
enemy, sought him in the narrow plain of Issus between the
mountains and the sea, is so in keeping with Oriental custom and so overwhelmingly attested by all the early histories, themselves founded on the accounts of Alexander's
own generals, that it is impossible to accept the conclusions
of a recent German critic, who is sure that the Persian army
was little, if at all, larger than the Macedonian. That the
really effective troops of Darius, however, did not exceed
ninety thousand, the outside number that the three-mile
battlefield could hold in the front line, and that the masses
behind, intended to overawe rather than fight, were useless
in battle and much worse than useless in retreat, may well
be acknowledged. We must admit, too, that the position
of Darius, so much criticized for its unfitness to the size
and character of his army, had one great advantage: he was
to the north of Alexander, between him and his base.
Beaten, the invader could have fallen back only into a hostile country and to certain destruction.

It was all or nothing, therefore, with the thirty thousand
Macedonians and Greeks and their young general, and there
may well have been sinking hearts among the officers whom
he called to a council of war. But when, after he had pointed
out to them that the gods had delivered the enemy into their
hands by inspiring him to take up such a position, and had
inflamed their pride as warriors and free Hellenes by com-
paring them with the enslaved and effeminate Persians, he
ended by reminding them of the exploits of Xenophon and
his Ten Thousand and calling upon them to beat that record,
they rushed up to him from all sides, grasping his hand and
calling upon him to lead them that very moment against
the foe.

This time, however, there was to be no impulsive rush

into battle. Alexander, with his whole fate hanging in the
balance, summoned all his faculties and for the first time
showed himself not only a clever and daring leader, but a
great tactician. Only after arranging and rearranging his
various troops to face the different points of the carefully
observed hostile line, did he, leaving the left, or defensive,
wing in charge of the reliable Parmenio, take personal command of the right and, leading his horse-guards, charge in
the famous oblique order that his father had learned from
Epaminondas. That charge could not, as at the Granicus,
settle the business; the Persian cavalry in their turn crossed
the stream to attack Parmenio's Thessalians, and the hired
Greek infantry, seasoned old campaigners, held the center
desperately against the Macedonian phalanx; but when
Alexander, wheeling to the left, drove straight for the royal
chariot, Darius turned and fled, and his whole army, discouraged and demoralized, followed him in headlong rout.
Only the disciplined Greeks, sticking close together, fought
their way slowly back to their ships and sailed away. Alexander, left master of the field, held in his hands the very
shield and mantle left behind by his terrified enemy, as well
as his family and his gorgeous camp. "So, this is royalty!"
laughed the hardy victor, as he refreshed himself after the
soil of battle in the sumptuous bathtub of Darius.

The victory of Issus opens a new era in Alexander's life.
Hitherto he had been nominally, and at first, undoubtedly,
in his own mind, the generalissimo of the Greeks, going
forth to avenge Hellas upon the empire of Xerxes and the
first Darius, and to deliver the Greek cities of Asia Minor
from the alien yoke. How it would have been if Greece had
really put her heart into the enterprise and if the Ionian
cities had leaped to meet him, we can but guess; as it was,
the venture showed itself more and more plainly as a personal one, and the crusader became the conqueror. With

the deliverance of Asia Minor and the crushing defeat of Darius, the task on which he had set out was really accomplished, but it never occurred to him to stop. That overwhelming defeat, proving the fact to which Xenophon had borne witness, the essential helplessness of the Persian empire, had opened a new field, and there was to be no rest for Alexander until he had explored and conquered it all.

Of course this change of aim could not fail to bring about some change in character. In some respects the alteration was for the better. At Issus, Alexander could still speak in the traditional Greek vein of utter contempt for the "barbarian" and all his ways; as he went on, he learned to approve and even to adopt many of those ways, to ally himself by the closest personal ties with men and women of alien race, and to make his great object as a ruler a mutual tolerance, understanding, and coöperation between East and West. On the other hand, he unquestionably became both harsher and haughtier, soiling his fame by indulgence in barbarian cruelties, and alienating his free-born brothers-in-arms by his demand for that prostrate, unquestioning obedience which is the mark of Oriental sovereignty.

The hardening of his character shows in his southward progress through Phœnicia and Syria, where at Tyre and still more markedly at Gaza he met for the first time that power of desperate resistance, that willingness to die to the last man rather than surrender which is fundamental in the Semitic race. The gallant resistance of a band of Greek mercenaries at Miletus, a year before, had won from him — traitors to the common cause of Hellas though in his eyes they were — admiration and mercy, but the heroic determination of the Phœnicians and Syrians to defend their freedom and their homes to the last gasp called forth not only his fullest resources of ingenuity, persistency, and skill, but his uttermost vengeance when those marvelous sieges were at last successful. Then indeed — though not, as the prophet expected, by the hand of Nebuchadnezzar — was the word of Ezekiel fulfilled against "the renowned city which wast strong in the sea": "And they shall destroy the walls of Tyre and break down her towers: I will also scrape her dust from her and make her like the top of a rock. It shall be a place for the spreading of nets in the middle of the sea . . . and it shall become a spoil to the nations." A more unpardonable act of personal cruelty was the dragging by the heels of the yet living body of Batis, the brave defender of Gaza, at the wheels of the conqueror's chariot, in unworthy imitation of the worst deed of Achilles. Stern and abrupt, too, though in no way base, was the reply he sent at this time to Darius' second request for the ransoming of his family, offering him the half of his kingdom and the hand of his daughter. The price dazzled Parmenio, who could not help saying, "I should accept, if I were you." "So should I," curtly remarked Alexander, "if I were you"; and he sent word almost as briefly to Darius that he intended to take the whole of his kingdom and to marry his daughter if he wanted to, whether or no.

Darius, indeed, was no longer a factor in his calculations. Having once tested his metal, he knew he could safely leave him to collect another army, while by securing Syria and Egypt he took the Persian fleet without a battle, as each squadron, hastening back to its threatened home port, went over, perforce, to the conqueror. In Egypt he had no occasion to be harsh, since the natives, who had always found Persian rule peculiarly unsympathetic, welcomed him at once. It was the other form of his increasing self-assertion which displayed itself in the famous and fantastic visit to the temple of Zeus Ammon, across two hundred miles of pathless desert. When the priest there saluted him as "Son of Ammon," he gave him the conventional homage due to every Pharaoh, and to an Egyptian the words meant no more, but among Greeks the reported recognition of his divine origin by an oracle the prestige of which had come to eclipse that of Delphi was sure to make a profound impression. Just what it meant to himself, or what passed between him and the priest in a private interview of which he speaks in a letter to his mother, we cannot know; there was a strong vein of mysticism in his character, which, mingling with his pride, tempted him to believe himself a man apart, akin to those demigods and heroes who in old days had been the founders of the Greek race; on the other hand, he had a saving sense of humor, as when once, being wounded, he pointed out to his friends with a rueful smile that what he was losing was real blood and not ichor "such as immortal gods are wont to shed."

Having settled the affairs of Egypt, and marked out with white flour on the black soil — for all the world like a tennis court — the plan of a new city, which on its well-chosen site grew to be the greatest and most famous of all the scores of "Alexandrias" he founded, he was ready, in 331, to go and try conclusions with Darius in his own country. It is a valuable experience to follow the route of Alexander on a map which includes Greece and to see that ragged little peninsula, so long the crowded center of historical interest, slip aside, as it were, almost out of one's sight, and become a mere speck in the northwestern corner, while the vast spaces of the East roll out before the resistless advance of the invader. It is then that one understands Alexander's remark, when news reached him of the battle of Megalopolis, in which Agis, the hero-king of Sparta, had fallen at the head of the Lacedæmonians, Arcadians, Eleans, and Achæans, in hopeless revolt against the Macedonian regent: "It seems that while we have been conquering Asia there has been a battle of mice back there in Greece."

At Gaugamela, near the crumbling mound which had once been Nineveh, the Persian empire followed the Assyrian down to final destruction. In this battle, the climax of his military career, we see Alexander more completely the general, less the personal champion, than in any other. A thousand miles from home and fronting with fewer than fifty thousand men, unshielded on either side by mountain or sea, a host made up from all the tribes of the empire and variously estimated at from half a million to a million, he took no chances — except the one great chance of battle. Even under the familiar swagger of his refusal to make a night-attack, because he would not stoop to "steal a victory," may be easily seen the sound judgment which rejected anything likely to bring but a confused and indecisive result. The care with which he rested his troops and surveyed the ground, and the sober and manly exhortations, very different from his "Hurrah, boys!" speech at Issus, with which he impressed upon his officers the extreme importance of the occasion and the need of absolute discipline, all show his full realization of the enormous risk he ran, as well as the sound night's sleep which he enjoyed after all the preparations had been made does the perfectly healthy state of his nerves and the quiet confidence in which he awaited the event.

In a general way and allowing for the difference of situation, which enabled the long Persian line to outflank Alexander's on either side, his tactics were similar to those at Issus — the oblique offensive with his own right wing while Parmenio held back the left. This time the victory was more hardly won; gaps in the line were penetrated from either side, and not till Alexander had once more directed his charge full on Darius' chariot and the royal coward had for the second time turned and fled, was the enemy's center routed, while even there the result was not so sure but that the victor, reached by a message from the hard-pressed

Parmenio,—whom he never quite forgave,—had to check his headlong pursuit and gallop back to succor his left wing. Thus, to his deep disgust, Darius escaped, but only as a beaten fugitive, and Alexander, resuming his pursuit on the morrow, found at Arbela his chariot, shield, and bow. It was not till several months later, after taking full possession of Babylon, Susa, and Persepolis, with their almost incredible treasures, and destroying, by a marvelous feat of strength and daring, the army with which the satrap Ariobarzanes held against him the apparently impregnable pass of the "Persian Gate," that he found time to follow up the unhappy king in the mountains of his ancestral Media. Still the Persian fled before the oncoming Macedonian, first as commander, then as prisoner, of his few remaining troops and the Bactrian Satrap, Bessus, and when at last, by mad riding, day and night, over rocky deserts, Alexander caught up with his rival, it was to find his murdered body left behind on the roadside. That Bessus, when he finally fell into the victor's hands, was put to death with Oriental tortures can hardly excite our compassion for him personally, though the manner of his execution was one of the incidents which more and more often shocked and disturbed the Greeks and Macedonians in Alexander's train.

For from the day of Gaugamela that change of attitude and outlook of which, as we noted, the victory of Issus marked the beginning, became obvious and even deliberately emphasized. Whether or not we regard the burning of the palace of Xerxes at Persepolis, when "the King seized a flambeau with zeal to destroy," as a symbolic act intended to mark the consummation of the vengeance exacted for the Persian destruction of Athens one hundred and fifty years before, we can hardly miss the significance of the discharge at Ecbatana of the Greek troops who, in the name of the Congress of Corinth, had followed him as General of the

Pan-Hellenic League. Henceforth, any who chose to re-enlist would do so with their eyes open, for a new and distinct enterprise, the creation of a world empire. In the prosecution of this, so far as it meant "glory and gunpowder, plunder and blood," — aye, and danger and heroic effort, too, — Greeks and Macedonians were willing enough to follow Alexander, but it was another matter to see him taking Persian nobles and governors into his favor, confirming some in their commands and giving others positions about his very person, — barbarians, born to be slaves, placed on an equality with free Hellenes! It was with disgust that his hardy warriors saw him adopt even a modified form of that eastern costume which they had always scorned as the very embodiment of effeminate luxury, and with profound anxiety and anger that they realized that the ceremony of prostration, that humiliation which free Greeks, even as solitary individuals in most pressing need of the Great King's favor, had made every sacrifice to avoid, was being not only performed as a matter of course by the Persians but welcomed and evidently soon to be exacted from the old comrades in arms who had been used to grasp his hand and call him by his name.

The view which Alexander had reached was undoubtedly the wiser and wider one: he was learning to understand, to use, and to respect races and customs which he had been taught, even by the great Aristotle, ignorantly to despise. It was certain, too, that the world empire of which he was now dreaming could be built only on a foundation of universal tolerant intercourse and swayed only by a sovereign who should identify himself with neither West nor East, but rule impartially, like a god, over both alike. Yet it is impossible not to sympathize with the feelings of the grizzled warriors in their bewilderment and pain, or to recognize that the change in their leader was not wholly a matter of policy or of mental growth, but partly also the intoxicating effect of absolute power upon a proud, imaginative nature, very impressionable for ill as well as for good. Philotas, who had been his right hand in every campaign and led the horse-guards at the Granicus and Gaugamela, may possibly have been guilty of more than carelessness in failing to notify his commander, to whom his rank gave him instant access, of a conspiracy against his life, but his haughty demeanor and unwise boasts of the share he had in Alexander's victories must have gone far to harden the king's heart before he could stand by and sneer at the outcries wrung by torture from his old companion in arms, and the once generous and trusting Alexander seems utterly lost in the cold and calculating despot who sends messengers to execute, without so much as a trial or even an accusation, Philotas's father, the faithful, tiresome old Parmenio.

It is not the orientalized monarch, however, but the true son of the hard-drinking Philip and the passionate Olympias whom we see in the tragic climax of this alienation between Alexander and his old friends. We seem again at the wild banquet in Pella where Philip so nearly slew his son, as we watch the drinking grow fast and furious; the comic songs in ridicule of the Macedonian veterans; the anger of these finding voice through the outspoken Clitus; the bandying of words between him and Alexander, more and more exasperated as the rude warrior, too far gone for any prudence, boasts of having saved his life at the Granicus and loudly asks him why he bids free men to sup with him if he is n't willing to hear them speak their minds; the fury of the king, casting vainly about for the sword his attendants have prudently concealed and shouting in the Macedonian patois of his boyhood for the trumpeter to sound the onset; the crazy Clitus, once safely dragged out of the hall, rushing in again at another door, derisively singing; the fatal blow at

last, when Alexander, snatching a spear from one of the
guards, runs it through the body of his oldest friend,
brother of the beloved nurse who had herself lost all her
sons in his service — and then the dead silence, the mad
attempt at self-destruction, and the outburst of inconsol-
able weeping that racked him all that night and all the
following day.

It was far away in Bokhara that this wretched scene took
place, for Alexander's pursuit of Darius had lengthened
itself, first into the hunting down of Bessus in his own
Bactria, and then into a thorough exploration and conquest
of the northeast provinces of the Persian empire — a region
quite unknown to the Greek charts, crossed by the mighty
mountain chain of the Hindu Kush and the broad streams
of the Oxus and Jaxartes, and inhabited by warlike, independent tribes of pure old Aryan stock. Some of these
proved friendly and were allowed to retain their own at the
price of a nominal submission; others fought to the death
for freedom, and it was in his forced marches and hair-
breadth adventures in the pursuit and slaughter of these
gallant hillfolk that Alexander showed how little his adop-
tion of Persian manners had affected his extraordinary
hardihood and willingness to take the greatest personal
risks. Here, too, he found a bride, falling in love, for the
first time in his life, with Roxana, the fair young daughter
of a Bactrian chief whom he had scaled the very skies to
conquer. This marriage was another thorn in the flesh to his
Macedonians, but he knew how to deal with them. In one
of his own letters, which Plutarch quotes "almost word for
word," he tells how he met the grumblings of even the
picked corps of twenty thousand foot and three thousand
horse with whom, after sorting out and placing in colonies
the war-weary, he planned to advance yet farther. They
were all free to leave him if they liked, he told them; "he

should merely enter his protest that when on his way to make the Macedonians the masters of the world he was left alone with a few friends and volunteers." This was entirely too much for the troops, who shouted that they would go with him anywhere he pleased.

It was now the spring of 327. For three years Alexander had been campaigning in the northern hills, while the vast plain behind him lay in perfect tranquillity and order, ruled, so far as possible, by its former laws and governors, under the supervision of a few trusted Macedonians and Greeks. He had reached the extreme northern limit of the Persian empire, the river Jaxartes, and he resolved to make it his limit also, though, dared by the jeering Tartar shepherds on the opposite bank, he had crossed the stream on stuffed sheepskins. and driven the nomads in terror before him. To the southeast, however, beyond the great wall of the Hindu Kush, lay a country which also had been a nominal part of the empire and which by its very remoteness and strangeness fascinated the explorer and adventurer in him. He could not rest till he had seen with his own eyes that land of the spices and the elephants and made his own name feared wherever those of Cyrus and of Xerxes had been heard.

With a great army, swelled as his forces now were by a constant stream of adventurers from Europe as well as by chosen bands of native horse, he crossed the mountains and began the conquest of the unknown Punjaub. Dividing his forces into two main lines of advance, he swept along, storming, sacking, and scattering, till he had fought his way through into the Indus valley and across the five rivers. The first great rajah whom he met prudently accepted his overlordship and was established as head of what the British in India call a Native Protectorate; the next, Porus, gave him perhaps the hardest battle of his life. Darius had used a few elephants at Gaugamela, but this was the first time that Alexander had had to face the problem of attacking, with horses that reared and screamed at sight and smell of the monsters, a line of two hundred living towers, drawn up at intervals of a hundred feet through which the enemy's infantry could be seen, a solid wall, behind. But his record was not to be broken; once more he seized the offensive, and by a furious flank attack upon the Indian cavalry forced Porus to come to the rescue by turning his elephants to the right and thus exposing their sides to the spears of the Macedonian light infantry. Porus himself, a superb figure of a man, fought his elephant to the last, and when taken captive asked only, with grave eastern dignity, to be treated "like a king." Like a king both policy and magnanimity dictated that he should be treated, for Alexander had no idea of establishing a direct rule over these distant regions; he was close upon the world's end, as he thought, and planned only to guard his eastern frontier by a row of semi-independent friendly provinces. At this point, however, a new vision dawned upon him,— beyond the Indus, he heard, were rich and fertile lands surpassing anything he had yet seen, and a great river (the Ganges) flowing eastward, surely into that "Ocean" which encompassed the earth and of which the Caspian Sea was but a gulf stretching southward. To explore that river and then sail around the north of Asia with one half of his fleet, while the other descended the Indus and circumnavigated Africa — that would be an achievement indeed. But now the world conqueror was to meet the disappointment of his life: his soldiers struck. Utterly worn and weary as they were, a great wave of homesickness suddenly broke over them; they clamored for the wives and children they had not seen for so many years, and utterly refused to go a step farther. In vain Alexander tried the reproach which had brought them round before;

the veterans hung their heads before his scorn, but they would not budge. Sick with grief and humiliation, he flung himself upon his couch and for two days spoke to no one; then he yielded, and his army pressed around him, weeping for joy that he who had conquered all the world had let himself be conquered by his adoring Macedonians.

In September, 326, began with pomp and circumstance the descent of the Hydaspes and the Indus in a great flotilla, a journey uneventful for the most part, save for the opposition of the Mallians, which gave Alexander a chance to show that the years were making no change in his dare-devil courage. Scaling a lofty wall in advance of all his men, he leaped down into the hostile fortress and fought single-handed till two devoted followers saved him, severely wounded, from almost certain death. But perhaps the finest single picture we have of him is in the midst of the terrible return journey which he took with twenty-five thousand of his best troops across the burning desert of southern Beluchistan, where, exactly like David in similar straits, he "poured out unto the Lord" the helmet-full of precious water which his young men had risked their lives to fetch him. With barely half this host, after incredible toils, he reached the western limit of a land which no European after him was to penetrate for more than two thousand years, and, joined by the army which he had sent ahead by a more northern route and by the fleet which had followed along the coast, he was ready at last to revisit Susa, which he had left five years before.

As soldier, explorer, conqueror, Alexander's work was done. For the fifteen months of life that remained to him, he was the statesman and administrator, correcting, with prompt and stern justice, the misgovernment of many of the deputies he had left in charge, and perfecting his great scheme of the amalgamation of races and civilizations. Even on the warpath and in the remotest parts of the earth, this idea had always been present with him; wherever he went, "cities" had sprung up in his footsteps, serving at once as asylums for disabled soldiers, garrisons of his rule, and centers of Greek civilization.[1] Following out the same policy, he would have transplanted bodily large groups of settlers from Asia into Europe and vice-versa, while to encourage intermarriage among his subjects he himself, adopting polygamy, espoused a daughter of Darius and bestowed some eighty or ninety other maidens, "the choicest daughters of the Persians and Medes," each with a dowry out of the royal treasury, upon his chief nobles and counselors, signalizing the occasion by a gorgeous spectacular banquet whereat all the brides appeared and seated themselves beside their respective husbands, who took them by the right hand and kissed them, Alexander leading the way. This great wedding, we are told, was the most popular thing he ever did, but another step in the amalgamating process caused a terrible commotion. For years he had maintained military schools at which Oriental youths were taught Greek tactics; now the time had come to take the graduates of these schools into his army, not as separate detachments, but mixed in, man by man, with the existing regiments. That was bad enough, but when he capped the climax by proposing to discharge and send home, with generous pensions, ten thousand Macedonians who had grown old in his service, the whole army broke out in open mutiny. "Send us all home!" they shouted; "you don't want us! Go and get your father Ammon to conquer for you!" It was the third time that Alexander had had to face his veterans; this time he had no idea of yielding. Leaping down from the

[1] One of the remotest of these was named Bucephala, in honor of the beloved horse he had tamed in his boyhood, which had carried him so often to victory and had finally died on the banks of the Hydaspes.

platform from which he had personally made them the offer of release, he pointed out with his own hand a dozen ringleaders and ordered them led away to execution; then, remounting, he addressed the rest in scathing terms, telling them flatly that it was thanks to Philip and to him that they were rulers of the world, wealthy and powerful, instead of wandering mountain shepherds clad in skins, reminding them that there was no peril or toil of theirs which he had not shared, no wound of which he could not show the fellow, and finally bidding them *all* go if they pleased, and tell the people at home that they had left him to the protection of barbarians. With that he shut himself up in his palace, and for two days the army, dazed and sullen, heard no word from him. On the third, it was announced that all the high commands were to be given to Persians and that new regiments of horse- and foot-guards, bearing the grand old Macedonian name of "Companions," were being formed of Oriental soldiers. It was too much. The men fairly stormed the palace doors, throwing down their weapons and themselves, weeping and praying to be taken back. When Alexander at last came out to them, he too broke down, and the whole episode ended in a grand love-feast of forgiveness and reconciliation.

It was perhaps the last really happy day of his life, for the next event was one which nearly broke his heart, the death of his dearest friend, Hephæstion, his Patroclus, as he loved to call him and as he mourned him, with all the passionate abandonment which characterized him to the end. That end was very near. At Babylon, whither he had gone in the early summer of 323 to preside over the final funeral ceremonies as well as to start out Nearchus and the fleet on a voyage around Arabia, he caught a fever in the swamps where he had been superintending an improved drainage-system, aggravated it by two late suppers with hard drinking, and found himself seriously ill. For several days he lingered, still able to offer the morning sacrifice and do a little business from his bed. On the twelfth of June the horror-struck army realized that he was dying — even heard that he was dead. Heart-broken, they clamored to see him once more, and a long line of weeping veterans passed silently through the room where their beloved commander lay, feebly waving his hand to them in a last farewell. The next day he died.

Into less than thirty-three years of existence and not quite thirteen of rule, Alexander had packed more life and accomplishment than stand to the credit of all the warrior-statesmen of the past. It is useless to wonder what more he might or could have done in another thirty years, or whether he ever really entertained those dreams which have been attributed to him, of adding the western world to his dominions. Early and sudden though his death was, it does not seem, somehow, inappropriate or wholly tragic, for an *old* Alexander is inconceivable; the phrase is like a contradiction in terms. His glorious strength and beauty, his generosity, his reckless valor, his vast, imaginative plans, his very faults of savage anger and overweening pride, are all qualities of a young man, and young he remains forever in the eyes of a wondering world.

That world has never forgotten him or ceased to feel the impress of his genius. The organization, it is true, which he had so newly created, failed to stand alone; the empire fell apart and was devoured, piece by piece, by oncoming Rome, but the seeds of Greek civilization which he scattered broadcast from the Mediterranean to the Indus sprang up a hundredfold and made possible the development of Christianity, the Eastern Empire, the Renaissance, and the modern world. All through the Middle Ages, the name and deeds of Alexander, in queerest mediæval transformation, were the familiar stuff of European minstrel and romancer, and far up in the mountains of Turkestan there lingers to this day the personal tradition of the fair-haired hero whom no precipice or raging torrent could hinder and no human valor could resist.

ARATUS

(Died 213 B.C.)

In the year 264 B.C., the prosperous manufacturing town
of Sicyon, not far from Corinth, went through one of the
periodical convulsions to which at that time her political
life was subject. Some years before, she had thrown off a
"tyranny" and elected two prominent citizens to manage
her affairs. Now the survivor of these, Clinias, was murdered, with as many of his kinsfolk as could be reached, by
a certain Abantidas, who proceeded to make himself tyrant
until the usual fate should overtake him in his turn. During
the confusion the seven-year-old son of Clinias managed to
hide in the house of an aunt who was also related to the
victor, and who succeeded in smuggling him away to his
father's friends at Argos. There the youthful Aratus grew
up like any other vigorous, healthy lad, well educated but
fonder of athletics than of study, yet always nursing in his
heart an undying hatred of not merely the individual tyrant
who had orphaned him, but the whole system of tyranny
which was crushing out the ancient liberties of Greece.

This Greece in which Aratus passed his youth was so
different from the Fifth or even the Fourth Century Greece
with which we are all so much more familiar, that it is well
to take a good look at it before going on with our narrative.
Two generations had passed since Alexander's death, and
his vast empire, after furious wars among his successors, had
settled into the three main kingdoms of Syria, Egypt, and
Macedonia, the latter including the control of Greece.
Monarchy, in short, was now the rule in the Hellenistic
world, and was for the most part surrounded with all the

elaborate, splendid ceremonial, the sickening flattery and deifying worship which marked the Oriental type of sovereignty. The Macedonians, however, still preserved a certain rough freedom of manners along with the pride of having been the conquerors of the world, and their present King, Antigonus Gonatas, was no despot by nature, but a moderate, sensible man, with a taste for literature and philosophy and a strong sense of responsibility. He had no desire to lord it over Greece as a matter of pride or to make his rule oppressive, but his rivalry with Egypt forced him to keep a firm hand on the peninsula, lest the rich and crafty Ptolemy, who loved to fight with moneybags, stir up trouble for him there. Just such had been the policy of Egypt a few years before, in financing the "Chremonidean" war, in which Sparta and Athens had joined hands in one last effort to shake off the Macedonian yoke. Now Athens, as an independent power, was no more; henceforth the "eye of Hellas" was, politically, a provincial Macedonian town. Old men yet lived who had listened to the burning words of Demosthenes when he foresaw and would have averted the doom of the imperial city; for the future those words were to be studied by schoolboys as models of pure rhetoric with no bearing upon any action that could ever be.

Sparta, on the other hand, still clung to her independence, but with her territory shrunk to Laconia, her citizenship limited to a few hundreds, and her ancient discipline long cast aside, she was but the ghost of her former self. Even so, however, it was the policy of Macedonia to keep an eye on her, and the two most trustworthy watchdogs were held to be her natural enemies — Argos, her rival from earliest days, and Megalopolis, which Epaminondas had founded in her despite. It was not necessary for Macedonia to garrison these towns; she found it cheaper and more convenient to control them through native tyrants who were sure of her backing so long as they governed in her interest. Equally convenient, though less important, was a similar state of things in the other cities, and accordingly we find the whole Peloponnesus dotted with small local tyrannies, on the best of terms with the great neighbor to the north.[1] Only three strongholds, significantly called the "shackles of Greece" — Piræus, Chalcis, and Acrocorinth — did Antigonus think it necessary to hold absolutely in his own hands.

To realize what this state of things meant to Greeks we have only to remember their peculiar horror of *tyranny* — that is, of arbitrary, irresponsible, unconstitutional government, apart from the crimes or merits of the individual tyrant. Enormously and in a hundred ways Greece had changed since the days of Harmodius and Aristogiton, but in this one respect her mind was the same: in her code the tyrant, having put himself above the law, was become an outlaw, and to kill him was the most virtuous act a patriot could perform. The lives of tyrants, therefore, were decidedly precarious; yet when one fell, it was usually to be succeeded by another, equally subservient to the dominant kingdom, for in the far larger and more complicated world which had taken the place of the clear-cut little Hellas of old, the small city republics, which so long had been the normal type of Greek life, were no longer capable of maintaining their independence. Yet republicanism was not dead; on the contrary, at this very time it was taking on fresh life and trying a new and very hopeful form. North of the Corinthian Gulf the rugged villagers of Ætolia, south of it the staid and provincial townsfolk of Achaia, were drawing together in federations which, each in turn, but seldom, unfortunately, in coöperation, were to lift once more the banner of a free Greece.

[1] The situation has been suggestively compared with that in Italy during the Austrian domination, before 1859.

Not since Homeric days had the Achaians played a prominent part. Their cities were small and had produced no geniuses in the arts of either war or peace. The general character of the people seems to have been conservative, peace-loving, mildly democratic, and eminently respectable. In old days there had existed among them some sort of a league, and now, almost unnoticed, the cities began to draw together again, until, by the time Aratus appears upon the political scene, all ten were united in a most interesting and promising federation, bearing much resemblance to our own and even more to our first attempt under the Articles of Confederation (1781–89). The city-states, that is, while preserving complete local independence, formed one nation in regard to the outside world, all questions of war, peace, treaties, and alliances being reserved to the national government. Coinage, weights, and measures were also uniform throughout the federation, and citizens of any state enjoyed full rights, including those of marriage, in every other. One point in which the Achaian League was much stronger than our Confederation was the provision for an elective executive, with great power. Where, on the other hand, it showed a similar weakness was in the system of requisitions, whereby the troops and the taxes were raised by the states separately on the demand of the central government instead of directly by that government, as well as in the equality of its members — one state, one vote, regardless of relative size or population. Of course there was nothing like the modern system of representative government; the national assembly, answering to our Congress, was but a town-meeting on a large scale, and, as attendance was unpaid, only the well-to-do were able or willing, except at times of rare popular excitement, to leave their homes and travel up to the sessions. This tended to keep the national government in conservative hands, while, on the other hand, the widespread opportunity to take part in local affairs made the general atmosphere healthily democratic. It is interesting to notice that our Constitution, in providing that the United States guarantee to every state a republican form of government, follows that of the Achaian League.[1]

Such, then, was the Greece of the Third Century: a collection of weak city-states, each separately helpless among the surrounding monarchies, many ruled by local despots in the interest of the nearest of those monarchies, a few cherishing their old self-government and drawing together in defense of it. For the rest, it was a time vastly more modern in tone than the great age of Greece, — softer in manners, more cosmopolitan in culture. Though wars were frequent, they were waged chiefly by professional soldiers in the pay of rival monarchs; neighboring cities no longer, as a matter of course and almost of sport, turned out their well-drilled youth for summer campaigns against each other. Consequently perhaps, when a city was taken, it was no longer usual to execute or enslave its inhabitants; in many ways, warfare was being modified in accordance with the scruples of a humaner time. In the world of thought, science had come to the fore; writings and speeches were less poetical, more realistic and everyday; a still more modern feature was the increasing prominence of women in social and public life. In other words, Alexander, by the enormous shaking-up and shaking together that he gave to East and West, had begun the modern world.

In this new world a great part was to be played by the boy-exile from Sicyon who had now, in the safe shelter of Argos, reached his twentieth year. It is an important and very significant fact that the intense hatred of tyrants, as such, which was the ruling principle of Aratus' life, did

[1] Madison, in preparation for the Constitutional Convention, made a careful study of the Achaian experiment.

not extend itself to legitimate kings, ruling over countries where monarchy was the native form of government. He does not seem, indeed, to have felt as much instinctive suspicion of such monarchs as would seem natural, but rather to have turned to them from the first, as possible helpers. His family was on terms of hereditary friendship with both Antigonus and Ptolemy, and his first idea was to get aid from one or other of them in freeing his native town. That failing, he went to the other extreme and concocted with a group of fellow-exiles a plot the success of which depended absolutely on individual quickness and daring. There is no more entertaining story in Plutarch than that of the night-raid on Sicyon. We seem present at every stage of the proceedings — the discovery that a section of the city wall was almost level with a rocky ledge on the inside; the purchase of folding ladders; the collection of a little band of desperadoes; the moonlight march; the vain attempt to shut up the "uncommonly savage and noisy" little dogs of a gardener just outside the point of attack; the breathless moment when the first climbers, clinging close to the shaky ladders, waited while the watchman went by above them ringing his bell, and a large hound within, wakened by the noise, began a tremendous baying; the final rush up and over the wall, just as the cocks were crowing and the first market-women coming in from the country; the overpowering, without a blow, of the tyrant's guard; and the triumphant announcement to the bewildered populace who gathered with the dawn, that "Aratus, the son of Clinias, invited the citizens to recover their liberty."

Never was such a successful or such an unstained revolution. The house, indeed, of Nicocles — the tyrant of the hour — was plundered and burnt, but not a life was taken, either during the attempt or after the victory. The citizens simply shook themselves free, chose their deliverer as chief magistrate, and recalled their exiles. Those exiles, however, presented a problem: some of them had been banished as much as fifty years before; their houses and lands had been confiscated, sold, passed from hand to hand; to restore them would be to raise up a fresh group of malcontents. What was needed was money, and Aratus resolved to seek it from the wealthy Ptolemy, who had already shown his approval of the exploit he had been too prudent to finance, by a gift of twenty-five talents, every obol of which the young leader had spent on the ransom and restoration of Sicyonian prisoners. Now he set forth on a voyage which proved extrahazardous, and after many adventures reached Alexandria, where he proceeded to win the good graces of the luxurious old dilettante who ruled Egypt by talking art and promising to collect for him good examples of the Sicyonian school of painting, then the most admired in Greece. With forty talents in hand and a definite contract for over a hundred more, Aratus returned, and applied the money so skillfully and honestly that Sicyon had no more to fear from internal troubles.

Against external dangers — that is, the certain ill-will of the neighboring tyrants and the very probable hostility of Macedon — the young statesman had already persuaded his fellow-citizens to take the fateful, unheard-of step of joining the Achaian League, not as an ally, but as a full member. This union is extremely important, for nothing like it had ever happened in Greece before. Such federations as had been tried had been strictly limited to peoples of kindred stock; now Sicyon, a Dorian city, voluntarily submerged herself in an Achaian nation. Again, though not a state of the first class, she ranked well in the second, and in population alone probably equaled at least five of the ten League cities; yet she consented to count as no more than one. On the other hand, the League itself took a great step outside of immemorial Greek custom and prejudice in admitting to its innermost circle a people of different ancestors, pieties, and guardian-gods, on terms of absolute equality. During the next twenty-three years it was to continue along this fortunate course, until it embraced so many states that Polybius could speak of the Peloponnesus as enjoying such absolute community of interests, laws, and standards as to be just like one city except for not being inside one wall. And the reason, he goes on to say, why the Achaians succeeded where all others had failed, was that they were unfalteringly true to "the two most unfailing expedients of equality and fraternity." Not all the Peloponnesian cities came in voluntarily; some had to be persuaded, a few forced; but each, no matter how acquired, was put immediately on an equal footing with all the rest; the great principle laid down by Burke, that the surest way for a nation to win the loyalty of its dependents is to share its rights with them, seems to have been first put into practice by the Achaian League.

For the greater part of these glorious years, Aratus was the very soul of the League. At first he was too young to lead the whole nation, though already recognized as chief citizen of his own Sicyon. At twenty-six, however, in 245 B.C., we find him chosen as President — or, as they called it, General (Strategus) — of the League, and from that time till his death, thirty-two years later, excepting once when he declined the office, he was elected every other year, the intervening terms which the constitution required being nearly always filled by his friends and nominees. This extraordinarily continuous influence and popularity, which only the severest shocks and failures were able to interrupt for very short periods, bears the strongest testimony both to his persuasiveness and to his personal character. Though he handled huge subsidies, no faintest shadow of suspicion

ever clung to him; his reputation was as clean as that of
Nicias or Phocion. Likewise, no amount of power ever went
to his head or tempted him for a moment to aim at a tyranny; like Washington, he was genuinely content to remain
all his life "the first citizen of a free commonwealth."

If the success of the Achaian League was largely due to
the wise and broad statesmanship, diplomatic skill, and
high character of Aratus, its ultimate failure was also to
be brought about, in great measure, by his characteristic
weaknesses — his tendency to lean on foreign aid, his military incapacity, and his bitter jealousy. The first of these
we have already seen foreshadowed; the second was bound
to appear after he became President, for it was a fundamental, fatal fault of the Achaian constitution that it required its chief officer to be not only, like our own President,
commander-in-chief of the army, but its actual leader in the
field. Now Aratus' warlike skill was limited to surprises
such as the taking of Sicyon; all his life he delighted in these
and certainly showed plenty of personal daring in carrying
them out; yet in field warfare he was cautious and hesitat-
ing to the point of positive timidity. Like McClellan, he
seems to have habitually overestimated his enemy, and
again and again, to the exasperation and despair of his
gallant officers, he threw away victory rather than attack.
Among historical commanders, he has the remarkable record
of never having won a battle.

Fortunately for the establishment of his influence, he
was not called upon for several years to betray this weakness. In his first term, to be sure, there was war among the
leagues, but the Ætolians, now rapidly expanding into a
first-class power, put down the Bœotians before the Achaians had fairly got going. Antigonus had paid little attention
to the growth of the League; his enemies were Egypt and
his own nephew Alexander, who had made himself master

of Corinth and held it in defiance of his suzerain. In 248, however, Alexander had died, and Antigonus, playing a trick on his widow, had seized Corinth with its invaluable citadel; in 244 he beat Egypt and divided with her the control of the Ægean. The "Old Man," as he was commonly called, was now in a very satisfactory position, at peace with the world and in possession of all he wanted. He had reckoned with every possible danger except one, — Aratus, with his burning ambition to liberate Greece. To him, as to Antigonus, Acrocorinth was the key to the whole situation; without it, further progress was impossible, In full peace, and in defiance of all international law, he plotted an attack upon that fortress as outrageous from a legal point of view as those of Phœbidas upon the Cadmea or Sphodrias upon the Piræus. The only difference — and to Aratus it made all the difference — was that those seizures had been made to enslave, while his was to set free. The exploit, told in full and exciting detail by Plutarch, who admires and approves to the highest degree, was of the same sort as that of Sicyon and an absolutely personal venture on the part of Aratus, who paid for it out of his own pocket and risked his own life in the attack — for this time success was not to be won without fighting and some bloodshed. When the high rock fortress was scaled and won, he came down to the theater and faced the assembled Corinthians, leaning, utterly wearied with his night's work, upon his spear and listening in grave silence to the shouts and acclamations of the waiting crowd. Then, straightening up, he addressed them, not in his own name but in that of the League, which he invited them to join, and ended by handing over to the Corinthians the keys of their own gates, "which had never been in their power since the days of King Philip."

Small wonder that Corinth enthusiastically entered the League and was rapidly followed by Megara, Trœzen, and

Epidaurus. The federation, now including fifteen cities, stretched from sea to sea and controlled the Isthmus; the "shackles of Greece" were broken. It was equally natural that Antigonus, who saw his whole "system" shattered by this blow, should be furious and enter into formal alliance with Ætolia, with which Achaia was still in a state of war. Aratus, in his turn, looked for help, and got money from Egypt and men from Sparta, led by the young and romantic Agis, so soon to meet a martyr's death. No two men, both patriotic and disinterested, could have been more unlike or less able to work together than Agis and Aratus; to one a pitched battle with the enemy was the first, to the other the last, resort. Aratus had his way; the Ætolians entered the Peloponnesus unopposed and ravaged the fields whence, as the canny commander of the Achaians had observed, the harvest was already almost all gathered in; Agis went home in disgust, and Aratus retrieved his reputation by a successful surprise attack on the enemy, driving them from the town of Pellene which he had allowed them to capture. Soon after, the fighting came to a standstill, and on the death of the old king in 239 the two leagues not only made peace with each other but entered into an alliance against his successor, Demetrius II. It was in this next war, the details of which are confused and unimportant, that Aratus lost his first pitched battle.

Meanwhile, the extension of the League over southern Greece was going merrily on. Arcadian towns came in one after another, though some preferred to enter the Ætolian confederacy, and Mantinea joined only to secede. Aratus' own heart was set upon Argos and Athens, one ruled by a tyrant, the other in fact if not in name by Macedon, and over and over again, openly and secretly, by plot and stratagem and actual war, he tried to free them. The populations themselves, however, of the two cities were too supine to seize the opportunities he offered, and it was not until the death of Demetrius and the accession of his nine-year old son reduced the influence of Macedonia to a minimum that Aristomachus, the tyrant of Argos, was persuaded to abdicate and bring in his city, and that Athens allowed herself to be freed at the expense of Aratus and other friends of liberty, who bought off the Macedonian commander of the Piræus. Even then, she who had once been the city of Pericles could not bring herself to become a part of an Achaian nation; she graciously consented to an alliance.

The greatest conquest of the republican spirit, however, had been over the mind and heart of one of the noblest men of the time, Lydiadas, the young tyrant of his native Megalopolis, who, unforced and unbribed, laid down his power and persuaded his great city — by far the most important acquisition since Corinth — to join the League. His magnanimity was gladly recognized, and for several years he alternated with Aratus in the presidency.

Thus, by the year 228, all Greece was free. South of Thessaly there was neither a Macedonian garrison nor a local tyrant. From the Pindus range to Mount Taygetus, every city-state was once more a republic and protected, through membership or alliance, by one or other of the two great democratic leagues. Who could have dreamed that in seven short years the whole work would be undone and Greece once more lying at the feet of a conqueror?

What deepens the tragedy is that it came about through what was in itself a glorious achievement, the reawakening of Sparta to one last, brief period of national greatness. Alone among Greek states, she stood wholly outside both leagues; alone, she had never, at her weakest and most helpless, bent the knee to Macedon, opened her gates to a conqueror, or submitted to a tyrant; proudly and silently, in her distant corner, she was withering away under the old

constitution which had been her glory and was now her
bane. Yet all around her lay reservoirs of strength, — the
Helots, the Periœci, the poverty-stricken, disinherited Spartans themselves, whom a fatal narrowness had shut out
from citizenship. The man who could break down the walls
of age-long caste prejudice and let in these floods of new
life might make unconquered Sparta once more herself a
conqueror. This Agis had tried to do, and had died a victim to the old régime. His widow, forced to marry his boy-
ish successor, had taken the noblest of revenges: acquiring
soon, by her beauty and her strength of character, a lifelong influence over the youthful Cleomenes, she imbued his
mind with the ideas of the martyred reformer, ideas which
with greater ability and fewer scruples he was for a brief
period to carry into effect.

The outline of his plan may be briefly stated: to get rid,
by violence if necessary, — and it proved necessary, — of the
Ephors, whose constitutional control paralyzed every effort
at reform; to restore the disinherited Spartan families to
their original rights by a re-division of the land, all wealth
being first put into a common stock; to increase the number
of citizens by admitting four thousand selected Periœci;
to revive the ancient discipline, including the common
tables; thus, finally, to take his place as a real king of a
vigorous and united nation instead of the puppet of a small
and decaying aristocracy. But inextricably, and probably
inevitably, bound up with this ideal was another; such a
reinvigorated Sparta would never be contented with the
minor and passive position which the dying Sparta had held
perforce; the new Lacedæmon must be once more the chief
power in Greece. Thus we see how the wills of Aratus and
Cleomenes were bound to clash; each saw the Peloponnesus as a whole, but one was determined to unite it as a
federation of equal republics, the other as an alliance under

the recognized leadership of Sparta. As Freeman sums it
up, " Sparta and Achaia, Cleomenes and Aratus, were shut
up within one peninsula, and that was enough."

Of course the war had to have immediate causes, and one
of them was the jealousy of the Ætolian League, which, to
check its rival, handed over to Spartan alliance three important Arcadian towns which formed a wedge running
right up into Achaian territory and specially threatening
Sparta's old enemies, Megalopolis and Argos.   The ex-
tyrants of these cities, therefore, Lydiadas and Aristomachus, now influential statesmen of the League, took the
alarm at once and were for hurrying on war with Sparta and
forcing her into the League before it was too late.   Cleomenes also, who had not yet taken his revolutionary step,
was eager for a chance to win the military prestige which
would help him to put through his scheme. Aratus, on the
other hand, as well as the Spartan Ephors, was for caution
and delay, but the seizure of a post actually within Megalo-
politan territory made peace impossible.

Unluckily, not Lydiadas, a dashing soldier and the logical
candidate under the circumstances, but Aristomachus, who
was much more under the personal influence of Aratus,
was chosen President by the same assembly that declared
war. The result was that, under strong pressure from his
political chief, he declined battle when it might have been
joined at great advantage. There was much indignation,
and at the next election Aratus had to meet, for the first
time, a strong opposition, led by Lydiadas as a rival candidate; long habit prevailed, however, and the trusted statesman was elected for a twelfth term. A bad defeat at Mount
Lykaion was partly atoned for by the successful surprise of
Mantinea, which, although a seceder, was treated with much
kindness and taken back into the League with full rights.
The next defeat, however, shook Aratus's popularity more

than any event had yet done, for it involved the death of
the valiant Lydiadas, who, disregarding the signal to halt
after a first repulse of the Spartans, pursued the enemy to
their trenches and there, unsupported by the main body,
was cut down with his men. Sparta gave royal honors to
her bravest foe, sending his body, robed and crowned, to
the city over which he had refused to rule, and all Achaia
was painfully stirred by the charges that the cowardice, if
not the deliberate treachery, of Aratus had sacrificed his only
serious rival.

So high ran the feeling that the Assembly in extraordinary
session passed the strange resolution that Aratus might go
on with the war if he pleased, at his own expense, — the
League would throw away no more men or money under
his leadership. Neither this pettishness, however, nor the
mortification of Aratus, who threatened to "lay down his
seal" and let the government run itself, lasted very long,
and we soon see him again at the head of the army and able
to dictate the choice of the next election. But a still greater
blow was in store. Cleomenes, in the flush of his victory at
Ladokia and his subsequent recapture of Mantinea, had
carried through his resolution, executed the Ephors, and
made himself King in fact as well as in name. With greatly
increased power and prestige he once more invaded Achaian
territory and at Hecatombeon inflicted on the League a
really crushing defeat.

It was a dark moment for Aratus. Not only was his personal popularity under a heavy cloud, but the dream of his
life now began to seem to him, for the first time, impossible
of fulfillment. On all sides rose the cry for peace. Sparta's
terms were moderate, from her point of view even generous.
She asked no territory, no garrisons, nothing but the en-
trance of the Achaian cities into an alliance of which she
should be head. But to grant these terms meant, of course,

the disappearance forever of the higher, freer type of union, the end of the federation. Citizens of Corinth, of Argos, of Megalopolis might lose nothing, might even gain, in local freedom and authority, but they would never again be citizens of a great Hellenic nation. On the other hand, it was quite obvious that the League could not, unassisted, maintain itself against Sparta; Ætolia, its fellow-federation, was aloof and hostile; there remained only Macedon. At first sight it seems almost incredible that Aratus, whose life-work had been the rescue of the Peloponnesus from Macedonian domination, should have voluntarily proposed its return to that control. That he did make this proposal, that he planned and plotted for its success, and finally bought the aid of Macedon at the price of that invaluable fortress of Acrocorinth which it had been his proudest personal achievement to snatch from her hands, is the great indelible blot upon his fame; the man who had done more than any one who ever lived to unite Greece made her union impossible. Yet it is unfair to judge entirely after the event. Almost always the near danger looks more terrible than the distant one. Cleomenes was close at hand; under his dominating personality the control of Sparta would be felt at every point and every hour. Moreover, to Aratus' essentially conservative mind the revolutionary Spartan was at once a tyrant and a socialist, vastly more dangerous than the steady, respectable, constitutional monarch, Antigonus Doson, who was quietly ruling Macedon for his boy-nephew, Philip. The demand for Acrocorinth, too, was still in the future, and a friendly alliance on equal terms between Kingdom and League was all, no doubt, that Aratus originally had in mind. Remembering how naturally he had turned, in his very boyhood, to the expedient of foreign succor, one begins to see that it was not as a traitor or a weakling, but as a self-deluded patriot, that the great statesman of the League took the fatal step.

Of course, no such proposal could be bluntly made to the Achaians. By a series of ingenious negotiations carried on in the name of the city of Megalopolis, they were gradually familiarized with the idea, even while peace parleys with Cleomenes were also proceeding. The Spartan terms were so attractive that only a most unlucky illness which prevented the king's appearance at the crucial moment postponed their acceptance. Aratus, who had by this time learned, but dared not tell his countrymen, the price Antigonus demanded, gained time by contriving to renew the quarrel with Cleomenes. It was impossible, however, to keep the secret long, and at the news that the cession to Macedon of the key of the Peloponnesus had even been considered, the whole League fell into the wildest confusion. A party favorable to Sparta sprang up everywhere and carried city after city into the Lacedæmonian alliance. The Spartans entered Corinth, detached her from the League and besieged the citadel with its federal garrison. In his own Sicyon, Aratus had to execute some "traitors," — the first civil bloodshed committed in the name of the League, — and soon only that city, Megalopolis, a few small Arcadian towns, and the original Achaians remained true to the Federation. In one way, Aratus was the stronger, for he had no rivals, and was now appointed dictator, with an armed guard. Nor was this the prelude to tyranny; at least, the Achaians knew they could trust him to consider their interests, however mistakenly, rather than his own. In vain did Cleomenes, by splendid offers, try to win him over. His decision was taken, and he was now able to impose it upon his people. After sending to Ætolia and Athens for the aid which there was no hope of their granting, the League formally requested the assistance of Macedonia at the price of Acrocorinth.

Soon the northern legions were in the Peloponnesus, and

Cleomenes, now the champion of Greek independence, was waging a magnificent but losing fight. Argos went back to her allegiance, Mantinea, which had twice seceded, was recaptured, stripped of her citizens and recolonized as "Antigonia." The final struggle came on the battlefield of Sellasia, in 222, when the hopes of Sparta went down in final defeat, and her king, losing the opportunity of a hero's death, fled from the field to a miserable end in Egypt. For seventy-five years more the Achaian League, now restored to nearly its greatest extent, maintained its existence and in some ways its usefulness, but its independence was over forever. As a member of what may be called a League of leagues, which included almost all Greece, it could manage its home affairs without interference and send delegates to a general congress which met under the presidency of the king of Macedon, but it could carry on no foreign policy of its own, and in war its contingents marched under the orders of the northern king.

Under these circumstances the latest period of Aratus' life is necessarily the least interesting. For eight years more he remained the unquestioned head of the League — his son usually filling his place between terms — as well as the trusted counselor of the youthful Philip V, now ruling for himself and as yet impressionable and unhardened. As President of the League, he had to wage war, as unsuccessfully as usual, against the predatory Ætolians and their allies the Eleans, and put up so poor a defense that at one time the three little old Achaian cities of Dyme, Pharæ, and Tritaia, getting no help from "an incompetent executive with a bankrupt treasury," refused to pay Federal taxes, holding the money for their own protection — a proceeding remarkably like that proposed by the New England States in the Hartford Convention of 1814. The extreme impudence of the Ætolians, however, had brought the whole

Macedonian Alliance down upon them, and as "minister of Peloponnesian affairs," so to speak, Aratus accompanied Philip on many successful campaigns, using the great influence which his years, experience, and personal charm gave him over the latter's yet unformed character to keep his policy moderate and merciful. His original idea, when he persuaded the Achaians to put themselves under the shield of the Macedonian King, had been that they should become not his subjects but his free allies; the vision with which he comforted himself was of a united Greece willingly following the lead of a powerful friend. It was therefore essential to his own self-respect as well as to the welfare of his countrymen that the intercourse between Philip and the Peloponnesians should be kept on this open and manly footing, and we see the line he took in the argument with which he dissuaded Philip from seizing the fortress on Mount Ithome, which dominated the southern part of the Peloponnesus as Acrocorinth did the northern. "Robbers," he said, "nest themselves in rocks and precipices, but the strongest fort a king can have is confidence and affection. These have opened to you the Cretan Sea, these make you master of Peloponnesus, and by the help of these, young as you are, are you become captain of the one and lord of the other."[1]

But Aratus was not Philip's only counselor. Close to his person and enjoying the right of free and familiar intercourse with their sovereign which was still tenaciously held by the old Macedonian nobility, were a group of men whose viewpoint was still that of the captains who had gone forth to conquer under Philip II and Alexander, who regarded Macedonians as born masters and Greeks as born subjects. To these "junkers" Aratus and his influence were simply insufferable, and they never rested in their efforts to dislodge him. At one time they made use of a passing wave of

---

[1] Again, cf. Burke, peroration to *Speech on Conciliation with America*.

popular discontent among the Achaians to secure the election of one of their creatures to the presidency, but his incompetence was such that Aratus came back stronger than ever. At another, they trumped up a charge before Philip which Aratus was luckily enabled to disprove by the mouth of the man he was accused of suborning. The curious fact which proves the immense pride and self-confidence of the old Macedonian stock is that the conspirators after each defeat became not less but more open and outrageous in their attempts, until actual rebellion led them one and all to disgrace and death.

Nevertheless, Aratus was playing a game in which he was bound to lose. As Philip grew older and more confirmed in power, the seeds of evil in his character came to fruit, and the increasing violence of his passions rebelled more and more against the restraint which his Achaian minister would have put upon them. Particularly, the way in which he had yielded, overawed for the last time by the higher standards and more far-seeing statesmanship of Aratus, in the matter of Mount Ithome, rankled in his proud heart, and from that time the two became more and more estranged. So obvious was the King's ill-will that when Aratus sickened and died of an illness the symptoms of which look exceedingly like those of consumption, it was commonly believed that he had been poisoned by royal order, and the dying man himself, looking at the blood he had coughed up, remarked, "That is the reward I have got for my friendship to Philip."

Aratus died in his seventeenth term as President and in the fifty-ninth year of his age. Whatever fault later critics have found with his career as a patriot statesman, his fellow-countrymen were united in his praise. The only controversy was between Ægium, the capital of the League, where he died, and Sicyon, where he was born, as to which should have the honor of being his final resting-place. Sicyon prevailed, and instituted two solemn sacrifices, performed yearly at his tomb to commemorate the day of his birth and that on which he had delivered her from tyranny. It was not long before Greece exchanged the position of a dependency of Macedon for that of a Roman province, yet "e'en in our ashes live their wonted fires," and three hundred years after the death of Aratus, some remnants of these observances still preserved the memory of the man who had cleared the Peloponnesus of tyrants and had been the guiding spirit of a great free federation.

SUMMARY OF GREEK HISTORY

PREHISTORIC PERIOD: 2500–1000.

I. *"Cretan Period"*: 2500–1350.

The Ægean Sea was the seat of an elaborate and splendid civilization, known to us by its monuments, especially those discovered in Crete. The people, a small, dark, skillful, industrious, and docile race, were governed by despotic kings of the Oriental type. They used bronze but no iron.

II. *"Mycenæan Period"*: 1500–1000.

The Greeks, a tall, fair, warlike race, invaded Greece and the islands from the north. Coming in small bands, they conquered different parts of the country and ruled as a superior class, mixing more or less with the original race and partly preserving the "Cretan" civilization.

"DARK AGES": 1000–800.

I. *Dorian Invasion* — about 1000.

The final wave of northern invaders, the peculiarly warlike Dorians, forced its way through Central Greece and settled mainly in the Peloponnesus, destroying the last remains of the older civilization. The art of writing was now forgotten and the Mediterranean trade was lost to the Phœnicians.

II. *First Era of Colonization:* 1000–900.

The general unsettlement caused by the Dorian invasion caused the migration of many peoples, driving out others in turn. In the midst of the turmoil the Greeks took possession of the western coast of Asia Minor, where they subsequently appeared in the north as Æolians, in the center as Ionians, and in the south as Dorians.

"MIDDLE AGES": 800–500.

Civilization gradually rebuilt. Revival of trade. Grouping of tribal villages in "city-states." Government of kings, with aid of council of tribal elders, gives place to that of nobles (*oligarchy*). Great misery and discontent of commons, often taken advantage of by ambitious adventurer who makes himself *tyrant* (i.e., ruler contrary to law). Second generation of tyrants usually overthrown and followed by *republics*, either *aristocratic* or *democratic*. During this period we may also note:

1. *Second Era of Colonization* : 750–550.

As a result of the increase of population, the expansion of trade, and the political disturbances, a great many cities sent out colonists who established Greek towns on the shores of the Black Sea, Sicily, Southern Italy, etc. These cities often surpassed their founders in wealth and population.

II. *Development of Sparta.*

Of the Dorian tribes which invaded Laconia and Messenia the Spartans proved the strongest. In time they conquered the others, retaining all power and all the best land. The inhabitants of the small Laconian towns (*Periœci*) kept *local* rights only. The rest of the population and the Messenians tilled the good land as state-serfs (*Helots.*) The Spartans themselves remained a small ruling caste, purely military. Their peculiar discipline and form of government was adopted and attributed to *Lycurgus*. They were the only Greek state to retain always the original monarchy (but divided between two kings), council of elders, and assembly of warriors who shouted assent or dissent. Later they added a board of five *Ephors*, annually elected to supervise the kings and the observance of the laws of "Lycurgus."

III. *Development of Athens.*

Small townships of Attica consolidated very early into city-state of Athens. Kings lost power to nobles in pre-historic times. By 682, nine *Archons* elected annually by and from the nobles (*Eupatrids*) who held all the power and most of the land. Popular discontent led to reforms by *Draco* (621) and *Solon* (594–93). Solon relieved debtors and tenants, re-classified citizens according to property, and established a modified democracy. New disturbances led to establishment of tyranny by *Pisistratus*, who reigned brilliantly. His younger son *Hipparchus* was assassinated by *Harmodius* and *Aristogiton*, and his elder son *Hippias* driven out by democratic revolution led by *Cleisthenes* (510). A new constitution divided all citizens, increased by inclusion of resident aliens (*metics*), into ten *tribes* (wards) each consisting of *demes* (districts), which formed the basis of the *Council of Five Hundred* and of the voting in the Assembly (*Ecclesia*).

PERSIAN INVASIONS: 492–479.

During the second half of the sixth century Greek cities of Asia Minor, previously subjected by *Lydia*, passed into power of *Persia*. In 500, the Ionians revolted, aided by Athens, but were put down. 492, *Darius*, resolving to conquer Greece, sent expedition along coast, wrecked off Mount Athos. 490, a second, under *Datis* and *Artaphernes*, crossed the Ægean and landed at *Marathon*. The Athenians, aided by Platæans only, won decisive victory. 480, King *Xerxes* renewed attack with huge army and fleet, following coast route. Most Greek states (*Thebes* and *Argos* holding aloof) formed league for defense, under Spartan leadership. A small force under *Leonidas* of Sparta was cut to pieces at *Thermopylæ*, and the Greek fleet after indecisive battle at *Artemisium* withdrew to *Salamis* where, through diplomacy of Athenian *Themistocles*, a great naval battle was won. Xerxes returned to Asia, leaving best troops in Thessaly under *Mardonius*, who advanced southward in 479 and was defeated at *Platæa* by combined Greek army under Spartan *Pausanias*. At same time, a Greek fleet and army, chiefly Athenian, won great victory over Persians at *Mycale*, Asia Minor,

During Persian invasions, Phœnician city of *Carthage* nearly overwhelmed Greek cities of Sicily, but was defeated at *Himera* (480) by *Gelon* of Syracuse.

ATHENIAN SUPREMACY: 479–431.

Athens chief naval power in Greece. After treachery of Pausanias, allies refused to serve under Spartan admiral, and Sparta and rest of Peloponnesians retired from war, leaving Athens head of *Delian League* of maritime states, established by *Aristides*. War with Persia continued until by victory of *Cimon*, son of Miltiades, at river *Eurymedon* (466) freedom of Ægean absolutely secured. Meanwhile, League developed into *Empire*, allies becoming subjects. At same time, Athens conquered several neighbor states but was obliged to give up attempt at land-empire. 445, Thirty Years' Truce signed with Sparta. Next fifteen years those of greatest prosperity, power, art, and literature. Time of *Phidias, Sophocles.* Chief statesman of whole period, *Pericles*. Athens now complete democracy and champion of democracies everywhere, as Sparta of aristocracies.

PELOPONNESIAN WAR: 431–404.

Peloponnesian League, headed by Sparta, at war with Athenian Empire. (1) Annual Spartan invasions of Attica. Plague at Athens. Death of Pericles. Rise of *Cleon*. Victories of *Demosthenes* (Athenian). Capture of Spartans at *Pylos*. (2) Death of Cleon and *Brasidas* (Spartan) at *Amphipolis.* "Peace of Nicias." War continued among allies. Disastrous *Sicilian Expedition* urged by *Alcibiades*. (3) Sparta renewed direct war and occupied *Decelea* (in Attica) continuously. Naval war in Ægean. Sparta betrayed Ionians for Persian aid. Brief oligarchical revolution ("Four Hundred") in Athens. Spartan victory under *Lysander* at *Ægospotami.* Athens surrenders, 404.

SPARTAN SUPREMACY: 404–371.

Sparta chief military power in Greece. Set up oligarchies, supported by Spartan garrisons and *harmosts* (governors) in almost every city. Renewed war with Persia. [Weakness of Persia proved by march (401) through interior of "*Ten Thousand*" Greek mercenaries, under Athenian *Xenophon*, left stranded by death of insurgent prince, *Cyrus*.] *Agesilaus* (Spartan King) after victories over Persians, recalled to Greece to put down revolting states.

THEBAN SUPREMACY: 371-362.

Thebes, led by *Pelopidas*, overthrew oligarchy and under *Epaminondas* refused to accept Spartan Supremacy as laid down by "King's Peace." At *Leuctra* (371) Theban infantry won great victory over Spartan. Epaminondas invaded Peloponnesus four times, depriving Sparta of *Messenia*, which set up as independent state, and helping to found *Megalopolis*, capital of new Arcadian League. In victorious battle of *Mantinea* (362), Epaminondas slain.

[During periods of Spartan and Theban supremacies in Greece, *Dionysius* of *Syracuse* rescued most of Sicily from Carthage and created a despotic empire.]

After a period of general exhaustion in Greece, during which *Philip of Macedon* was building up a great military state, came

MACEDONIAN SUPREMACY: 338-146.

I. *Philip*. Athens and Thebes, roused by the orator *Demosthenes*, fought Philip at Chæronea (338) and were beaten. Philip was chosen by Greek congress at Corinth to lead general expedition against Persia, but was assassinated.

II. *Alexander: 336-323*. Alexander, after putting down revolts in Greece, invaded Persian Empire, winning battles of the *Granicus* (334), *Issus* (333), and (after conquest of Syria and Egypt), *Gaugamela* (*Arbela*) (331). After pushing his conquests as far as the Indus, and laying the foundations of a great Asiatic-European empire of *Hellenistic* culture, he died in 323.

III. Wars of Succession: 323-280. The empire was divided among his generals and their successors, who fought long wars with each other. Finally, the principal divisions became *Syria* (about the old Persian Empire), under the *Seleucidæ*, *Egypt*, under the *Ptolemies*, and *Macedonia*, under the descendants of *Antigonus*.

IV. Period of Federations: 280-146. The Greek states, now very weak, were subject to Macedon, but under *Aratus* the *Achaian League* united most of the Peloponnesus in a *free federation*. The revival of Sparta under *Cleomenes* led Aratus to put the League under the protection of Macedon (222), which also conquered Sparta. Later, the *Ætolian League*, in northern Greece, called in *Rome* against Macedon. Finally, after the battle of *Pydna* (168) the kingdom of Macedonia was broken up into small states tributary to Rome, and in the battle of *Corinth* (146) the Achaian League was easily defeated. Thereafter Greece was a dependency of Rome.

INDEX

Achaian League, characteristics, 226; constitution, 226–27; receives non-Achaian members, 230; success and ultimate failure largely due to Aratus, 231; makes peace-alliance with Ætolian League, 233; extension over southern Greece, 233; at war with Sparta, 236; unable to stand alone against Sparta, 238; falls into confusion at news of cession of Acrocorinth to Macedon, 239; requests aid of Macedon, 239; restored in extent, exists 75 years under supremacy of Macedon, 240.

Acragas, sacked by Carthaginians, 126.

Admetus, King of Molossians, gives refuge to Themistocles, 33.

Æschines supports Eubulus, 173; goes on embassy to Philip, 181; accused of corruption and disloyalty by Demosthenes, but acquitted, 183; denounces sacrilege of Amphissa, 185; gains influence after Chæronea, 188; blocks vote of crown to Demosthenes by indicting Ctesiphon, 189; oration "On the Crown," 191–92; unable to pay fine, goes into exile, 192; teacher of oratory, 192.

Ætolian League, formed, 225; expands into first-class power, 231; alliance with Antigonus, 233; peace and alliance with Achaian League, 233; hands over Arcadian towns to Sparta, 236; its predatory raids, 240.

Agariste, grand-niece of Cleisthenes, mother of Pericles, 37.

Agesilaus, normal Spartan, 103; chosen king by Lysander's influence, 105–06; his pleasantness, 106; lameness, 106; generosity, 106; courtesy to Ephors and Elders, 106–07; tries to play part of Agamemnon, 108; takes army to Asia, 108, gets rid of Lysander, 108; most powerful Spartan king for 100 years, 109; campaign vs. Tissaphernes, 109–10; drills army at Ephesus, 109–10; takes Sardis, 110; alliance with King of Paphlagonia, 111; meeting with Pharnabazus, 111–12; humanity, 112–13; height of power, 113; appoints Pisander to command fleet, 114; plans invasion of Persia, 114; recalled to Greece, 114; reception of news of Spartan victory, 115; at battle of Coronea, 115–16; goes to Delphi and Sparta, 116; leads two expeditions against Corinth, 117; anecdotes of, 117, 118; influence over Spartan policy, 118; refuses to let Thebes sign for Bœotia, 120, 151; defends seizure of Cadmea, 120; fondness for his children, 120; mingling of public and private considerations, 120–21; leads army twice into Bœotia, 121; receives victorious army, 121; defends Sparta against Epaminondas, 122; goes to Asia to get money for Sparta, 122; takes field against Epaminondas, 123, 165; saves Sparta, 123, 166; general at battle of Mantinea, 167, 169; hires out to Tachos of Egypt, 123; surprises the Egyptians, 123–24; goes over